First Edition

Common Core
Support Coach

TARGET → Reading Comprehension **6**

Common Core Support Coach, Target: Reading Comprehension, First Edition, Grade 6
T229NA   ISBN-13: 978-1-62362-008-0
Cover Design: Q2A/Bill Smith   **Cover Illustration:** Scott Balmer

Triumph Learning® 136 Madison Avenue, 7th Floor, New York, NY 10016

Contents

Tools

Graphic Organizers and Close Reading Worksheets

Fiction

Fiction is your ticket to imagination. Fiction is made-up stories that might have some basis in reality but mostly come from an author's imagination. These stories can be set in any place or time in the past, present, or future. Good fiction stories contain plots with drama or suspense that hold a reader's attention from start to finish. They also contain characters that seem like they could be real people. Imagine you found an old book with this picture on the cover. What would you expect to read about?

Skills Focus

Aaron's Future Friend
Draw and Support Inferences
Story Elements: Plot

La Festival Calabaza
Theme   **Story Elements: Characters**

Practice the Skill

Authors often express their ideas directly, telling you exactly what they mean. Sometimes, they imply, or hint about, those ideas. In those cases, you need to infer, or figure out, what the author means. When you **draw an inference**, you decide what the author is stating indirectly in the text. Drawing inferences requires you to look for clues, or the facts and details in a text that show what the author wants to communicate. Following these clues helps you interpret the author's message. You can then point to these clues to support the inferences you make. For instance, if you encounter a character packing a bag with summer clothes and a swimsuit, and it is snowing outside the window, you can infer that she is about to go on vacation.

Try It   Read the following paragraph.

> Amanda sat wide-eyed in her seat and waited for the bus to pull out of the station. It wasn't an ordinary station, nor was it an ordinary bus. This bus could travel on land, in water, in air, and even in outer space. Amanda had read about vehicles like this and had been thrilled to sign up for a tour so she could experience it. "It's a little scary," her friend Kris had told her after he came back from the tour he'd taken a few months earlier.

Discuss   **What sort of person is Amanda? Underline the parts of the text that support your inference.**

Read on, looking for more clues to support your inference about Amanda.

> Amanda wasn't the least bit concerned about that. The tour was advertised as "the adventure of a lifetime," and Amanda had no doubt it would be. She could hardly contain her excitement.

Discuss   **How does Amanda feel about the tour? How do you know? Underline words and phrases that help you know how she's feeling.**

> **As you read, record your answers about drawing and supporting inferences on the Close Reading Worksheet on page 257.** 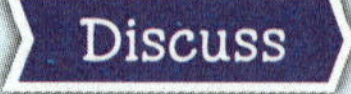

Practice the Skill

 Story Elements: Plot

The **plot** of a story is the series of episodes that move the story from start to finish. These episodes can be ordinary, true-to-life events or fantastic events that turn reality upside down. In many works of fiction, the plot unfolds in five parts.

- **Exposition:** the story's beginning, where the characters and setting are presented

- **Rising action:** the point where the story's main problem or conflict is introduced

- **Climax:** the turning point, which may involve great physical danger or strong emotions

- **Falling action:** the point where the story begins to wind down

- **Resolution:** the story's end, where conflicts are resolved and loose ends are tied up

Try It Read this very short story, and think about what happens.

My brother and I landed on Nyancia by accident when our spaceship ran out of fuel. The planet Nyancia wasn't on any star chart because it had only recently been discovered. It was dark and cold when we landed. We were frightened and nearly freezing, but we searched for something to use as fuel. After about an hour, we discovered a tunnel in the rock. Much to our surprise, a different world was on the other side: bright, warm, and colorful! We made friends in Nyancia, and they eventually helped us get back home. But first, we stayed awhile to get to know these kind people and their beautiful planet.

Discuss What is the story's conflict? Is it resolved? How well does this story follow the five-part plot structure? Reread the story, and box and label each part: *E* for *Exposition*, *RA* for *Rising Action*, *C* for *Climax*, *FA* for *Falling Action*, and *R* for *Resolution*.

As you read, complete the Plot Sequence Chart on page 258.

Aaron's Future Friend

How would you describe Aaron? Underline clues that support your answer.

Who are the characters, and what is the setting of the story? What do you know about them? Record your answers under Exposition on the **Plot Sequence Chart.**

Why did Aaron most likely keep the Icealia guide even though he had never thought about going there?

1   Aaron Eisely got the news on Friday afternoon by what his generation calls "the AM" (Ancient Mail). It was a printed letter in an envelope, hand stamped by the Bellmont postmaster and delivered by robot express. "It's from TTEP!" he cried out, thrilled, although not a soul was around to hear him. He tore open the envelope, and sure enough, it was a welcome letter to new members. "Congratulations, time traveler!" it read. "You have been selected for membership in the Time Traveler's Exchange Program (TTEP). As a new member, you have been awarded an opportunity to travel in time and space to Icealia for the upcoming school year. Once we receive your signed letter of acceptance, travel to Icealia will be arranged immediately. Welcome to TTEP, and happy travels in time!"

2   He had done it. Although the competition was admittedly fierce, he had created a first-class video application that had earned him his spot in TTEP. Aaron had wanted to time travel for as long as he could remember. He had watched every vidclip he could get his hands on about time travel, and he had read everything he could find on the topic—and Aaron was an **avid** reader.

3   But . . . Icealia? He had never thought of bare, lonely Icealia as a potential destination. Of all the worlds in the galaxy he could visit, past and present, Icealia was so **desolate** that it had never crossed his mind. Now, though, his mind was racing like a comet. He logged on to his reader and pulled up a guide about Icealia that he had read several years ago and stored in the hard memory, and began reading.

4   "Icealia is one of the most remote worlds in the known universe," Aaron read. "Found light-years from Earth, the primary Icealian civilization exists seven centuries in the future. Communication is accomplished through a complex system of coding, rather than formal spoken or written language. Because most communication is done remotely, Icealians have very little contact with one another and have adjusted to a **solitary** existence. Humans have learned much from the Icealians about remote communication and technology."

5   Aaron never even considered rejecting the offer. He sent off his letter of acceptance and contacted the TTEP office for his interview. Aaron would travel by space-time ship, traveling at sublight speed, making one short stop in Lunaria, then arriving at the Icealia landport ten days, two hours, and twenty-three minutes after his departure from Earth. The year of his arrival would be 2915.

6   Once he arrived, his strict directions were to log in at the landport with his name, his TTEP travel number, and his destination coordinates. He would then receive a card with driving directions written in code. His mind spun.

7   "Don't worry if you can't read the directions," Ms. Vanelli from the TTEP office explained to him. "Just take the card and feed it into the slot by the tramport door. The card will signal the tram doors to open and permit you to enter, then program the tram to deliver you directly to Hiz's homeport. If you follow the directions, then there really shouldn't be a problem." Hiz would be Aaron's Icealian host in the TTEP program.

8   Aaron still felt doubtful. "But . . . what if the doors *don't* open, or what if the card gets stuck in the slot, or what if anything like that happens—then what?" he asked nervously.

How does Aaron feel about his upcoming trip? <u>Underline</u> the parts of the text that support your inference.

How would you describe the rising action in this part of the story? Record your answer on the **Plot Sequence Chart**.

How does the author build suspense in this part of the story?

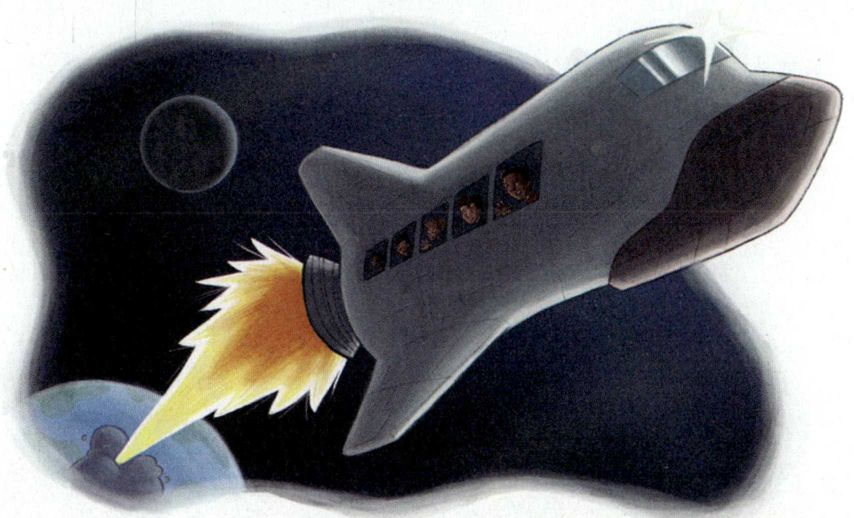

9   "And . . . I should still be able to communicate with Hiz, though, right, if I need to?"

10   "You can code him as soon as you land and exit the tramport. Let's get you set up with your codigraph, so you'll have time to familiarize yourself with it before you leave. The device won't be functional until you land in Icealia, but you will be able to see how it works, how to receive and submit code, and that sort of thing. How **fluent** are you at coding?"

11   "I have been getting better at it over time," Aaron replied.

12   "Good, because Hiz won't likely be completely fluent in English. Although he's studied our language, without actually speaking it aloud and communicating with another English speaker, his pronunciation is unlikely to be very understandable."

13   Aaron made a vow to practice coding at every opportunity right up to the day he left—and that day came quickly. For the next six weeks, Aaron bustled around the house getting ready to enter LearningPort 361X, where he would log in to his classroom, code in his assignments, and never speak a word to his teacher or classmates. For the next nine months, Aaron's sole companion would be Hiz Handler, a boy whose holographic images looked like those of any ordinary boy. However, Hiz would be a puzzle to figure out. Alien in mind but not in form, Hiz would be Aaron's only guide in his future life.

14   As Aaron had expected, when he finally arrived on Icealia, he found Hiz to be rather mysterious. As unused to company as Hiz must have been, he greeted Aaron warmly and extended his hand. Aaron noted that Hiz was also smaller than expected. He smiled and listened when Aaron spoke. He asked how Aaron enjoyed his trip and whether he had any trouble at the tramport. Most surprisingly, however, Hiz was **compassionate**, which Aaron learned once they started coding.

15   *Curious*, Aaron thought, *he has developed the ability to care about others, although he's been alone since he was a child.*

16   Hiz showed Aaron around his homeport, completely unfazed by the fact that it was cluttered and unkempt. Strange tools and stray pieces of metal covered every table and chair in sight. Hiz's profile in the TTEP program had explained that he was a builder, so Aaron had an idea that he'd find something like this. But the funniest thing was that amid the clutter of metal and electronics, images of other Icealians were projected on the walls. The images were of Hiz's family and friends, his classmates and teachers—all the people Hiz coded with every day but never spent time with in real life.

17   *The mind works more efficiently alone,* Hiz told Aaron in code, *when thoughts are allowed to flow freely, without interruption, in one continuous stream.* Aaron stared at the pictures, trying to digest them. He wondered how Hiz felt about these people he had chosen to commemorate.[1] He wondered if they shared secrets and coded about their dreams.

18   "Share?" Aaron asked in English. "I have holos to share with you." Aaron pointed to the images on Hiz's wall, and then he pulled up holograms from his reader—images of his mother, his father, his sister Cassidy, and his dog, Aloysius.

19   "My family," Aaron explained, pointing again to Hiz's family, projected on the walls. When Hiz saw the images of Aloysius and Aaron playing together, tears welled up in his eyes.

20   Aaron was perplexed, and so for a few minutes, he said nothing. He watched Hiz stare longingly at the hologram. *My best friend,* Aaron finally coded. *His name's Aloysius, and we play together. I talk to him. I* know *he understands me.*

21   Hiz continued to stare at Aloysius, and he touched the image wistfully. He coded, *There are no animals in Icealia. They've been extinct for a long time.*

[1]**commemorate** to honor the memory of someone

22. In this cold, isolated world, no one spoke aloud, no one played physical games, and no one built friendships anything like those Aaron had known. It occurred to him at that moment that Hiz knew about those things only from his studies. He had no real experience of companionship at all. Aaron was bringing that part of Earth culture to Icealia, but what would happen to Hiz when he left at the end of his nine-month exchange program?

23. That night, as Aaron lay in bed thinking, Hiz stayed up late viewing the images of Aaron playing with Aloysius that were projected on his walls. Eventually, Hiz slept, but Aaron remained awake, thinking. In this strange, barren world, this boy somehow had the capacity to love someone truly, someone who could bring joy and energy to his life and who could offer him love in return.

24. Aaron came up with a plan that was fully developed in his head by morning, probably because his thoughts flowed freely, without interruption, in one continuous coded stream.

25. *Hiz*, Aaron coded early the next morning, *I have an idea. How would you like your own Aloysius?*

26. *I would*, Hiz responded with curiosity, *but Icealia prohibits the import of animals.*

27. *Then how about the next best thing?* Aaron replied. *With your talent as a builder and the number of spare parts lying around here, we could build you a dog.*

28. Hiz looked stunned. The idea had never even crossed his mind. Wonder filled Hiz's eyes, and, perhaps for the first time in his life, a joyful impulse overwhelmed him. He sprang toward Aaron and hugged him awkwardly.

29. Over the next nine months, Hiz and Aaron worked together on Aloysius II whenever they weren't studying. As they built a companion for Hiz to bond with, they bonded and became true companions themselves. And companionship, Aaron knew, would make any world, even bare, lonely Icealia, a kinder place.

Vocabulary: Context Clues

You do not have to know the meaning of every word in a story to understand and enjoy it. Often, the meaning of an unknown word becomes clear when you look at the word's **context**, or the words and sentences that surround it. For example, synonyms and antonyms are good **context clues**. The unfamiliar word may be similar or opposite in meaning to a word or phrase nearby that you know. Or, context clues may define or restate the unfamiliar word. Use context clues to expand your vocabulary and improve your understanding of whatever you read.

Try It Read this excerpt from "Aaron's Future Friend."

> Most surprisingly, however, Hiz was **compassionate**, which Aaron learned once they started coding.
>
> *Curious,* Aaron thought, *he has developed the ability to care about others, although he's been alone since he was a child.*

If you did not know what *compassionate* meant, you could look at the words and sentences around it for context clues.

Discuss **What words help you determine the meaning of *compassionate*?**

The following words appear in "Aaron's Future Friend." Locate the words in the story, and look for context clues to determine their meanings. Write your own definitions, and then confirm or correct them using a dictionary.

1. **avid,** p. 8 ____

2. **desolate,** p. 8 ____

3. **solitary,** p. 9 ____

4. **fluent,** p. 10 ____

Practice the Skill

First Read **Theme**

The **theme** of a story is a general idea that is expressed through the story's characters, setting, and events. Often, a theme explains some universal truth about the human experience or teaches a lesson about life. Usually authors do not directly state the themes of their stories; instead, the themes must be inferred by readers based on what they read and on what they already know about life. You can come to understand a story's theme through details that are revealed as the story progresses. Note that there can be more than a single theme in a story.

Try It Read the following paragraph.

> Madelyn would never have volunteered to live with her great-aunt for the summer. It was her mother's idea. Aunt Nella had moved into a house that needed a lot of work, and Madelyn's mother thought sending Madelyn there to help out would be a good way to teach her daughter responsibility. After the first week, she was ready to leave.

Discuss ▶ **What has happened in the story so far? What message about life do you think the author is working toward? Double underline details that support your thinking.**

Read on to see if you were right about this story's theme.

> After two weeks, however, Madelyn wouldn't have left for the world, and she was already dreading summer's end. Aunt Nella was so much fun and full of stories that Madelyn would remember all her life. In return for the strength of her youth, Aunt Nella gave her niece the wisdom of her years.

Discuss ▶ **What do you think the theme of the story is? One theme could be "It is always good to try new things." Another could be "Everyone, young or old, has something to offer." Double underline details that helped you reach your conclusion.**

As you read, record your answers to questions about theme on the Close Reading Worksheet on page 259. ✏️➡

Practice the Skill

Fictional stories revolve around a cast of **characters** that participate in the main action. The protagonist of a story is often the main character, but other characters may play important roles in advancing the plot or developing the theme.

Authors may describe their characters directly: *Madelyn was a selfish girl.* However, they also reveal character traits indirectly through thoughts, actions, reactions, and what other characters think and say about a character: *"I sometimes think that girl is incapable of thinking about anyone but herself."*

Well-developed, realistic characters respond to events and change as a story moves toward the resolution. Well-developed characters both affect and are affected by the plot.

Try It Read this excerpt from the story about Madelyn and her great-aunt.

Aunt Nella had argued with Madelyn's mother about how Madelyn should spend her summer. While Madelyn's mother insisted that her daughter do her part to help the family, Aunt Nella thought that Madelyn should be allowed to spend the summer at home with friends. Madelyn had taken her aunt's side, of course, but once her mother made up her mind about something, she rarely changed it.

Discuss The author does not tell you directly what these characters are like; instead he or she lets their thoughts and actions show you. What words helped you understand Aunt Nella's character? What about Madelyn's mother? Circle the details that helped you draw your conclusions.

As you read, complete the Character Webs on page 260.

La Festival Calabaza

Based on the first two paragraphs, what theme do you think this story might develop?

What three words would you use to describe Papa and Tía Olga? Record your answers in the **Character Webs**.

What unstated reason might Tía Olga have for moving to Nuevo Laredo?

1   I had lived on a farm in Mexico since the day I was born, and life was never what I would call easy. There was a lot of work to be done on a farm, and Papa insisted that we work together as a family. That part was nice—we did most things as a family. I had three brothers and two sisters, and our **bond** was much closer than that of most families I knew.

2   In addition to my brothers and sisters, Tía Olga and my cousins lived nearby, and we saw them every day and worked together on the farm. All that changed about a year ago, when my *tía*—that's Spanish for "aunt"—decided to move north. Drought had devastated much of the land where we lived, and Tía Olga could no longer support herself and her children. For years, she had made a living by making sweet corn cakes and selling them at the market. As the drought got worse and worse, however, my tía decided to move in with her husband's sister, Marta. Marta had a successful *dulcería*, or candy shop, and Tía Olga said she needed help in the kitchen. Everyone knew that Tía Olga made the best *dulces* in the world.

3   The day my tía moved north was a difficult day for my mother. She and her sister had never been separated by more than a mile or so, and Nuevo Laredo[1] seemed like a world away from our village in the far south of Tamaulipas. Papa had offered to let my tía and my cousins move in with us, but Tía Olga knew we had very little room and insisted that she follow through with her plans.

[1]**Nuevo Laredo** a Mexican city in the state of Tamaulipas, across the Rio Grande from Laredo, Texas

4   "Thank you, but no, my sister," she said to my mother. "Marta needs help in *la dulcería*, and I must go north to help her," she continued in Spanish. "I must go where I can be of some use. It is time to move on."

5   I was saddened when my tía left and missed my cousins more than I could have imagined, but I had a feeling that we, too, would be moving north before long. There was no sign of relief from the drought and heat, and our distressed fields were nearly bare. My papa **mentioned** a few times that he might find work in Nuevo Laredo or Reynosa, as well. "I know a man there," he said, his words heavy with sadness, "who has a *zapateria*." For me to hear him utter those words was heart wrenching. My papa loved to work the land, and I couldn't imagine him selling shoes in a zapateria.

6   The days wore on and on, with no promise of rain, as if the heavens had shut their doors and refused to let even a droplet out. The corn had died, the beans were **sparse**, and Papa began to lose his last threads of hope. Every day he walked the fields with great sadness, as if he were preparing to leave them, until one day, as I watched him from the window, I saw him fall to his knees. He lowered his face to the ground and then cried out to the heavens. When I ran to the fields to comfort him, I was shocked at what I saw.

7   "Look! *Las calabazas!*" my papa cried excitedly, as he pointed to the ground. Despite the stubbornness of the heavens, the fields had awakened, and in one small area the earth sprouted pumpkins. It seemed nothing short of miraculous, but tiny seedpods sprang up from the soil.

8   "Oh, Papa, I see!" I said. "Pumpkins!"

9   We had never grown pumpkins before, so I wondered how they got there and to what we owed our good fortune. I desperately hoped against hope that they would produce enough so that we wouldn't have to move from our farm to the city.

10   Recharged by this discovery, my papa began to research all about growing calabazas and became convinced that soon enough he could grow them as well as anyone else. He scraped together the money to buy some more pumpkin seeds, and he planted them and cared for them. His study and tireless work paid off, because before too long, they started to grow.

11   "How can we have pumpkins with no rain?" my mother asked, perplexed at the sight. My father assured her that we could afford to irrigate the field in the small area where the pumpkins grew. "We can do it," he said to my mother with certainty, and my mother agreed that we had nothing to lose by trying.

12   For the next few months, my father continued to care for his calabazas. He worked the soil, and he watered it until the vines grew aggressively over the ground. To the surprise of all of us, the pumpkins flourished. By October, the fields seemed to have exploded. We had more calabazas than we had ever imagined! We sold some of them; then we sold some more.

13   Soon after, my mother started making *empanadas*.[2] Empanadas calabazas. She made mouthwatering *papadzules*,[3] too. And we made *pepitas*[4]—lots of pepitas! My brothers and sisters and I took overflowing bagfuls of pepitas, and we sold them at the nearest tourist market, where shoppers gobbled them up greedily. "We need Tía Olga," my mother decided, "and we need her now." Her sister could make empanadas calabazas better than anyone my mother knew. Yet Tía Olga had grown accustomed to her work at the dulcería, and for the time being, at least, she insisted that Marta needed her.

[2]**empanadas** baked pastries with filling
[3]**papadzules** a soft taco dish filled with hard-boiled eggs and a pumpkin seed–tomato sauce
[4]**pepitas** toasted pumpkin seeds

14   Still, Tía Olga had an idea that neither my mother nor my father had considered. "A pumpkin festival," she suggested. My father loved the idea of a pumpkin festival, or *la festival calabaza*, and my mother agreed. Tía Olga promised that if they planned it, she would come home to help. So over the next six weeks, we made preparations for the festival. By day, my father and my older brothers spent long hours in the field, while at night we all planned the festival for the harvest moon, the day at which the moon would be its biggest and brightest. My young sisters, Pilar and Elena, made signs to post in the streets and at the tourist market, while I had chosen something different to do.

15   I had decided to make a pumpkin patch by clearing out a circular area of land on the side of our house and next to our fields. I carried hay from the barn to my pumpkin patch, and I spread it around on the ground. Then I rolled in a few hay bales. I took the fencing from the garden, enclosing three sides of my pumpkin patch. Then I sat down on a hay bale and imagined what it would look like filled with pumpkins. In southern Mexico, the pumpkins come in all shades of green, yellow, orange, and even white.

16   Once Tía Olga was convinced that we were working hard and carefully to prepare for the festival, she packed up her children, and just as she promised, they took the bus from Nuevo Laredo back home. She brought with her a recipe for *dulces de calabazas*, pumpkin candy, from the dulcería.

17   "A gift from Marta," she told Mama. Mama was visibly touched by the gift. She had never known Marta to give her recipes to anyone; she considered her dulces de calabazas her prize.

What theme about family do the first two paragraphs on this page express? 

Do you think the pumpkin festival will be a success? Why or why not?

18   "Thank you to Marta," my mother said, smiling, with a **delicate** laugh in her voice that I remembered from long ago and hadn't heard in ages. Mama and Tía Olga together made dulces de calabazas, while the rest of us carried pumpkins to the pumpkin patch and set up an impressive display. We carved some of them into jack-o'-lanterns, while Mama and Tía Olga made more and more dulces de calabazas. In the twilight, our whole family gathered in the cozy kitchen and made bags and bags of pepitas. We talked and laughed like old times, and we marveled at the thought of the seeds that had miraculously sprung from the seemingly barren ground.

19   Mama said that the seeds *were* miraculous because they brought her so much joy—they allowed us to save our farm, and they brought her sister and her family back home. Tía Olga had to laugh because she was never good at keeping secrets for very long. And because Mama could read her like a book, she knew exactly what was on her mind.

20   "You planted those seeds, didn't you?" she asked Tía Olga knowingly.

21   That was when I remembered: Tía Olga had planted the seeds. It was sometime back in July, late at night when she thought all of us were sleeping, dreaming of better times. I had been **restless** and unable to drift off like the rest of them. From my bed, I had heard something in the yard. It was Tía Olga. I had watched her from the window and seen her planting seeds and heard her talk to them. "Grow, little seeds, grow," she had said. "Bring the family together again."

22   Tía Olga must have had faith that the seeds would grow and flourish and that everything would work out in the end, when she would bring her family back home to stay. When the rains returned, we knew that no future drought could harm what we had grown: both pumpkins and stronger family ties.

Vocabulary: Denotation and Connotation

All words have **denotations**, which you can find in their dictionary definitions. They might also have **connotations**. These are the positive, negative, or neutral thoughts and feelings that you connect with the words. For example, Tía Olga not telling anyone about planting the pumpkin seeds was *mischievous*. The word has a positive, sweet, playful connotation. How would it be different if the writer said she was *tricky* or *sneaky*?

Try It Read the following sentence from "La Festival Calabaza."

> My papa **mentioned** a few times that he might find work in Nuevo Laredo or Reynosa, as well.

Discuss **What is the denotation of the word *mentioned*? What thoughts and emotions does the word bring up? Is its connotation positive, negative, or neutral?**

Find these words in "La Festival Calabaza." Using a dictionary, write each word's denotation. Then write its connotation: positive, negative, or neutral.

1. **bond,** p. 16 _______________________________

____

2. **sparse,** p. 17 _______________________________

____

3. **delicate,** p. 20 _______________________________

____

4. **restless,** p. 20 _______________________________

____

Respond to Text: Comparing Themes

"Aaron's Future Friend" and "La Festival Calabaza" are both fiction. "Aaron's Future Friend" is a science fiction story because it imagines a future full of advances in science and technology. Some characters may not even be human, and the settings and events are astonishing. "La Festival Calabaza" is realistic fiction. The characters, settings, and events are true to life, even though the author has made them up.

Even though a story's theme is expressed through its characters, setting, and events, science fiction and realistic fiction can often have similar themes. Elements that greatly influence the themes of "Aaron's Future Friend" and "La Festival Calabaza" are the geographic location and cultures in each of the stories.

Try It Think about the themes of each story.

> **Discuss** **What themes might you find in science fiction stories? What themes might you find in realistic fiction? Include in your discussion the culture and the physical settings in both "Aaron's Future Friend" and "La Festival Calabaza," as well as the events that make up the stories' plots.**

On Your Own Compare the themes of "Aaron's Future Friend" and "La Festival Calabaza." Include details from both stories to support your comparison. Use the next page to help you plan your response. Then write your paragraph on a separate sheet of paper.

Checklist for a Good Response

A good paragraph

✔ states the themes found in each story.

✔ explains how the themes are similar and different.

✔ includes discussion of how the geographic locations and cultures affect the themes.

✔ uses details from the stories to support the response.

✔ includes a topic sentence, supporting ideas, and a concluding statement.

My Comparison of Themes

1. **Topic Sentence** Your first sentence should include this information: A

    major theme of "Aaron's Future Friend" is _________________________,

    while the major theme of "La Festival Calabaza" is _________________

    ____.

2. **Detail Sentences** These sentences should give details that support the
    themes you've chosen. Use this chart to organize your ideas.

	"Aaron's Future Friend"	**"La Festival Calabaza"**
Setting (including geographic location)		
Culture		

3. **Concluding Sentence** Your concluding sentence makes a final statement
    on the themes of the stories.

    ____

    ____

    ____

On a separate sheet of paper, write your paragraph.

Read on Your Own

Read the story independently three times, using the skills you have learned. Then answer the Comprehension Check questions.

First Read — Practice the first-read skills you learned in this lesson.

Second Read — Practice the second-read skills you learned in this lesson.

Third Read — Think critically about the story.

High Hopes

Theme Think about the details of the grain elevator and how they might contribute to the life lesson the author wants to convey.

Story Elements: Characters Think about how Natalia's thoughts and actions reveal what she is like. Circle details that show her personality. Details in the first paragraph have been circled for you.

1   Natalia was a country girl, but she was thrilled to be moving to the city. In her eyes, New York was the city of all cities. People dreamed big in New York City because the city inspired them, but Natalia dreamed big because she was full of ambition. She dreamed of being a famous architect someday and imagined designing towering skyscrapers.

2   In her town in southern Illinois, the tallest building around was the grain elevator by the railroad tracks that had ceased to operate nearly twenty years earlier. And as Natalia learned later, it wasn't even big in grain-elevator terms. Still, Natalia walked by that grain elevator every day on her way to school, and every time she passed it, she imagined how she could improve it.

3   Natalia had found a creative outlet in designing a garden, and if she and her family had stayed in Illinois, she would have expanded the plans into something magnificent by creating the actual garden. Knowing that she would have no use for the plans in New York, however, she crumpled them up and tossed them into the recycling bin. "I would never have thrown those away," her mother said when she saw what her daughter had done. "I still have that adorable poem about a kitten you wrote when you were in first grade."

4   Natalia rolled her eyes. Like her father, she was not a saver. Her mother most definitely was. Natalia could hardly believe her mother had gotten rid of all the things she did in preparation for their move. It must have killed her! As far as Natalia could tell, she had sold or given away most everything but the furniture and dishes.

5   "There simply isn't room for anything but the necessities," Natalia's father had explained to his wife. And he was right. Natalia was shocked when she arrived in New York and saw the size of their apartment. Her mother walked straight into the kitchen and started sizing up the **pantry** to figure out where she would fit groceries.

6   Natalia wasn't concerned about the groceries, but she was concerned about the tiny park nearby, in the middle of the city, surrounded by pavement. "Wait till you see Central Park. It's one of the largest urban public parks in the world," Natalia's dad said. "We'll go there later this week."

7   In time, Natalia began to visit Central Park more and more. Once she began to make friends at school, they went with her. Usually, they walked rather than take the subway so they could see all the city sights. Twice, they took a ferry to Staten Island to view the Statue of Liberty, and they even went to the top of the Empire State Building once to get a bird's-eye view of all the skyscrapers in Manhattan.

8   Alima Sharif became Natalia's closest friend, and before very long, the two were inseparable. Alima had lived in the city all her life. Natalia **confessed** her dream of becoming an architect and designing a skyscraper, and Alima shared her own dream of living off the land. When Natalia told her about the garden she designed in Illinois, Alima seemed almost sad, and she said that life in the country sounded so relaxed and carefree.

9   Natalia started to get used to the city, but she still fondly remembered her plans for her garden and wished that she had kept them. She shared that thought with her parents one night, and her mother and father smiled at each other. Natalia sighed dramatically and stormed out of the room. When her parents smiled at each other without talking, that usually meant they had a secret—or they were suppressing the urge to say, "I told you so."

Draw and Support Inferences How do you infer Natalia feels when her mother and father smile at each other? Underline details that clue you in to her feelings. The first one has been done for you.

10   "Natalia, there's something I want to show you," her father said later, "something I discovered just the other day." Natalia, her mother, and her father took the stairs to the rooftop, and they looked out over the city. They could see many of the skyscrapers of midtown Manhattan. The sunlight poured down, and the air felt fresh.

11   "I don't get it. The view's fantastic," said Natalia, "but there's nothing remarkable about this rooftop."

12   "Not yet," her father said, smiling ear to ear, "but let me tell you what once was. During World War II, most of our money went to the war effort, and food was in short supply. So, many Americans decided that they would grow their own food, to allow more money and food to go toward the war effort. They built gardens, which they called Victory gardens, anywhere they could make space. Well, the manager of this building told me the other day that one of the most successful Victory gardens in New York City was right here on this roof."

13   Natalia grew wide-eyed, and her heart began to race excitedly.

14   Her father continued, "You know what else the building manager said? He said he's been wanting to honor the memory of that garden by building another one just as grand."

15   "Are you saying we could help him build it?" asked Natalia.

16   "That's what I suggested," her father replied, "and he loved the idea."

17   "Now I wish I hadn't thrown away my garden plan!" Natalia exclaimed.

18   "Oh, I wouldn't worry about that," her mother remarked, turning to exchange that silent smile once again with her husband. This time, however, instead of annoying Natalia, the smile thrilled and delighted her. Maybe that smile wasn't an "I told you so" smile after all. Perhaps this time the smile concealed a secret. Natalia had a feeling her garden plan was waiting in their apartment, and she could hardly wait to tell Alima. It looked like Alima wouldn't have to wait long to experience "living off the land" herself after all.

✔ Comprehension Check

1. Write two or three sentences to summarize the story's plot.

2. What is the climax of the story?

3. Describe one major theme of the story.

4. What is the most likely reason Natalia dreams of redesigning the grain elevator? Provide a detail from the story to support your response.

5. How do Natalia's feelings about designing a garden change over the
   course of the story?

____

____

____

6. Read this sentence from the story.

   **Natalia confessed her dream of becoming an architect and
   designing a skyscraper, and Alima shared her own dream of
   living off the land.**

   The word *confessed* has both a denotation and connotation.

   What is the denotation? _______________________________________

   What is the connotation? ______________________________________

   What does the author suggest about Natalia by saying that she *confessed*
   her dream?

____

____

____

7. Read this sentence from the story.

   **Her mother walked straight into the kitchen and started sizing
   up the pantry to figure out where she would fit groceries.**

   Circle the context clues that help you figure out the meaning of the
   word *pantry*.

Drama

Drama is the name for stories written to be performed by actors on a stage. Dialogue is very important to drama, since the stories are told mostly through words the actors speak. The actors also follow stage directions, which tell them where to move on stage and how to speak and physically behave. These directions are usually in parentheses in the text. Dramas are broken into acts and scenes, which structure the stories. Like other types of fiction, dramas can be tragic, comic, romantic, or any combination of these. What sort of drama do you think is pictured here? How can you tell?

Skills Focus

The Love Story of Ch'unhyang, Act 1

Draw and Support Inferences

Figurative Language

The Love Story of Ch'unhyang, Act 2

Summarize   **Dramatic Structure**

Practice the Skill

 Draw and Support Inferences

An **inference** is a conclusion you draw from the details of a text. For instance, if a character in a story dresses warmly before stepping outside, you might infer that the weather outside is cold. An inference can also be made from more subtle clues. Suppose a character scowls at the words another character speaks. You can infer that the person who is scowling disagrees with what is being said. When you make an inference, you should be able to support it with evidence from the text.

Try It Read this paragraph.

Alec grew more terrified with every thump of the approaching robot. But then he pulled out the glittering box the old man had given him. Touching the golden buttons, he knew he had nothing to fear.

Discuss **Think about drawing inferences. What inference can you draw about the "glittering box"? What support from the text can you find for this inference? Underline the support.**

Read on to find another example of inference.

Alec stood on the jagged rock, high above the smoking ruin of the fortress. He gripped the box tightly in his fist as a slow smile spread across his lips.

Discuss **What can you infer about Alec's feelings about the ruined fortress? What evidence is there in the text to support this? Underline the evidence.**

As you read, complete the Draw Inferences Chart on page 261.

Practice the Skill

Figurative language is language used in a special way to convey an idea. The most common types of figurative language are metaphor and simile. **Metaphors** compare two unlike things by saying that one *is* the other. For example, *Her smile is a ray of sunshine* is a metaphor. **Similes** compare two unlike things by using words such as *like* or *as*. For example, *The runner sped down the track like a cheetah* is a simile. Another type of figurative language is **hyperbole**, in which exaggeration is used to make a point or for humorous effect. For example, *Losing the match hurt worse than a thousand bee stings* is an example of hyperbole. Figures of speech can be more than just one thing. For example, *Patrick jumped away from the cookies like a frightened cat* is both a simile and hyperbole.

Try It Read this paragraph.

The Gryphons' defeat at the state soccer championship was like the end of the world to them. Their striker had been a lightning bolt, but his attempts all missed the net. Meanwhile, the other team's defense had been as solid as the Great Wall of China.

Discuss What figurative language is used in this paragraph? Circle the examples of figurative language, and then tell what type of figurative language each example is. Remember that a figure of speech can often be more than one thing. For example, a simile can also be an exaggeration, or hyperbole.

As you read, record your answers to questions about figurative language on the Close Reading Worksheet on page 262.

The Love Story of
Ch'unhyang,
Act 1

CAST OF CHARACTERS

LEE DORYONG, a law student

PANGJA, servant of Lee Doryong

CH'UNHYANG, a young woman

WOLMAE, mother of Ch'unhyang

PYON, the new magistrate

AIDE, assistant to Pyon

GUARD

BEGGAR

Scene 1

Find two examples of figurative language on this page. Circle them.

SETTING: *A lane in a medieval Korean city. Through the fence that runs along one side of the lane, a girl can be seen sitting on a swing—Ch'unhyang, the beautiful young daughter of a great court official, Wolmae. Walking up the lane is Lee Doryong, a young law student and the son of the county* **magistrate**—*a sort of combination judge and chief of police—with his servant, Pangja, at his side.*

1 LEE DORYONG: Whew, I've been at those books so long, Pangja, it's like my brain has turned to cheese!

2 PANGJA: Too much study—it's unhealthy, my lord. The mind craves . . . my Lord Doryong?

3 LEE DORYONG: (*He's seen Ch'unhyang and stands staring, not hearing Pangja.*) What is this girl's name, who is so beautiful the sight of her could melt stone?

4   PANGJA: I know not, my lord, but I'll ask her if you wish—you seem quite stricken.

5   LEE DORYONG: Wait, give me pen and paper, quickly. (*scribbles something down*) Give her this, and we'll see what it conjures. (*winks*)

(*Pangja appears on the other side of the fence and hands the note to Ch'unhyang. She smiles as she reads it and then strolls over to Lee Doryong, who is standing in the lane.*)

6   CH'UNHYANG: So, I see you are a poet: (*reading*) "Hair like summer rain, face unruffled as a pond, skin like dew—I must see more of you."

7   LEE DORYONG: A trifle . . . not equal to its subject, I assure you.

8   CH'UNHYANG: (*smiling*) A trifle, yes, to be sure. How much time did you spend on it?

9   LEE DORYONG: (*looking at Pangja, who shrugs*) Not as long as I should have, clearly.

10   CH'UNHYANG: (*looking down at the poem*) It's very . . . watery. And unless summer rain is black as a raven, my hair isn't like it. Still . . . (*handing him the poem*) revise it now that you know me better, and when I feel you've got the hang of love poetry, I will have my mother, Wolmae, summon you.

11   LEE DORYONG: (*to Pangja, as Ch'unhyang walks away*) Who knew she was a poet?

Scene 2

SETTING: *Inside the house of Ch'unhyang's mother, Wolmae, several weeks later. Lee Doryong and Pangja stand before Wolmae, who is seated.*

12   WOLMAE: My daughter says you have become quite the romantic poet.

13   LEE DORYONG: If I have become anything in these past weeks, madam, it is humble.

Make an inference about how Ch'unhyang has judged Lee Doryong's poetry, and write it in the first circle on the **Draw Inferences Chart**. Then list the details that support the inference in the box below it.

What similes does Lee Doryong use in his poem?

Why do you think Ch'unhyang is so critical of the figurative language Lee Doryong uses?

14   WOLMAE: Indeed, Ch'unhyang can be a harsh critic—but I believe a fair one.

15   LEE DORYONG: None fairer, Madam Wolmae, and it is that fairness in every sense that has brought me here to ask for your daughter's hand in marriage.

16   WOLMAE: (*smiling*) So quickly. It is enough to make one wonder who here has mastered the art of courtship. (*Pangja smiles, too.*)

17   LEE DORYONG: Without any question it is your daughter who has mastered me, but then, I have not the looks or tongue or skill with a pen to win anything but a law degree. However, I promise to get that degree and to look after your daughter as she deserves. She might wish me a better poet, but I assure you, Ch'unhyang will never find a better protector, Madam Wolmae, than him who trembles before you now. *He*, I mean. *He* who trembles before you now.

18   WOLMAE: (*rising*) Then consider that you have my permission to ask for my daughter's hand, though that hand is a gift that only Ch'unhyang herself may grant.

19   LEE DORYONG: Then I'll lose no time in asking. Can you tell me where I might find her?

20   WOLMAE: Today she was to visit the Gwanghallu Pavilion.

Scene 3

SETTING: *The Gwanghallu **Pavilion**. Lee Doryong and Pangja are searching this public square for Ch'unhyang, and they finally spot her gossiping and laughing with some other young women.*

21   LEE DORYONG: (*rushing up to Ch'unhyang*) Ch'unhyang, I'm so happy I found you … I've just been to see your mother and …

22 CH'UNHYANG: (*to the ladies*) Does any among you know this **uncouth** young man? (*The ladies laugh behind their fans.*) To speak to a young woman in a public place is so uncivil. Where are his manners?

23 PANGJA: (*seeing Lee Doryong's face fall*) You must get her alone, my lord, it's the only way. (*to Lee Doryong, so all can hear*) Let us go see the peacocks, my Lord Doryong, for I believe they are in full feather this afternoon. (*Pangja and Lee Doryong walk away.*)

24 LEE DORYONG: (*whispering to Pangja*) Full feather? What on earth are you babbling about?

25 PANGJA: (*whispering*) Trust me, my lord, it doesn't matter.

(*Moments later, at the peacock cages, Lee Doryong and Pangja are pretending to admire the birds.*)

26 CH'UNHYANG: (*arriving with a smile on her face*) Thank heavens your servant has some idea of proper manners. Imagine if you had—

27 LEE DORYONG: (*taking her hand*) I understand I'm uncouth and no poet, though I imagine I've improved, if only because I was so horrible when I commenced. Be that as it may, I love you, Ch'unhyang, and I must ask your hand now or I may never have the chance again.

28 CH'UNHYANG: (*looking genuinely upset*) Never have the chance again? What? You ask for my hand, yet you steal yours away so soon?

29 LEE DORYONG: My father has been appointed to the capital, to the court at Hanyang, to serve the king as chief inspector.

30 CH'UNHYANG: Stay and marry me, and we can live with Mother.

31 LEE DORYONG: Ch'unhyang, my father needs my help, and I must complete my education. We leave as soon as the new magistrate arrives to replace my father, but you would do me the greatest happiness by—

32 CH'UNHYANG: (*kissing him*) You mad fool, of course I'll be your wife. We will marry the moment you return . . . which will be when?

33 LEE DORYONG: (*looking into her eyes*) As soon as can be humanly arranged, but it may be a year or more. My father wishes to grant me work that will advance me faster than any studies, so I may become an actual investigator. But I will write you, day and night, and as a special gift to you, I will not try to make it rhyme.

34 CH'UNHYANG: (*speaking loud and defiantly*) I swear by these full-feathered peacocks, before your good servant Pangja, and before everyone in Gwanghallu Pavilion, that I will wait for you, Lee Doryong, and that no other man will claim me. (*They embrace, weeping.*)

Scene 4

SETTING: *The Gwanghallu Pavilion on the following day. The new magistrate, Pyon, splendidly dressed, is arriving in a chair carried by servants. The important people of the city have gathered in the pavilion to greet him, including Ch'unhyang and her mother, Wolmae.*

35   PYON: (*to an aide*) Who is that lovely girl?

36   AIDE: Her name is Ch'unhyang, Lord Magistrate, the daughter of the great court official Madam Wolmae—the woman beside her.

37   PYON: Hmm, what better match could she desire for her daughter than myself, the county magistrate?

38   AIDE: They say she is betrothed, Lord Magistrate. A love match. A bad poet but a good man, the son of—

39   PYON: (*looking angrily at the aide*) **Betrothals** mean nothing. A betrothal is merely a promise of marriage. Who should know the law better than a judge? (*looking back at Ch'unhyang*) She will be mine, I tell you, whether her beloved be a wicked man and a marvelous poet or a silly peacock. I swear I will have this woman to be my wife or she will wind up in chains in the city's deepest dungeon.

40   WOLMAE: (*to her daughter*) See how Magistrate Pyon gazes at you.

41   CH'UNHYANG: Like some wolf, I think, who's missed his lunch, or a hungry beggar dreaming of a banquet he'll never get to enjoy.

42   WOLMAE: You'd be best beware of that one, daughter. From the way he carries himself and that pack that swarms around him, I'd say he intends no good for anyone.

Vocabulary: Context Clues

When you come across a word or term that you don't recognize, you may be able to find clues to its meaning in the words or sentences nearby. Such clues are called context clues. **Context clues** are any words or phrases in a reading that help you determine a new word's meaning.

Try It Read this setting description for a scene in *The Love Story of Ch'unhyang.*

SETTING: *The Gwanghallu* **Pavilion.** *Lee Doryong and Pangja are searching this public square for Ch'unhyang, and they finally spot her gossiping and laughing with some other young women.*

Discuss **Look for clues to the meaning of the word *pavilion* as it is used in the play. What clues did you find? What do you think *pavilion* means?**

The following are some difficult words found in *The Love Story of Ch'unhyang.* Find the words in the play. Look for the context clues that help you understand what each word means. Then write a definition of the word and use it in a sentence.

1. **magistrate,** p. 32 _______________________________

____

2. **uncouth,** p. 35 _______________________________

____

3. **betrothal,** p. 36 _______________________________

____

Practice the Skill

When you write a **summary**, you identify the important details in a story and put them in the proper order to briefly state what happens. First, look at the text carefully and decide what the most important events are. Then, consider how things begin, how they end, and the most important things that happen in the middle that connect the beginning to the end.

A summary should include only the most important details. Important details are those without which your summary would not make sense or would fail to convey the point the author intended. A summary should never include your personal opinion or bias on a topic.

Try It Read this scene.

Orlando's Big Break

SETTING: *a baseball game in a small town. The afternoon is sunny and warm. Cliff is the catcher, and Orlando is the pitcher. They are talking on the mound between pitches.*

CLIFF: I heard that guy outside the right-field fence is a talent scout. (*struggling to conceal his envy*) He's been watching you like a hawk.

ORLANDO: (*shaking his head*) Get real. He's just there because his truck axle broke on that bump like everyone's does.

CLIFF: So you don't think he's here for you? I'm just saying—pitch like you mean it.

(*The other team cannot get a hit. By the ninth inning, the small crowd is anxious to see local history made. A pitcher finishing a game with no hits against him is rare. The final batter hits the ball straight up.*)

CLIFF: (*looking up*) I got it! (*He catches the ball and looks at it. He saved Orlando's no-hitter despite his jealousy of Orlando. He holds up the ball in triumph.*) We won!

Discuss **What words would you use to create a summary of this scene? Which details would you include, and which would you leave out? Why?**

As you read, complete the Summary and Important Details Chart on page 263.

Practice the Skill

 Dramatic Structure

Dramatic structure refers to how a writer shapes and tells the story in a play, or drama. A play is made up of acts, which are like chapters in novels. Each act is broken up into a series of scenes that advance the story in some way. Each scene helps the author move the story forward, heighten the drama, further develop the characters, or communicate the key themes of the play. Some scenes will contribute more to introducing the setting of the play, while others will introduce the conflict, resolve it, and show the conclusion.

Playwrights use acts and scenes, among other things, as intervals between which the play's setting can change, whether that involves location, time, or the characters on the stage. As you read, notice act and scene numbers that indicate a change in place or time.

Dialogue tags tell you who is speaking, and elements such as stage directions tell you how characters say their lines and what they are physically doing as they talk. Setting descriptions help you visualize what the setting looks like and any physical information the actors are meant to communicate. Don't forget the larger picture, too; as the play unfolds, there will be themes to follow and characters to keep an eye on.

Try It Reread the drama about a baseball game on the previous page.

Discuss **What aspects of dramatic structure did the author use? Is this a whole play, an act, or a scene? How does knowing this help you understand what to expect from the information you read? What information do you get solely from the stage directions? Put a box around that information.**

As you read, record your answers to questions about dramatic structure on the Close Reading Worksheet on page 264.

The Love Story of
Ch'unhyang,
Act 2

Scene 1

What is the setting of scene 1? How does this scene add to the development of the story?

SETTING: *The courtroom of new county magistrate Pyon. His hangers-on surround him on his raised platform, while servants fan him. He has summoned Ch'unhyang's mother, Wolmae, who stands before him.*

1   PYON: This has gone on for longer than I care to discuss, so I have brought you to my court to make it clear that I can no longer tolerate your daughter's behavior—or yours.

2   WOLMAE: Our behavior?

3   PYON: You have failed to honor my repeated **requests** for your daughter's hand in marriage. If I, the county magistrate, desire a thing, then it stands to reason it should be so, don't you think? (*His courtiers nod vigorously and his fanners fan harder.*)

4   WOLMAE: (*seething*) Ch'unhyang's hand is already promised to another, so even if she wished to, she could not possibly comply with your demand.

5   PYON: (*looks to either side, shrugs*) If she's already promised to another, as you say, why do I not see this oh-so-fortunate suitor? Surely the whole world knows by now that it is my desire to wed Ch'unhyang, and yet this devoted young man is nowhere in sight. Perhaps he has changed his mind.

6   WOLMAE: I will go to my daughter and try to convince her, but if she decides against you—

7   PYON: If she decides against me, Ch'unhyang will be thrown in the darkest prison in the city. (*rubbing his hands together*) And that's the least of it—things will not go well for her.

8   WOLMAE: Magistrate Pyon, although I cannot say how, I vow that if even a tiny measure of harm comes to my daughter, things will not go well for *you*.

9   PYON: (*sneering*) We'll see whose threat has teeth. You have a week to convince her, and I suggest you don't dally for one instant, as her future is at stake.

Scene 2

SETTING: *Inside a filthy prison. Ch'unhyang is alone.*

10   CH'UNHYANG: (*looking out a barred window*) Oh, how I would love one of your poems right now, Lee Doryong. I'd simply read it over and over until the paper was worn smooth and the ink faded, and then I'd read it again. Pyon can starve me and beat me, but he cannot drive out my love for you.

11   WOLMAE: (*entering the cell with a guard at her side*) Ch'unhyang, my daughter, you look absolutely terrible.

12   CH'UNHYANG: (*smiles, a little bitterly*) Really? I'd have thought that Pyon's filthy prison would be as excellent for the complexion as any mud bath.

13   WOLMAE: Listen, my daughter, I was wrong to leave the decision to you and to abide by whatever you chose, no matter the danger. It's obvious now that Pyon will stop at nothing to make you his wife, and in truth, you are merely pledged to Lee Doryong—he has not taken your hand in marriage.

14   CH'UNHYANG: Stop, Mother, I refuse to listen to another word.

15   WOLMAE: (*shaking her head*) The whole county is alive with stories of Pyon's cruelties—he is no servant of the people. I only pray that word spreads to Hanyang, that the king hears of your situation, and that you may be released.

16   CH'UNHYANG: Yes, well, I believe it's too late for me, but if someone should profit from all this misery, let it be the enemies of that beast Pyon. That fat troll must be vanquished!

(*Mother and daughter hug.*)

Scene 3

SETTING: *The prison laundry. Ch'unhyang and several other women are cleaning clothes in big vats beneath barred windows.*

17   GUARD: (*dragging in a raggedly dressed beggar who's raving like a maniac*) You women, listen up, this mad beggar was found wandering the city streets—see that his clothes are deloused. But mind you, he's crazy as a loon and twice as loud.

18   CH'UNHYANG: (*to the beggar*) Relax, we'll be gentle with you.

19   BEGGAR: Oh wah di doo, doo di dee, wah di doo di dee. (*keeps chanting until everyone leaves, then whispers to Ch'unhyang*) Please, you must help me. I'm looking for a girl named Ch'unhyang—and I swear to you, I'm not mad, nor am I a beggar.

20   CH'UNHYANG: (*suspicious*) What do you want with Ch'unhyang?

21   BEGGAR: That I cannot tell you.

22   CH'UNHYANG: In honor of the one I truly love, I'll do anything to help another. Especially one so direct, so honest.

23   BEGGAR: And yet clearly, I am attempting a deception.

24   CH'UNHYANG: (*laughing and kissing him*) Your deception is no more **sophisticated** than your poetry, Lee Doryong. Why on earth are you here?

25 LEE DORYONG: I'm serving undercover for my father, the chief **inspector**. He gave me this badge. (*shows her the badge and gives her a sneaky smirk*)

26 CH'UNHYANG: That's wonderful, but I'm afraid you are too late, for tomorrow night is Pyon's birthday banquet. He plans to give me one last chance to marry him, and when I don't . . . he'll execute me. Lee Doryong?

27 LEE DORYONG: Yes, my love?

28 CH'UNHYANG: How is it possible you didn't recognize me, Lee Doryong?

29 LEE DORYONG: You know how you never hid your opinion of my poetry? (*Ch'unhyang nods.*) Well, to be equally blunt, you look awful— what has Pyon done to you in this dreadful place?

30 CH'UNHYANG: Nothing you couldn't undo . . . (*sniffling, hugs him*) . . . if I weren't doomed.

31 LEE DORYONG: You've already told me everything I need to save you, but you must put your faith in me. Do nothing to reveal my identity, and go along with everything Pyon says, right to the last moment. Listen, there are things I must arrange—my servant Pangja will do everything I ask, and everything will soon be in order. (*rubbing some filth from her face*) We make quite the couple, don't we?

Underline details you would use to summarize scene 3. Then, write the summary and the details on the **Summary and Important Details Chart**.

How might the reappearance of Lee Doryong in this scene affect the events of the play?

Underline important details from the text and record them in your **Summary and Important Details Chart.** Then write a summary of scene 4.

SETTING: *The courtyard of the Hall of Justice. Pyon's birthday banquet is in full swing. Prisoners are being used as servants—including Lee Doryong, still dressed as a beggar. The guests are chanting for Pyon to make a speech.*

32 PYON: Guards, bring in my biggest present! (*Ch'unhyang is hauled before him in chains.*) Now, my girl, the time has finally arrived for you to grant me your willing hand in marriage.

33 CH'UNHYANG: Never.

34 PYON: You understand that if you refuse me, you will be executed instantly. (*Ch'unhyang nods.*) Then let the execution proceed!

35 LEE DORYONG: (*pulls back his hood and whips out his badge*) Magistrate Pyon, I hereby arrest you in the name of the king!

(*Pangja enters, leading the king's troops, who seize Pyon.*)

36 PYON: What? I *am* the law—you cannot arrest the law!

37 LEE DORYONG: (*snaps out a scroll*) According to Article 19A of the Legal Code, it is a crime for a magistrate to condemn any prisoner to death without the king's agreement.

38 CH'UNHYANG: (*runs to Lee Doryong*) Lee, you saved me!

39 LEE DORYONG: No, you saved yourself. By staying true right to the end, you forced that evil villain to convict himself.

40 CH'UNHYANG: I promise to stay true to you always, but you must never leave me again.

41 LEE DORYONG: Never. (*kisses her*) I swear by all the peacocks of Gwanghallu, I will honor and protect you every day of your life . . . but the poetry I leave to you.

Interpret

Why does Lee Doryong say that he will leave the poetry to Ch'unhyang?

Vocabulary: Understand Common Latin and Greek Roots

Common **Latin and Greek roots** are basic word parts that come to us from these ancient languages. Often we don't even notice these word parts are there. In the word *patronize*, for instance, the Latin word *pater*, meaning "father," is present in the root *patr* and helps create its meaning—to "grant something," as a powerful father would do. Likewise, the word *matronly* means "to appear or behave like an older woman or a mother." You can probably guess the root here—it is *matr*, from the Latin word *mater*, which means "mother."

Try It Read this sentence from *The Love Story of Ch'unhyang*.

> CH'UNHYANG: (*laughing and kissing him*) Your deception is no more **sophisticated** than your poetry, Lee Doryong.

The word *sophisticated* has a Greek root, *soph*, meaning "wise."

> Discuss **Brainstorm all the words you can think of with the root *soph*.**

The following words appear in *The Love Story of Ch'unhyang*. Underline the Latin or Greek root in each word, and see how the word is used in the drama. Then explain how the meaning of the root leads to the meaning of the word. Use a dictionary to look up the word's root and meaning.

1. **requests,** p. 40 (root *ques*) ______________________________

____

2. **maniac,** p. 42 (root *mania*) ______________________________

____

3. **inspector,** p. 43 (root *spec*) ______________________________

____

Respond to Text: Compare and Contrast

In *The Love Story of Ch'unhyang*, both Lee Doryong and Ch'unhyang use figurative language, but they tend to use it for different purposes.

Try It Think about how the two main characters use figurative language in the drama.

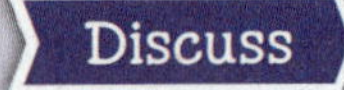

At which point in the play does Lee Doryong first use figurative language? Whom does he address, and what is he trying to accomplish? About whom does Ch'unhyang use her own figurative language? What do these uses of figurative language have in common? How do the sentiments that each character expresses by using figurative language differ?

On Your Own Write a paragraph that compares and contrasts the ways Ch'unhyang and Lee Doryong use figurative language in *The Love Story of Ch'unhyang*. Include details from the drama to support your conclusions. Use the next page to help you plan your response. Then, write your paragraph on a separate sheet of paper.

Checklist for a Good Response

A good paragraph

✔ clearly states the comparisons being made.

✔ explains the ways in which the use of figurative language is similar or different.

✔ defines the type of figurative language being used.

✔ includes details from the text to support your conclusions.

✔ shows your understanding of the information.

✔ includes a topic sentence, supporting ideas, and a concluding statement.

My Comparison and Contrast

1. **Topic Sentence** Include this information in your first sentence:
   Based on what I read in *The Love Story of Ch'unhyang,* I conclude that

   ____

   ______________ and also that ___________________________________

   ____.

2. **Detail Sentences** The sentences of your paragraph should provide details
   that explain your conclusions. Use this chart to organize your ideas.

Conclusion	Details That Support My Conclusion

3. **Concluding Sentence** Your final sentence should restate your conclusions
   with a new twist.

   ____

   ____

   ____

On a separate sheet of paper, write your paragraph.

Read on Your Own

Read the drama independently three times, using the skills you have learned. Then answer the Comprehension Check questions.

First Read — Practice the first-read skills you learned in this lesson.

Second Read — Practice the second-read skills you learned in this lesson.

Third Read — Think critically about the drama.

Lost and Found

CAST OF CHARACTERS

MOTHER, mother of Keisha and Leo

GRANDFATHER, father of Mother, grandfather to Keisha and Leo

KEISHA, daughter of Mother

LEO, son of Mother

Scene 1

Summarize Think about how you would summarize the first scene of the play.

SETTING: *A grandfather, his daughter, and her two children are making their way through the winding streets of Cancún, Mexico, but they are hopelessly lost.*

1 MOTHER: (*quietly, to her father*) Dad, we've got to get back to the ship—the cruise director said Cancún was only a stopover! We've only got an hour to return to the dock and—

2 GRANDFATHER: (*handing her a GPS device*) It's a little messed up, but do what you can with it. I think I may have punched in the wrong coordinates, although I can't understand a word that lady says in the first place.

3 MOTHER: (*shaking the GPS*) She's speaking in Spanish, Dad, but it's OK—I think I remember enough Spanish to pull this off.

4 GRANDFATHER: Fine. In the meantime, I'll do what I can to help. (*turning to the children*) Now where was I? Forty years ago it was, forty years or *more*, I dare say—

5 KEISHA: No one says "dare say" anymore, Gramps!

6   LEO: (*giggling*) No one says "Gramps," either, Keisha!

7   GRANDFATHER: (*a little stung*) All right, kids, all right. As I was saying, I've been tangled up in some pretty tight spots before. So there we were—outmaneuvered, outmanned, and out of gas, drifting toward a great sucking whirlpool <u>as deep as a canyon</u>. I remember watching the bits of wood from our wrecked mast speeding toward that swirling pit of water. It was like a living thing, and we could feel its cool breath on our cheeks. I'd never been so terrified in my life—I was a trembling mouse!

(*Keisha and Leo now riveted*)

Scene 2

SETTING: *They all head down a dark and winding street.*

8   MOTHER: (*taking Grandfather aside*) Dad, the GPS just died, and I have zero idea where we are.

9   GRANDFATHER: Well, did you see a landmark, anything?

10   MOTHER: (*as they hunch over the GPS*) No, I've just been staring at this screen, and now it's completely blank.

11   GRANDFATHER: (*flicking the screen*) It's dead, all right, so I say we keep heading downward—whatever streets we take, they should get us to the waterfront.

12   MOTHER: But the streets are level here.

13   GRANDFATHER: Then keep your eyes peeled for anything we saw from the ship.

Lost and Found   49

(*Keisha comes up and tugs Grandfather's shirt impatiently.*)

14 GRANDFATHER: But for now I've got business to take care of. Right?

15 MOTHER: (*winks*) Right, Dad.

16 KEISHA: Did you have the GPS programmed right *that* time, or were you as doomed then as we are now?

17 GRANDFATHER: I assure you, Keisha, I had every intention of putting in the right numbers, only the batteries had mysteriously died when the shark crashed into the cabin two days before.

18 LEO: But how did you end up escaping the whirlpool? Maybe whatever you did then could help us *now*.

19 GRANDFATHER: Yes, yes indeed. (*looking up, as if remembering*) Or maybe that story's not the best example after all, now that I think of it.

20 KEISHA: How about the time you were stuck at the top of a giant redwood tree?

21 LEO: Right, and it was on fire, as hot as lava, and you made a parachute out of a picnic blanket to escape, but then there was that grizzly bear lurking below . . .

22 MOTHER: (*peering at the GPS as if it's still working*) If I remember my Spanish at all, I think we should take a left here.

23 LEO: It just stands to reason that someone who can get out of a jam like that can get out of almost any kind of trouble.

24 GRANDFATHER: Well, Leo, there was the episode in the ancient temple not unlike the one we visited today—those passages were every bit as twisty as these streets! (*Mother is clearly leading, as she consults the GPS and nudges everyone around corners and down streets.*) So there I was—nearing the last row of temple steps, the ancient stone crumbling beneath my very feet as the jaguars circled and the jungle throbbed with—

<h1 align="center">Scene 3</h1>

SETTING: *They enter a plaza where a church can be seen in the distance.*

25 MOTHER: Hooray! The cathedral! I remember seeing it when we sailed into the harbor.

26 GRANDFATHER: (*gazing into the distance*) That's rather a long way away . . . how did we wind up this far from the port?

27 MOTHER: We just lost track of time . . . it doesn't matter. (*looks at her watch; then, as an aside to her father*) The thing is, now we only have half an hour to get back before the ship leaves port—we can do it, Dad, but I'm going to need you to keep it up with the kids. Until I saw that spire just now, I had no idea where we were . . .

28 GRANDFATHER: You can count on me, honey, but keep your eyes on that church . . .

29 MOTHER: This way, everyone! Toward that steeple! (*Everyone follows Mother, but the children are only paying attention to Grandfather.*)

30 LEO: (*to Grandfather*) The end of your story?

31 GRANDFATHER: (*gathering his wits*) Oh, yes. My story. Hmm, um . . .

32 KEISHA: You were getting chased by jaguars, up a rotten old temple.

33 LEO: So did they catch you? (*Grandfather just looks at Leo.*) Oh, right . . .

34 GRANDFATHER: Apparently the jaguars regarded the top of the temple as holy because, once we reached the summit, they went howling back into the jungle like scared kittens—but we were still lost.

35 LEO: So was there a map carved into the temple stones, or maybe from the top of the temple you could see your way out?

36 GRANDFATHER: Um, yes, something like that, but we had to creep along very quietly, don't you know—the jaguars and all.

37 KEISHA: Like we're creeping along now?

38 GRANDFATHER: Exactly so. Because sometimes the thing that saves you isn't a picnic blanket parachute or a strong breaststroke—that was how I escaped the whirlpool!—but sheer, calm **persistence**. Must keep going and not lose your nerve, not even for a moment.

39 KEISHA: Kind of boring, huh, Leo? (*looks at Leo, who nods his head in agreement*)

Summarize Think about how you would summarize the play to this point. Which details would you include? Which would you leave out?

Draw and Support Inferences Think about why Leo says, "Oh, right . . . ," when Grandfather looks at him.

Figurative Language <u>Underline</u> the simile on this page. Think about how it helps you picture the scene Grandfather is describing.

Dramatic Structure
Think about how each scene contributes to the drama as a whole.

Critical Thinking
Think about how the family might have avoided getting lost in the first place.

40 GRANDFATHER: Imagine right now that there are jaguars in every alleyway we pass . . . and they're hungry.

41 LEO: (*passing an alley*) Like this one? (*Grandfather nods, finger to his lips, as they follow behind Mother.*)

42 MOTHER: (*pulls Grandfather aside*) Dad, I lost sight of the cathedral.

43 LEO: (*overhearing*) That's no big deal—look at that! (*An old fort with winding stairs looms a couple blocks away.*) We'll just go up there and look around like you did on the jungle temple!

44 KEISHA: (*only half joking*) Safe from jaguars, too.

45 GRANDFATHER: (*looking doubtful*) Not a half-bad idea . . . but I'm not as young as I used to be . . .

46 MOTHER: You stay here, Dad, and rest.

(*Mother climbs quickly up to the top of the fort, smiles, and points toward a street corner.*)

47 MOTHER: Hey, everyone. That way!

(*She rejoins them and they all turn the corner, and a wide **vista** opens up in which they can see the harbor and the cruise ship.*)

48 LEO AND KEISHA: Hey, there's the ship—good job, Mom!

49 MOTHER: (*quietly, to Grandfather*) Thanks, Dad, we couldn't have done it without you!

✔ Comprehension Check

1. How can you tell the grandfather is making stories up on the spur of the moment?

____

____

____

2. How do each of the three scenes contribute to the drama as a whole?

____

____

____

3. Summarize the action in this drama. Include only the most important details.

____

____

____

4. Read these lines from the drama.

   Because sometimes the thing that saves you isn't a picnic blanket parachute or a strong breaststroke—that was how I escaped the whirlpool!—but sheer, calm persistence. Must keep going and not lose your nerve, not even for a moment.

   Circle the words that help you understand the meaning of *persistence*.

5. Read this line from the drama.

   **… drifting toward a great sucking whirlpool as deep as
   a canyon.**

   "Deep as a canyon" is a simile because it uses *as* to make a comparison.
   What other kind of figurative language is this? Why?

   ____

   ____

6. What inference is supported by the detail of the mother thanking her
   father at the end of the drama?

   ____

   ____

7. How do the stage directions help you understand what the mother and
   grandfather are doing in the drama?

   ____

   ____

8. Read these lines from the drama.

   **(She rejoins them and they all turn the corner, and a wide vista
   opens up in which they can see the harbor and the cruise ship.)**

   The word *vista* comes from the Latin verb *videre*, meaning "to see."
   Looking at the sentence, what do you think the noun *vista* means?

   ____

   ____

Poetry

Poetry is a form of literature based on rhythmic language. Poets organize language in lines and stanzas to create rhythm, tension, and surprise. They sometimes use rhyming words to make their writing more musical. Sometimes they even invent new words! Poets use interesting language and sounds to express vivid imagery and strong feelings. Suppose you read a poem about the first day of summer vacation. The poem might tell a story or express images of summer beauty or feelings of joy and freedom. How might you begin a poem about the girl in this picture?

Skills Focus

The Glove and the Lions

Poetic Structure

Figurative Language

Ozymandias / A Sphinx

Visualize

Compare and Contrast Poetic Forms

Practice the Skill

Poetic structure is the way a poem is built. The most common building block for poems is the stanza, which is a group of lines of similar style or length.

In a poem that tells a story, called a **narrative poem**, each stanza has a particular purpose. The stanza may develop the setting, plot, or theme of the poem's story. To determine what a stanza contributes to the poem, look at what the stanza describes. Is it giving details about time or place? If so, it is developing setting. Is it describing the main action? In that case, it is developing plot. Is it explaining a truth or insight about life? This means it is developing theme.

Try It Read the following stanza.

> The sun shone bright in the cloudless blue sky,
> The day was warm and our spirits were high.
> The first day of summer had finally arrived
> After a long, lonely winter that we had barely survived.

Discuss **How many lines are in the stanza? Does this stanza focus on setting, plot, or theme? Explain your answer.**

Read on to analyze the poetic structure of the next stanza.

> Like knights' loyal horses, three bikes stood eager and tall
> To start our adventures, and to heed every call.
> So we set off to conquer on that beautiful day
> The overgrown park on the hill by the bay.

Discuss **What purpose does this stanza have? Does it focus on setting, plot, or theme? Underline the details that support your answer.**

As you read, record your answers to questions about poetic structure on the Close Reading Worksheet on page 265.

Practice the Skill

Figurative language makes poetry, along with other kinds of writing, come alive. Figurative language creates word pictures by describing or comparing one thing in terms of something else. Figurative language often expresses something other than the words' literal definitions.

When a poet describes "the long arms of the tree reaching to the sky," he or she gives the tree arms, which are human qualities. Giving human qualities or characteristics to something that is not human is called **personification**.

Figurative language can also help you to imagine certain sounds. When you read about a campfire's "pop and sizzle," you can hear the fire in a way that feels very real. Using words that make the sound being described is called **onomatopoeia**. Words like *buzz*, *chirp*, *slurp*, and *hiss* are examples of onomatopoeia.

Try It   Read the poem below.

> The first BOOM of the fireworks lit up the night
> And the crowd oohed and ahhed its grateful delight.
> The rockets squealed as they skipped and leapt in the sky
> Then painted the heavens with colors that made the moon cry.

Discuss   **Which words give human qualities to nonhuman things? Circle the examples of personification. Which words make the sounds they describe? Underline the examples of onomatopoeia.**

As you read, complete the Figurative Language Chart on page 266.

The Glove and the Lions

By Leigh Hunt

Underline the rhyming words in this stanza. Does this stanza develop setting, plot, or theme? How do you know?

Why do you think the Count de Lorge is specifically mentioned?

King Francis was a hearty king, and loved a royal sport,

And one day as his lions fought, sat looking on the court;

The **nobles** filled the benches, with the ladies in their pride,

And 'mongst them sat the Count de Lorge, with one for whom he sighed:

5   And truly 'twas a gallant thing to see that crowning show,

Valour and love, and a king above, and the royal beasts below.

Ramped and roared the lions, with horrid laughing jaws;

They bit, they glared, gave blows like beams, a wind went with
their paws;

With wallowing might and stifled roar they rolled on one another,

10 Till all the pit with sand and mane was in a thunderous smother;

The bloody foam above the bars came whisking through the air;

Said Francis then, "Faith, gentlemen, we're better here than there."

De Lorge's love o'erheard the King, a **beauteous** lively **dame**

With smiling lips and sharp bright eyes, which always seemed
the same:

15 She thought, the Count my lover is brave as brave can be;

He surely would do **wondrous** things to show his love of me;

King, ladies, lovers, all look on; the occasion is divine;

I'll drop my glove, to prove his love; great glory will be mine.

She dropped her glove, to prove his love, then looked at him and smiled;

20 He bowed, and in a moment leaped among the lions wild:

His leap was quick, return was quick, he has regained his place,

Then threw the glove, but not with love, right in the lady's face.

"By god!" cried Francis, "rightly done!" and he rose from where he sat:

"No love," **quoth** he, "but vanity, sets love a task like that."

Vocabulary: Using a Dictionary

Some poems use unusual words or older forms of words that you might not recognize. When you are uncertain about the meaning of a word, a dictionary will help you determine the word's exact definition. A dictionary can also help you see how the same word can have different uses and meanings. Remember to look at all of the meanings of a word listed in a dictionary. Then, reread the poem to decide which meaning of the word the poet intends.

Try It Read this line from "The Glove and the Lions."

> De Lorge's love o'erheard the King, a **beauteous** lively **dame**

You might wonder if *beauteous* means the same thing as *beautiful* because they look similar. A dictionary confirms the meaning with this definition of *beauteous*: "a poetic word for *beautiful*."

Discuss **Using the word's context in the poem, brainstorm definitions of the word *dame*. Then use a dictionary to confirm the meaning.**

The following words are found in "The Glove and the Lions." First, write down what you think each word means. Then, look up its dictionary definition and confirm or correct your definition.

1. **noble,** p. 58 ____

____

2. **wondrous,** p. 59 _______________________________________

____

3. **quoth,** p. 60 ____

____

Practice the Skill

To **visualize** means to make and see images in your mind as you read. When you visualize, you become like a movie director or an artist by creating your own pictures and scenes. This process can help you understand the events or images in a poem. Poets use figurative language and language that appeals to the senses to allow you to visualize.

Imagine you are reading a poem about horses galloping across a field in the early-morning mist. Now picture the horses with their manes and tails flying as they speed over the green grass. You might also see the trailing white mists and the sun burning on the horizon. You are visualizing both the action and the subtle sensory details of the poem.

Try It Read the following poem.

Fall

A rainbow shower of leaves flutters down
Crowning me with their red and yellow glory
As I climb the sunlit forest path.

The crunch of leaves beneath my boots
Reminds me that the brilliant glory
Of my rainbow crown
Will not last.

I feel a sudden chill
And zip my jacket,
Quicken my steps
And head for the glowing campfire,
The sizzling dinner, and my laughing friends
That will greet me at trail's end.

Discuss What pictures did you create in your mind as you read the poem? What images stand out? Underline the details you visualized.

As you read, complete the **Visualization Chart** on page 267.

Practice the Skill

Poems come in many forms that are defined by either content or structure. For example, an **ode** is a lyric or musical poem that expresses strong feeling toward its subject. An **epic poem** is a long poem that tells the story of a great hero or cultural event.

Some poetic forms follow specific rules regarding their structure. **Sonnets**, for example, have fourteen lines of similar length and words ordered into a particular rhythm and rhyme scheme. **Free verse** poetry does not fit a specific form. In free verse, some lines may be short and some may be long. A free verse poem may have stanzas of different lengths or no stanzas at all. If a free verse poem contains rhyming words, they are often in unpredictable places and patterns.

Try It Reread "Fall" on the previous page. Then read the following poem.

> The amber harvest moon has risen high
> To welcome fall and bid August away.
> A nip in the air, cranes across the sky
> Bring sadness that the warmth's not here to stay.
> Changes that chilling autumn always brings
> Will gladden some hearts as the heat's released.
> But thinking back on summer's glorious things
> Makes my heart weaken, my soul feel displeased.
> Yet soft on my skin is the gentle night wind
> And fragrant the fire that welcomes me home.
> Golden and warm are the gifts that fall sends
> So to summer my mind no longer must roam.
> The joys of dear autumn I suddenly know
> So into her beauty I'm now ready to go.

Discuss **What are the poetic forms of the two poems? What features, such as line length, stanza, rhythm, and rhyme, can you identify?**

As you read, record your answers to questions about poetic forms on the Close Reading Worksheet on page 268.

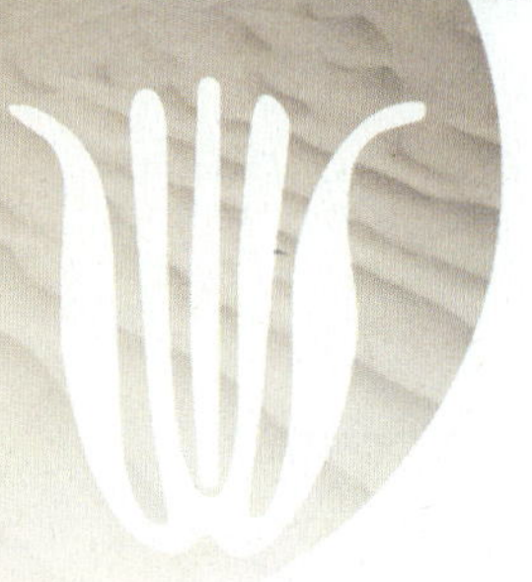

Ozymandias

by Percy Bysshe Shelley

What images can you visualize from the poem? Draw what you visualize and write the poetic phrase that inspired you in the **Visualization Chart**.

Is this poem a sonnet or free verse? How do you know? Circle words that rhyme. Does this poem have a rhyme scheme?

How does the traveler feel about Ozymandias? How do you know?

I met a traveller from an **antique** land

Who said: "Two vast and trunkless legs of stone

Stand in the desert . . . Near them, on the sand,

Half sunk, a shattered **visage** lies, whose frown

5   And wrinkled lip, and sneer of cold command,

Tell that its sculptor well those passions read

Which yet **survive**, stamped on these lifeless things,

The hand that mocked them, and the heart that fed:

And on the pedestal these words appear:

10   'My name is Ozymandias, king of kings:

Look on my works, ye Mighty, and despair!'

Nothing beside remains. Round the decay

Of that **colossal** wreck, boundless and bare

The lone and level sands stretch far away."

A Sphinx

by Carl Sandburg

Close-mouthed you sat five thousand years and never let
  out a whisper.
Processions came by, marchers, asking questions you answered
  with grey eyes never blinking, shut lips never talking.
Not one croak of anything you know has come from your cat
  crouch of ages.
I am one of those who know all you know and I keep my questions:
  I know the answers you hold.

Vocabulary: Academic Vocabulary

Academic vocabulary refers to words that are commonly used in discussing and writing about school subjects. Academic vocabulary can include challenging language. As you study and read, you will come across words you don't know. At times, you will need to use a dictionary to determine a new word's meaning.

Try It Read this sentence from "Ozymandias."

> I met a traveller from an **antique** land

Antique means "very old" or "not modern." It can be used as an adjective to describe things, like *land* in the poem. It can also be used as a noun to refer to old objects. A dictionary can help you understand the different forms of a new word.

Discuss **Brainstorm some things that might be described as *antique*. Now use the word as a noun in a sentence to refer to an old object.**

The following words appear in "Ozymandias." Write a definition for each and then answer the question to show that you understand the word.

1. **visage,** p. 64 Definition: _______________________________________

Name three things that have a visage: ___________________________________

2. **survive,** p. 64 Definition: _______________________________________

What are two events a person would be happy to survive? ___________________

____

3. **colossal,** p. 64 Definition: ______________________________________

What is a synonym for *colossal*? ______________________________________

Respond to Text: Compare and Contrast
Reading and Listening to Poetry

"Ozymandias" describes the ruins of a large statue in the desert. You have read the poem, and now you will listen to an audio version of it.

Try It Think about what you saw and heard as you read the poem to yourself. Then think about hearing the audio version of the poem.

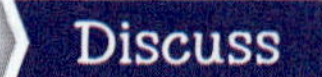 **Discuss** **What images from the poem could you easily visualize? What sounds could you imagine as you read it? List specific details from the poem that struck you as you read it. What new understanding did you gain about the poem from listening to it being read? How was the experience of reading the poem similar to and/or different from hearing it?**

On Your Own Write your own paragraph comparing and contrasting the experiences of reading and listening to the poem. Describe how the different experiences affected your understanding of the poem. Include details from the poem that support your points. Use the next page to help you plan your response. Then write your paragraph on a separate sheet of paper.

Checklist for a Good Response

A good paragraph

✔ describes the experiences of reading and listening to the poem.

✔ compares and contrasts the experiences using specific examples.

✔ includes specific details from the poem.

✔ shows your understanding of the poem.

✔ includes a topic sentence, supporting ideas, and a concluding statement.

Comparing and Contrasting Reading and Listening to a Poem

1. **Topic Sentence** Include this information in your first sentence: When I read

    "Ozymandias," I was able to ____

    ______________, and when I listened to the poem, I was able to ___________

    ____ .

2. **Detail Sentences** The sentences of your paragraph should provide details
    that compare and contrast reading and listening to the poem. Use this
    chart to organize your ideas.

	Reading	Listening
What did I visualize and hear easily from the poem?		
What parts of the poem did I enjoy most?		
What did I understand about the poem?		

3. **Concluding Sentence** Your final sentence should restate how reading and
    listening to the poem affected your understanding.

    ____

    ____

On a separate sheet of paper, write your paragraph.

The Children's Hour

by Henry Wadsworth Longfellow

Poetic Structure What details help establish the setting? Underline the details. The first one is done for you.

Between the dark and the daylight,

    When the night is beginning to lower,

Comes a pause in the day's occupations,

    That is known as the Children's Hour.

Figurative Language What example of onomatopoeia is in the second stanza? Circle the word.

5   I hear in the **chamber** above me

    The patter of little feet,

The sound of a door that is opened,

    And voices soft and sweet.

From my study I see in the lamplight,

10   Descending the broad hall stair,

Grave Alice, and laughing Allegra,

    And Edith with golden hair.

A whisper, and then a silence:

    Yet I know by their merry eyes

15   They are plotting and planning together

    To take me by surprise.

A sudden rush from the stairway,

    A sudden raid from the hall!

By three doors left unguarded

20   They enter my castle wall!

They climb up into my turret[1]

    O'er the arms and back of my chair;

If I try to escape, they surround me;

    They seem to be everywhere.

25   They almost devour me with kisses,

    Their arms about me entwine,

Till I think of the Bishop of Bingen

    In his Mouse-Tower on the Rhine![2]

[1]**turret** a small tower, usually attached to the corner of a larger building
[2]**Bishop . . . Rhine** an evil ruler swarmed and eaten by mice in a tower after acting cruelly toward his people and calling them mice

Do you think, O blue-eyed banditti,[3]

30 Because you have scaled the wall,

Such an old mustache as I am

  Is not a match for you all!

I have you fast in my fortress,

  And will not let you depart,

35 But put you down into the dungeon

  In the round-tower of my heart.

And there will I keep you forever,

  Yes, forever and a day,

Till the walls shall crumble to ruin,

40 And moulder in dust away!

[3]**banditti** bandits

Rain Music

by Joseph S. Cotter, Jr.

On the dusty earth-drum
Beats the falling rain;
Now a whispered murmur,
Now a louder strain.

5   Slender, silvery drumsticks,
On an ancient drum,
Beat the mellow music
Bidding life to come.

Chords of earth awakened,
10   Notes of greening spring,
Rise and fall triumphant
Over every thing.

Slender, silvery drumsticks
Beat the long tattoo[4] —
15   God, the Great Musician,
Calling life anew.

[4]**tattoo** a fast and rhythmic tapping

Dust of Snow

by Robert Frost

Visualize Think about which lines help you visualize the scene.

Compare and Contrast Poetic Forms Think about how the rhyme schemes of "Rain Music" and "Dust of Snow" are different.

Critical Thinking Think about how you would compare the poets' attitudes about nature.

The way a crow

Shook down on me

The dust of snow

From a hemlock tree

5   Has given my heart

A change of mood

And saved some part

Of a day I had **rued**.

1. What details in the third stanza of "The Children's Hour" help to develop the setting?

2. What details in the eighth stanza of "The Children's Hour" describe the daughters' and father's appearance?

3. Why do you think the speaker tolerates these attacks by his daughters?

4. Read this stanza from "The Children's Hour."

> **I hear in the chamber above me**
> **The patter of little feet,**
> **The sound of a door that is opened,**
> **And voices soft and sweet.**

The word *chamber* is an old-fashioned word that probably means what?

5. Read these lines from "Rain Music."

    Beats the falling rain;
    Now a whispered murmur

    What is an example of onomatopoeia, and what is an example of personification?

    ____

    ____

6. What similarities in poetic structure do all three poems share?

    ____

    ____

7. What kind of music does the speaker in "Rain Music" think the rain sounds most like? Use details from the poem to support your answer.

    ____

    ____

8. Read this entry from a dictionary.

    rue (ro͞o) **verb. 1:** to feel remorse or regret; **2:** to wish a thing away; **noun. 3:** strong-scented shrub; **4:** family of herbs

    Which meaning of *rued* is used in the poem "Dust of Snow"? Explain how context helped you to know.

    ____

    ____

Historical Fiction

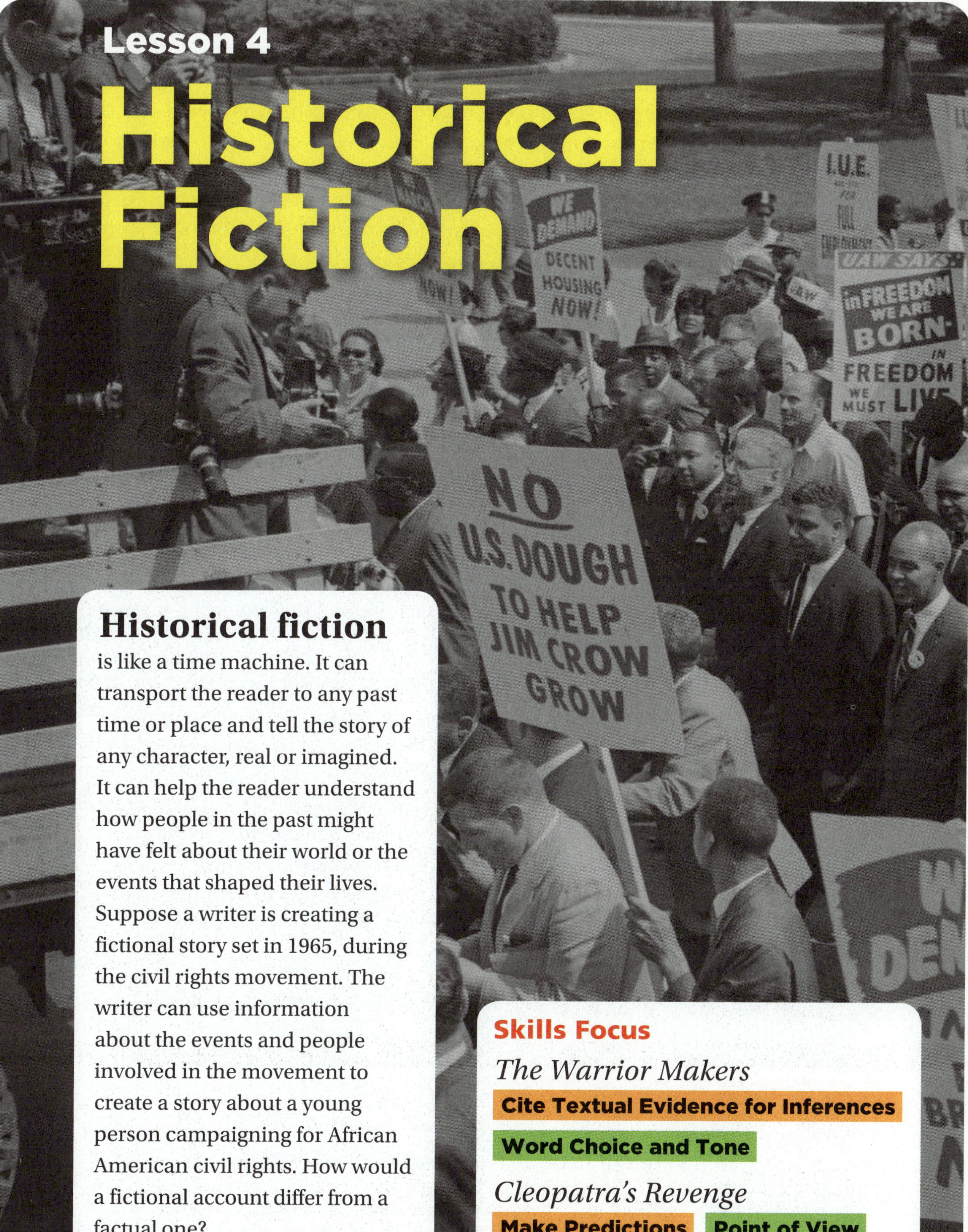

Historical fiction

is like a time machine. It can transport the reader to any past time or place and tell the story of any character, real or imagined. It can help the reader understand how people in the past might have felt about their world or the events that shaped their lives. Suppose a writer is creating a fictional story set in 1965, during the civil rights movement. The writer can use information about the events and people involved in the movement to create a story about a young person campaigning for African American civil rights. How would a fictional account differ from a factual one?

Skills Focus

The Warrior Makers

Cite Textual Evidence for Inferences

Word Choice and Tone

Cleopatra's Revenge

Make Predictions   **Point of View**

Practice the Skill

Writers sometimes express ideas directly, stating exactly what they want you to know. But sometimes writers express ideas indirectly, and you have to make an inference to fully understand what is meant. An **inference** is an educated guess that you make based on textual evidence and on what you already know. **Textual evidence** includes words, facts, details, or ideas in the text. When you talk or write about what you have read, you can **cite textual evidence** by pointing out the specific words and ideas that support your inferences.

Try It   Read the following paragraph.

Leroy gently brushed the dust away from the fossil. "This is an awesome find!" he thought. He couldn't wait to tell someone about it, but he knew his first responsibility was to carefully remove the object that had been buried underground for millions of years.

Discuss   **How would you describe Leroy's personality? Underline the textual evidence that supports your idea.**

Read on and look for more textual evidence to support what you think about Leroy's personality.

Leroy worked under the hot sun for hours. Sweat soaked his shirt and he was hungry, but he didn't stop even for lunch. He was too busy using a tiny paintbrush to carefully remove the layers of dirt around the fossil. This discovery would be big news at the museum, but first it had to be removed from the ground in one piece.

Discuss   **How do you think Leroy is feeling as he works? The writer does not say directly, so how do you know? Underline the textual evidence that helps you know how he is feeling.**

As you read, complete the Textual Evidence Chart on page 269.

Practice the Skill

Tone shows how a writer feels about the subject of a text—sad, earnest, and so on. A writer's tone isn't stated directly but is reflected in his or her words. The writer thinks not only about the words' meanings but also about the positive or negative feelings the words communicate to the reader. These feelings are part of a word's **connotation**; they tell more about the word than just its dictionary definition, or **denotation**. For example, to describe how a person laughs, a writer could use the word *chuckled*, which has a positive connotation. Or the writer may say that the person *cackled*, which has a negative connotation. Understanding words' connotations will help you correctly identify a writer's tone as you read.

Try It   Read this paragraph, and think about its tone. Is it positive or negative? How does the writer feel about this subject?

> General Washington sat tall and straight astride his chestnut warhorse, Nelson. His confident and commanding presence calmed the men as they waited their turn to board the boats. No one would guess from watching Washington how dangerous it was to take his army across the Delaware River.

Discuss | **How would you describe the writer's tone toward General Washington? Circle the words that help create that tone.**

In works of fiction, the tone is expressed through the narrator. What tone can you identify here?

> Jessie huddled miserably under her blankets and tried to ignore the wailing of the wind. "Mama," she squeaked, "how long will the storm last?" The walls of the one-room wooden cabin where she lived with her family seemed thin and fragile compared to the might of the storm outside.

Discuss | **How would you describe this narrator's tone? Circle the words that communicate the tone.**

> **As you read, record your answers to questions about tone on the Close Reading Worksheet on page 270.**

The  Warrior Makers

1   Yun's father gently shook him awake and handed him a bowl of rice. As the boy ate, his father built a fire to warm the hut. "Eat it all. You will need your strength today. The inspector is coming to view the warriors," his father said. Yun worked for his uncle and the other master craftsmen who were creating warrior statues to be placed in the emperor's tomb.

2   When he was finished, Yun handed the empty bowl to his father. His father took the bowl in his large, rough hands and said, "Hurry. Your brother and uncle are already at the workshop."

3   Yun put on his jacket and slipped out the door. The spring air was cold, and he could see his breath as he ran toward the caves. Caves were excellent workshops, because they were warm in the winter and cool in the summer. While his brother Gao did the hard work of digging the **clay** out of the riverbed and hauling it to the cave, Yun worked inside with his uncle. His job was to prepare the clay for the master craftsmen, and he hoped that he, too, would be a master one day.

4   When Yun arrived at the cave, the workshop was humming with activity. On his way to his workbench, Yun took stock of the work. Some warriors were only half finished: they had legs and a torso, but no head or hands. Some were almost complete, with unique heads, ears, hands, mustaches, and decorated uniforms. These warriors were ready for the masters' review. Yun knew that few people would ever see the marvelous warriors, despite the enormous amount of work that was being done to create them.

5   The warriors were the inspiration of the emperor, Ying Zhen, who had become ruler when he was only thirteen—Yun's age. Within a few years, he had unified all of China and then renamed himself "Qin, the First Emperor." Qin was the most powerful man in the world, and he wanted people to remember him long after his death. So he planned an elaborate tomb, or burial place. Covering acres of land, the tomb would contain a palace surrounded by rivers of poisonous mercury for defense. For protection in the afterlife, the emperor wanted an army of soldiers buried with him. Yun's uncle and the other masters were making the soldiers—all molded out of clay, fired in the kiln, and painted. Yun felt honored to be working on such a noble and grand project.

6   The warriors were large and lifelike, each standing about six feet tall and weighing more than six hundred pounds. Workmen crafted each soldier by hand, forming feet and legs from clay pressed into **molds** and then creating a torso fashioned from strips of clay. The warriors' hands, heads, ears, and hats were formed separately in different molds. Masters used dozens of molds to create variety in the warriors' appearance. The pieces would then be fired in a **kiln**, a huge oven in which the clay would be fired until it hardened. After all the pieces had been fired, the masters attached the heads to long, stemlike necks, like putting stoppers into the tops of bottles. Finally, the masters would paint the figures with bright colors and cover them with a shiny substance called **lacquer**. When a clay warrior was completed, everyone in the workshop would gather to admire it.

7   At his bench, Yun grabbed a lump of clay, threw it on a stone slab, and pounded it with his fists until it became soft like bread dough. Then he cut it into sections and rolled them into narrow coils for the masters to work with. As Yun worked, he realized that the mood in the room had become tense. Then he remembered that the emperor's inspector was coming that very day. Surely there was nothing for the masters to worry about; they had already completed 1,500 statues, and hundreds more were in various stages of assembly, firing, and painting.

8   Yun's uncle called, "Yun, we must assemble the last warrior before the inspector arrives. Go with Buwei and bring the head to me."

9   Yun ran with Buwei to the area where the fired warrior heads were cooling. The boys were directed to pick up a splendid head that a master had just finished checking for cracks; its face had high cheekbones and frowning eyes. Yun thought it would make an excellent warrior. When the boys lifted the wooden slats the head rested on, they were surprised by its great weight.

10   The boys secured their grip and were headed to the main workshop, when suddenly Buwei tripped, nearly dropping his end. The head wobbled on the slats.

11   "Buwei!" barked Yun. "Be careful, you clumsy oaf! What would happen to Uncle if he showed a warrior with no head? The inspector could send him to jail—or worse!" Yun shivered at the thought.

12   The boys carried the head through the narrow corridors, and the other assistants created a small procession behind them. Yun felt proud to be carrying the head. But then his nose began to itch. He tried to call out to Buwei, but it was too late! In front of everyone, he sneezed violently and lost his grip. The assistants watched in horror as the warrior's head rolled off the slats and hit the floor with a crack. The handsome molded face was now a pitiful pile of shards.

13   The apprentices scattered like mice. Yun was paralyzed with fear and shame. He kept his eyes down as the masters gathered to look at the shattered clay head.

14   Finally, Yun's uncle spoke. "This is very bad."

15   Yun squeaked. "Wh-what can I do?"

16   "Quickly, go back and get another clay head!" growled Yun's uncle.

17   Yun and Buwei ran back to the part of the workshop where the heads were made. There were no extra heads there! With a groan, Yun returned and told his uncle the terrible news. Yun's uncle frowned at the other masters and said, "Surely, one of us will lose his own head for this." Their faces were taut with anxiety.

18   "I will tell the inspector that it was my fault," pleaded Yun.

19   His uncle said sharply, "We are the masters, so we are responsible. Go away from me now, but do not leave the workshop."

20   Yun bowed miserably and stumbled out of the workroom. Buwei grabbed him and pulled him aside. He said, "The masters will figure something out. That's why they are the masters." But Yun did not feel comforted.

21   The masters did devise a plan, and it was both bold and risky. They had one warrior body with no head, so they decided to put that body at the farthest end of the workshop. After the inspector had seen the first row of soldiers, the masters would remove a head from one of the warriors and quickly take it to the back of the workshop, placing it on the headless body.

22   Yun was chosen to act as the inspector's attendant, whose job was to carry the hem of his robes as he walked around the workshop. This meant that Yun would be a witness if the inspector discovered the masters' trick, and the thought terrified him.

23   When the inspector arrived, Yun's uncle led him to the rows of waiting warriors. The inspector walked slowly by them, seeming to take in every detail.

24   "These are . . . acceptable," said the inspector as he moved past the first row, pressing his cold, bony hand into Yun's shoulder for balance. "Now let us see the rest."

Circle words and phrases the author uses to establish the tone of the scene after Yun drops the clay head. What is the tone of the scene?

25   As the official made his way down the rows, Yun was aware of two masters lifting a head from a body in the first row and struggling to carry it to the back of the workshop without being noticed by the inspector. Yun did the only thing he could think of: he pretended to sneeze, loudly, and the inspector turned to look at him with distaste. Yun trembled at what might come next, but the inspector merely turned away with a sniff and continued walking. Yun noticed the two masters moving away from the last row, small smiles of relief on their faces.

26   When they reached the last row, the inspector stopped and squinted at the warrior who had just received a head. "There is something about this one," he said. Yun held his breath. "He looks like me, don't you think?" The inspector laughed, and all of the masters and workmen laughed with him. Yun sighed with relief.

27   Once the inspector had left the workshop, Yun's uncle placed his hand on his nephew's shoulder. "We are lucky that only a clay warrior lost his head today. But Yun, I am afraid that you have lost your place in this workshop."

28   Yun left the workshop and went to work with his brother. He did not mind the heat in the summers or the cold in the winters as he harvested great slabs of yellow clay from the riverbed and then dragged them up to the cave. As he worked, he daydreamed happily about the day when an army of warriors would guard the emperor's tomb. Yun had no way of knowing that the masters would eventually create more than seven thousand warriors. After their burial with the emperor in 210 BCE, the warriors would remain undisturbed for more than two thousand years. They would become objects of fascination in the twenty-first century, a time Yun could not even imagine.

Vocabulary: Domain-Specific Vocabulary

Domain-specific vocabulary refers to words and phrases that are commonly used by people involved in a particular field of work or study. The words have specific meanings and are often included in work-related documents and conversations. For example, people who work with computers use words such as *cursor*, *motherboard*, and *menu bar*. Cooks and others in the food service industry use words such as *reduction*, *julienne*, *mince*, and *braise*.

Try It The table below lists some domain-specific words from the story "The Warrior Makers." Find context clues from the story and use your prior knowledge about the words to write a definition for each. Then, check your definition in a dictionary and complete the table.

Word	Context Clues	Definition
1. **clay,** p. 80	digging the clay out of the riverbed; pounded it with his fists; rolled	
2. **molds,** p. 81		carved forms that clay is pressed into for shaping
3. **kiln,** p. 81		
4. **lacquer,** p. 81		

Discuss Think about a topic that you know a lot about. What domain-specific words are important for that topic? Discuss the words below.

Practice the Skill

When you **make predictions**, you use your own prior knowledge along with story details to guess at what might happen next or how a character will behave. Making predictions can help you think about what has happened, what is happening, and what will happen in a story. It is important to repeatedly check your predictions while you read—and you won't always be correct. When that happens, revise your predictions using new information from the text.

Try It Read the following paragraph.

Henry David Thoreau wasn't like most people who lived in his hometown of Concord, Massachusetts. He liked to do things his own way. He would wander through the woods and spend whole days walking and thinking. As he walked, he took great pleasure from his surroundings, from the smallest creature to the tallest tree. He kept a journal of what he observed. Some of his neighbors thought that he was lazy and told him he should spend more time working and less time thinking.

> **Discuss** **Make a prediction. Do you think Thoreau will listen to his neighbors? Underline the textual evidence that you used to make this prediction.**

Read on to see if your prediction is correct.

Thoreau loved nature so much that he decided to do an experiment. He built a small cabin in the woods and decided to live there for two years by himself. He would survive only on what he could find in nature. When the neighbors heard about that, they thought he was not only lazy but crazy. But Thoreau did it anyway.

> **Discuss** **Was your prediction correct? Underline details in the paragraph that show whether your prediction was correct or incorrect.**

> **As you read, record your answers on the Make Predictions Chart on page 271.**

Practice the Skill

The narrator of a story is the voice telling the story, and the **point of view** is the narrator's perspective. The most common points of view are

- **first person:** In first-person point of view, the narrator is a character in the story. The narrator uses words such as *I*, *me*, *my*, *we*, and *us* and can tell about events in the story only as he or she experiences them. The reader knows only what the narrator thinks and feels, not what other characters think and feel.

- **third person:** In third-person point of view, the narrator is not a character in the story. The narrator uses words such as *he*, *she*, *they*, *them*, and *their* to refer to the story's characters. A **third-person omniscient** narrator can tell the thoughts and feelings of all the characters in the story. A **third-person limited** narrator tells the thoughts and feelings of only one character in the story.

Try It Identify the narrator's point of view in each passage below.

I ran home from school as fast as I could. As I turned the corner on my street, I nearly ran into our neighbor, Mrs. Soo. "Sorry!" I yelled as I raced past. "Mom!" I said as I banged through the door. "Is it here? Did my birthday present come?"

Matt and Sean stood on the grass, nervously waiting. Coach Clark chuckled to himself as he crossed the field. He knew it had been a difficult wait for the boys, but now he was ready to announce his choice of the team's starting goalkeeper. "Me, me, me," Matt thought as Coach Clark walked toward them. "Not me, not me, not me," pleaded Sean silently.

Discuss **What is the point of view in each passage? Circle the words in each passage that indicate the point of view. Now choose one of the passages and rewrite it from a different point of view.**

As you read, record your answers to questions about point of view on the Close Reading Worksheet on page 272.

What prediction can you make about Cleopatra from the details in paragraph 1? Record the prediction and supporting details on the **Make Predictions Chart.**

What point of view does the author use, and who is the narrator of the story? Circle the clues that tell you.

Why do you think Cleopatra likes the idea of the royal family being gods in human form?

1   When I was a girl, I dreamed of becoming queen of Egypt. I never doubted that it would happen, since I believed myself to be the daughter of a god. Yet even I am surprised by how it actually came about. I will tell you the story of how I became the most powerful woman in Egypt, and you can decide whether truth is stranger than fiction.

2   My father was King Ptolemy[1] XII, and he was a descendant of Ptolemy I, the first king of Egypt, appointed by Alexander the Great himself. As children, my brothers and sisters and I heard many stories about this famous relative. Oh, how we all wanted to be like him! Like Alexander the Great, Ptolemy I was Greek. However, he wanted to rule Egypt as had the ancient pharaohs—rulers who built the great pyramids and believed themselves to be gods in human form. While I liked that idea, Ptolemy I had another idea that I thought very strange. He believed that brothers and sisters in the royal family must marry one another. One day I realized that this meant that I too might have to marry one of my younger brothers!

[1]**Ptolemy** (TAH-luh-mee)

3   We lived in Alexandria, which is a wonderful city with beautiful, wide streets, stadiums, gymnasiums, and concert halls. Most amazing of all the city's wonders is the Museum, which houses the finest library in the world—it contains over 700,000 papyrus **scrolls**! Philosophers, poets, and scientists come from all over the world to study there.

4   I was fortunate that my father believed in educating his daughters as well as his sons. While I was not allowed to go to the Museum to study, I had my own tutor who taught me philosophy, literature, art, music, and medicine. I especially loved languages and happily learned to speak six of them.

5   I thought Alexandria was the center of the universe, but when I was eleven my father took me to Rome. I learned that Rome was the greatest city in the world and the center of the greatest empire in history. The marketplace was filled with delicious foods, beautiful clothing and jewelry, and exciting performers of every kind. One day, as I was at a shop admiring a lovely golden bracelet, I noticed people outside running and shouting, "Hail, Caesar!" My father pointed out Julius Caesar, the most powerful man in the world. I thought he looked rather old, but there was something exciting about the way everyone cheered when he walked by. I wanted to know more about him, and I had a strange feeling I would see him again one day.

6   After visiting Rome and seeing the great Caesar, I was more determined than ever to become queen of Egypt. I studied even more than I had before, wanting to learn everything I would need to know when I became queen.

7   My destiny was fulfilled sooner than I had expected. My father died when I was seventeen, and since I was the oldest child, I became queen of Egypt. My name, Cleopatra, means "the one who brings glory to her father," and this is what I had always dreamed of doing. Unfortunately, my dreams were quickly dashed; my father's advisers declared that Egypt's chief ruler had to be male, and they made my ten-year-old brother, Ptolemy XIII, king and co-ruler with me. Even worse, they insisted that I marry him! I knew in my heart I couldn't trust Ptolemy; he and his advisers would never be content with me as a co-ruler. My brother had become my **enemy**, and I knew I had to go to war with him in order to win back my throne and rule alone.

8   I went to Syria and raised an army, then led it back to Egypt. Ptolemy raised an army of his own and marched out of Alexandria to meet us. While all this was happening, Julius Caesar came to visit Alexandria. I remembered being impressed by him when I was a young girl visiting Rome, yet now he was even more powerful. I knew that he could be a valuable **ally** in my plans to defeat my scheming brother.

9   When Caesar heard that Ptolemy and I were going to war, he asked us to return to Alexandria and make peace. Ptolemy went right away—he feared that I might convince Caesar to side with me. In addition to my intelligence, I was known for my sweet voice and my many charms. So Ptolemy surrounded the palace with soldiers and ordered them to kill me if I tried to get in.

10   Not only was I older than my brother, I was far more clever. I hatched a plan of my own. First, I sailed back to Alexandria and anchored my ship offshore. When darkness fell, my faithful servant and I took a small boat and slipped into the harbor. Once we were safely ashore, my servant wrapped me up in a rug, carried me into the palace in secret, and delivered the rug directly to Caesar as a gift. When Caesar unrolled the rug, he found quite a surprise! Never will I forget the smile on Caesar's face when he saw me. I think he fell in love with me right then and there.

What do you think will happen now that Cleopatra and Caesar have met? Record your prediction on the **Make Predictions Chart**.

If this story were told in the third-person point of view, how would the scenes on this page be different?

Why do you think Caesar falls in love with Cleopatra?

11   Despite our age difference, Caesar and I had much in common, and we spent long hours talking about how we could rule the world together. Caesar tried to convince Ptolemy and me to **compromise** and rule Egypt together, but such a **bargain** wasn't possible. Instead, we started a civil war and fought sister against brother. The palace was seized, the water was poisoned, many **ships** in the Egyptian **fleet** were destroyed, and even some of the books in my beloved Museum were burned. Finally, with Caesar's help, I defeated my brother's army. He drowned in the Nile River, weighed down by his own golden armor, and I was again crowned queen of Egypt. Unfortunately, I still had to share the throne with my next-youngest brother. My brothers were nothing but a thorn in my side! But I didn't let that get in the way of my plans.

12   Julius Caesar and I were the most powerful couple in the world. He had eyes for no one but me, and I had him eating out of the palm of my hand. There was no stopping us! In the end, my plans didn't turn out exactly as I would have liked, but that's a story for another day.

Vocabulary: Use Word Relationships to Understand Words

When you encounter a difficult word in a reading, you may be able to understand it better by figuring out how it relates to other words close by. Common **word relationships** that you might see include

- **synonyms:** two words that have similar meanings (*delay* and *postpone*)
- **antonyms:** two words that have opposite meanings (*clean* and *filthy*)
- **part to whole:** one word is part of another (*country* and *empire*)
- **cause and effect:** one word leads to another (*earthquake* and *damage*)
- **item and category:** one word is a subset of another (*juice* and *beverage*)

Try It   Read this part of a sentence from "Cleopatra's Revenge."

> . . . the Museum, which houses the finest library in the world—it contains over 700,000 papyrus **scrolls**!

If you were unsure of the meaning of the word *scrolls*, you could still understand that it was something found in the library at Alexandria, and that part-to-whole relationship would give you important clues.

Discuss   **What is a scroll? Why would so many be in the library in Alexandria?**

The following related words appear in "Cleopatra's Revenge." Read the sentences from the story that contain the words. Then tell what relationship the words have to each other.

1. **enemy/ally,** p. 90 ____

2. **compromise/bargain,** p. 92 ______________________________________

3. **ships/fleet,** p. 92 ____

Respond to Text: Point of View

"The Warrior Makers" and "Cleopatra's Revenge" are told using different points of view.

- "The Warrior Makers": third-person-limited point of view

- "Cleopatra's Revenge": first-person point of view

Try It Think about how each story uses point of view and how the point of view affects the reader.

 **Discuss** **How did the point of view from which each story is told affect your understanding and enjoyment of the story? How did the point of view influence your connection to the characters?**

On Your Own Write a paragraph about the effect of the narrator's point of view on each story. Describe how the point of view affected your reading experience and feelings about the main characters. Give examples from the texts to support your response. Use the guide on the next page to help you write your response. Then write your paragraph on a separate sheet of paper.

Checklist for a Good Response

A good paragraph

✔ describes the point of view used to tell each story and convey its central message.

✔ discusses the effect of the point of view on the story itself, using specific textual examples.

✔ describes how the point of view affected your reading experience.

✔ describes how the point of view affected your feelings or insights about the main characters.

✔ includes a topic sentence, supporting ideas, and a concluding statement.

How Point of View Affected My Reading

1. **Topic Sentence** Include this information in your topic sentence:

   "The Warrior Makers" is written from the _______________ point of view, and

   "Cleopatra's Revenge" is written from the _______________ point of view.

2. **Detail Sentences** Describe how point of view affected the story and your experience with it. Use this chart to organize your ideas.

	"The Warrior Makers"	**"Cleopatra's Revenge"**
How did the author's choice of point of view affect the story and its outcome?		
How did the point of view affect my understanding and enjoyment of the story?		
How did the point of view affect my feelings about the main character?		

3. **Concluding Sentence** Your concluding sentence should restate in a fresh way how the point of view affected your reading.

____

____

____

On a separate sheet of paper, write your paragraph.

Farewell to Vinland

Cite Textual Evidence for Inferences
Think about how the narrator feels about the native people. Underline details in the text that are clues to his feelings. Details in the first paragraph have been underlined for you.

Word Choice and Tone
Circle the words that describe the narrator's impressions of Vinland. Think about the feeling these words express.

Norse sagas, or long stories written during the Middle Ages, tell of an explorer named Leif Eriksson who in the late 900s founded the first Viking settlement in North America. It was called Vinland, after the wild grapes that grew there. In 1013, the settlers fled. Some people think that recent discoveries of a Viking settlement in Newfoundland, Canada, may be Leif Eriksson's Vinland.

1   It was a cool evening in late summer in the year 1013, but I was sweating as I ran through the vineyard toward the longhouse in the settlement. I knew I should not be out alone at night. People from the settlement had become edgy, as attacks by the native people had increased lately. Just the previous week, one of the outbuildings had been set on fire; it was a clear sign that our time was running out.

2   My people are Norse, and we had come from our native Iceland to this new place after hearing tales about a land rich with majestic trees and abundant purple berries—grapes. Neither timber nor grapes grew in our cold homeland. So three years ago, my parents and siblings and I sailed with twenty other families over rough seas for three weeks to get there. This new land was as beautiful and bountiful as we expected. It was a paradise, and so we called this settlement Vinland.

3   But the native people did not welcome us, and who could blame them? Why would they want to share their land, trees, and fruit? Relations did improve for a while. The native people were impressed by the strength of the iron tools we Norse used to cultivate fields, chop trees and sod, and build houses. But we did not have enough tools to share, and the native peoples grew hostile. My father had been killed in a surprise attack in the vineyard. He died under a grape arbor and was buried nearby.

4   So I was running alone on my way back to the longhouse from visiting my father's grave. The grave was a small mound in the woods near the vineyard, marked only by a wooden slat with our family name carved on it. Two years had passed since my father's death, and because we were considering returning to Iceland, I felt uneasy about leaving my father behind. "Someday I will come back," I promised.

5   In the vineyard, the grapes were nearing harvest. Some were as big as my thumb and deep purple, but in the spring, they had been the size of peas and the color of the dawn sky. As I reached the end of a row, I heard a rustling sound, and then a figure appeared. It was a native boy about my own age. I stopped short to avoid crashing into him.

6   "What are you doing here?" I cried, more in surprise than in anger.

7   The boy shouted something in his own language that sounded fierce but also pleading. He was carrying a knife but not wielding[1] it.

8   We eyed each other suspiciously, both of us breathless from running. I did not know what to do or what he wanted, but I thought perhaps he wanted some grapes. So I raised my hands to show him they were empty and then pointed to the grapes, saying, "Take some."

9   The native boy, who wore a cloak of soft fur, looked at me and then at the grapes. Suddenly he lunged at the vines, cutting some grapes free with his knife. But instead of tasting them, he threw them down and smashed them with his foot. He repeated the words he had said earlier and then vanished. I waited a moment until my heart stopped racing and then hurried back to the settlement.

10   I finally reached the longhouse, my community's meeting and living space. In the dark, it looked like a grassy mound, but it was a sturdy structure with a frame built from tall, strong trees from the forest. Around the wooden frame we laid hundreds of squares of **turf**, or grassy sod, that provided insulation from winter's bitter cold.

[1]**wielding** using as a weapon

11   Stepping over the threshold, I ducked my head and entered the main room, a long narrow space with fires burning at both ends. The firelight made the room appear bright and cheerful, but the faces of the men were gloomy and somber. I took my place among them on one of the benches that lined the walls. As a fatherless son, I was invited to sit in my father's place but was not expected to speak.

12   Thorfinn Karlsefni was the leader of our settlement. His once vibrantly red beard was now threaded with white hairs. He stood and said, "As you know, the attacks by the native people have increased. They consider us invaders on their soil and will not let us rest easy. It is no longer safe to walk in the fields or vineyard. We have worked hard on this settlement, but it is time to consider returning home to Iceland."

13   Some of the men said, "No, it is impossible!" and others burst out with, "Yes, let's return home!"

14   Thorfinn raised his hand to command silence and said, "I know that we are divided on this issue. We have built this longhouse, and our grapes will be ready to harvest in weeks. But we are in constant danger. We must consider our future."

15   Bjarni Herjulfsson, a man about my father's age, interrupted. "It is our own fault," he said. "We had friendly relations with the native people, but when they asked us for tools, we refused. Why couldn't we have shared what we have?"

16   "Nonsense," cried another man. "They would only have used any tools as weapons against us. They don't want us here."

17   Then Thorfinn pointed to me and said, "Snorri, what do you have to say?"

18   My eyes widened, and I sputtered, "I . . . I . . . uh . . ." I knew that I should tell my people about my unexpected encounter with the boy in the vineyard—and the boy's warning. It was a warning, wasn't it? I could still smell the sweetness of the smashed grapes. It mingled with the scent of the wood smoke in the longhouse.

19   I thought about my dead father, and I thought about the look of anguish on the boy's face. I looked around the longhouse, taking in the faces of our people, some angry, others hopeful—but many fewer than had made the long voyage to Vinland. And then I knew what I would say. I was ready to go home.

✔ Comprehension Check

1. Identify the narrator and the point of view from which this story is told.
    How does the point of view affect the reader's experience with the story?

2. How do you think the other Norsemen will respond to Snorri's suggestion?
    Cite textual evidence to support your prediction.

3. What is the narrator's tone in this story? Which words does the author use
    to help you identify the narrator's tone?

4. Do you think the native boy was giving Snorri a warning? On what textual
    evidence do you base your answer?

5. What could the Norse have done to improve their relationship with the
   native people?

   ____

   ____

   ____

6. Do you think the Norse in Iceland will make more attempts to settle
   Vinland? Why or why not?

   ____

   ____

   ____

7. Read this sentence from the story.

   **Around the wooden frame we laid hundreds of squares of turf,
   or grassy sod, that provided insulation from winter's bitter cold.**

   Circle the words that help you understand the meaning of *turf*.

8. Read this sentence from the story. Some words below have a part-whole
   relationship.

   **It was a cool evening in late summer in the year 1013, but I was
   sweating as I ran through the vineyard toward the longhouse in
   the settlement.**

   Which word describes the whole? ________________________________

   Which words describe parts of the whole? ________________________

   Write a sentence using the words. ______________________________

   ____

Literary Nonfiction

Literary nonfiction

tells true stories while using some of the devices of fiction. Biographies and historical narratives are examples of this type of writing, as are many books about politics, the arts, popular culture, sports, science, and technology. Literary nonfiction is informative and fact based, but it can also be exciting, humorous, and suspenseful. For example, an author might use the literary devices of dialogue, suspense, or figurative language in a magazine article to tell a story. What might a piece of literary nonfiction tell about what is happening in this photograph?

Skills Focus

Shackleton: An Enduring Leader

Central Idea and Supporting Details

Secondary Sources

from *Escape from the Antarctic*

Ask and Answer Questions

Primary Sources

Practice the Skill

The **central idea** of any piece of writing is the main or most important idea the author wants you to understand. Even though literary nonfiction contains elements of fiction, it will still have a central idea. Authors often state their central idea directly, but sometimes they do not. In those cases, you must identify the details that seem to support an unstated key idea. **Supporting details** are facts, statistics, quotations, examples, and anecdotes an author uses to reinforce the central idea.

Try It   Read the following paragraphs.

A seed turning into a fresh tomato, a rose, or a soaring oak may seem an almost magical process, but it is one that biologists understand well. Once a seed is planted, the moisture and heat of the soil trigger the process of growth. The seed bursts into action. It unspools a single strandlike root even as its tiny stem and leaf buds surge upward toward the sunlight.

Once the seedling is established, the process of photosynthesis begins. The young seedling works furiously at both ends. Above the soil, leaves unfurl from the stem like flags. Like tiny green solar panels, their cells capture and transform the sun's energy. Below ground, the seedling knits a network of roots that provide ballast and soak up needed water and nutrients to fuel the factory of growing and dividing cells inside.

Discuss   **Underline the sentences that state the central idea of each paragraph. Double underline the details that support each central idea.**

As you read, complete the Central Idea and Details Web on page 273.

Practice the Skill

A **secondary source** is a text about a real person or event that is based on information from primary sources: eyewitness accounts, diaries, personal letters, official records, and so on. Secondary sources are written after the fact, looking back at their topic. The author of a secondary source gathers a variety of information from primary sources, which, taken together, provides the author with a broad perspective on the topic. Secondary source authors often draw on other secondary sources as well as primary sources.

As you read a secondary source, analyze it to understand both the information and the author's perspective. For example, look for citations that tell where information comes from. The author should give the source of any quotations or ideas included in the text that are not his or her own.

Try It   Read this paragraph.

The city square was filled with thousands of people holding signs and chanting in unison. A city official described the crowds as "restless and swarming," but videos captured by cell phones showed an enthusiastic but surprisingly calm crowd. The demonstrators knew they had numbers on their side. According to official police reports, the crowds had doubled in size since the first day of demonstrations. Unlike a swarm and more like a hive, the people had one purpose—to work together to preserve their community.

Discuss   How do you know the paragraph is from a secondary source? Circle the sentences or phrases that tell you. Does the author cite any primary sources? What is the author's perspective on the event described in this paragraph?

As you read, record your answers to questions about secondary sources on the Close Reading Worksheet on page 274.

Shackleton:
An Enduring Leader

What central idea about Shackleton does the author express? Record your answer in the largest oval on the **Central Idea and Details Web**.

How do you know this selection is a secondary source?

1   The Antarctic is one of the least hospitable places on Earth. Frozen and windy most of the year, it is one of the world's coldest, driest, and wildest regions. Even during summer, the weather is unpredictable, and irregular ice **formations** make sea travel dangerous for a **vessel** of any size. At the beginning of the twentieth century, the Antarctic was one of the last unexplored places in the world, and people were hungry to go there. Men from all over Europe and North America **engaged** in a fierce contest to be the first person to stand at the South Pole and to mark it with his nation's flag.

2   Among those who tried and failed was Ernest Shackleton, an Irishman of English ancestry with a restless sense of adventure, ambition, and a natural ability to lead. Shackleton traveled to the Antarctic several times during his life but never reached the South Pole. Yet his name lives on in history because of an amazing odyssey. From 1914 to 1916, he and his crew survived being shipwrecked and stranded on ice floes, sailing hundreds of miles in open boats over stormy waters, and scaling ice-covered mountains before they reached safety. And not a single man died. Most historians now believe Shackleton's leadership skills, concern for his men, and stubborn persistence were the reasons he and his men survived their ordeal.

To the South Pole!

3   Shackleton's first journey to Antarctica happened in 1901, when he was twenty-seven years old and joined an **expedition** led by Robert Falcon Scott. An Englishman known for charm and competitiveness, Scott was determined to become the first to reach the South Pole. But he was not an effective leader, and the expedition was plagued with problems. In Antarctica, Scott and his crew would wait out the winter on their icebound ship, the *Discovery*. It seemed a good plan, but Scott was unprepared for life on the coldest continent. He had brought along equipment that turned out to be useless. A hot air balloon provided a unique view of the horizon but little else of value. The crewmembers had skis, but no one knew how to use them. They also had dogs, but no one knew how to harness them into teams to pull sledges.[1] Arguments erupted, including one in which Shackleton called his leader the worst "fool of the lot." Food ran short, which contributed to an outbreak of scurvy, a disease caused by a lack of vitamin C. In addition, many of the men Scott had selected suffered from illnesses, such as tuberculosis or, as in Shackleton's case, heart disease.

4   To Scott's frustration, the expedition was still more than 500 miles from the South Pole when harsh conditions caused the men to turn back. Shackleton was so weak that Scott sent him back to England. Shackleton felt they had failed, but on his way home, he began making plans for his own expedition to the South Pole.

5   In 1907, he and a crew sailed again for Antarctica, where he had more success than Scott. Shackleton's team was only 111 miles from the South Pole on January 9, 1909, when supplies ran out. Knowing his men's lives were more important than reaching the pole, he turned back. "We have shot our bolt,"[2] Shackleton wrote, yet he would not give up.

---

[1] **sledge** a large sled, usually pulled by horses or dogs, to transport people or goods over snow
[2] **shot our bolt** British expression meaning "done all that we can"

Ernest Shackleton and his wife, Emily Dorman

The South Pole Is Taken

6   After the 1907 expedition, Shackleton was made a knight, and as Sir Ernest, he spent the next few years traveling, lecturing, and raising money for another Antarctic expedition. But then came the news: Norwegian explorer Roald Amundsen had reached the South Pole on December 14, 1911. His expedition had been a secret and a success.

7   Amundsen's expedition had benefitted from several advantages over Scott's and Shackleton's. His crewmen could ski and run dogsleds. As a result, they covered ground quickly and did not run low on supplies. Scott had staged an expedition, not knowing that Amundsen's team was weeks ahead of him. Amundsen left the Englishman some cast-off supplies and a note that teased: "Dear Captain Scott: As you probably are the first to reach this area after us, I will kindly ask you to forward this letter. . . ." When Scott reached the South Pole, he was devastated to see the Norwegian's footprints in the snow. In his diary, he wrote about his smashed dreams, calling the South Pole "an awful place . . . Now for the run home and a desperate struggle. I wonder if we can do it." They could not. Scott and two others froze to death in a tent in Antarctica. Despite his failure, Scott was mourned as a national hero.

8   No evidence survives that tells what Shackleton felt about the death of his **rival**, but he sent a gracious note of congratulations to Amundsen and then—ever persistent—changed his plans. Instead of striving for the South Pole, he would lead a team on an "Imperial Trans-Antarctic Expedition." He would cross the continent of Antarctica. It would be a feat far more dangerous and daring than reaching the South Pole. He called it "the last great Polar journey that can be made." By 1914, he had a ship, the *Endurance*, and a crew of twenty-eight men. They sailed from London on August 1, 1914, just three days before England entered World War I.

The *Endurance*

9   Shackleton's ship's name proved to be an omen, since during their voyage on the *Endurance*, Shackleton and his crew would undergo tremendous hardship, and Shackleton's leadership skills would be sorely tested. While still hundreds of miles from Antarctica, the ship encountered drifting pack ice. Pack ice is deadly for a ship; it traps a vessel and forces it to drift off course. Then, over time, like a voracious python, the ice builds up around the ship's body and crushes it. Shackleton and his crew had no choice but to wait out the winter on the icebound ship.

10   For months, the ship's hull, or body, withstood the pressure of the ice. To keep the crew feeling upbeat, Shackleton stayed calm and established a strict routine. Though there was no sailing to be done, there was still plenty of work, including cooking meals and caring for the dogs. Crewmembers took the animals out on the ice for sled races. Frank Hurley, an avid photographer, took photos of life on the trapped ship. His images show the men enjoying their adventure. Mrs. Chippy was also in some of the pictures. "She" was the carpenter's cat, but it was discovered early in the journey that she was a he.

11   In July 1915, the ship's sides began to **buckle** and collapse, and Shackleton warned the ship's captain, "The ship can't live like this, Skipper . . . what the ice gets, the ice keeps." Shackleton formulated an escape plan and ordered the men to set up a camp on the ice around the collapsing ship. They offloaded small boats, food, tools, sleds, and tents. Hurley saved more than one hundred photographic negatives and a small camera. Then on November 21, 1915, the twisted shell of the *Endurance* was finally destroyed by the ice.

12   The men camped on ice floes for five months. The weather was cold, food grew scarce, and because the ice began to break up beneath them, the men were constantly on the move in search of solid "ground." When the ice melt was nearly complete on April 9, 1916, Shackleton ordered the men into boats. Their only hope was to row across the open sea to the nearest land.

The *Endurance*, trapped in the Antarctic pack ice

The Fight for Survival

13   For a week, Shackleton and his men rowed three small boats through rough seas, fierce winds, and subzero temperatures. When they reached Elephant Island on April 15, they had not stood on solid ground for 497 days. Although they were momentarily safe, the men were sick, hungry, exhausted, cold, and no closer to rescue. Shackleton had to do more than rally his men; he had to save them.

14   Shackleton announced a daring plan: He and five volunteers would sail 800 miles northeast to South Georgia Island, the site of a whaling station. The chances of success were slim, but the men pulled together to **outfit** a boat and set up a camp where they would await rescue.

15   Surviving on the open sea in an open boat is unlikely even with good weather conditions. Overcast skies prevented reliable navigation, and as a result, the men sailed blindly through some of the worst weather ever recorded in the region. After sixteen days, they reached land, but not help. They had to cross the mountainous island in order to reach the whaling station.

16   Shackleton and two men continued on foot over the mountains. At one point, they were stranded, their descent blocked by ice. In wet clothing and without sleeping bags, they would surely freeze to death. Shackleton urged the men to slide down the slope on their backs. Within minutes, they stood at the foot of the mountain, and soon after, they staggered into the whaling station. The whalers, rough men used to hardship, were stunned by Shackleton's story. They dispatched ships to collect the waiting crewmen, all of whom survived.

17   Shackleton never relinquished his dream of the transcontinental journey. In 1921, he sailed again for Antarctica, but he died of heart failure off the coast of South Georgia. The explorer was buried there in a whaler's cemetery on March 5. He never reached the South Pole, but he is remembered for his persistence, strong leadership, and dedication to his crewmen that carried them all through a harrowing polar adventure.

Shackleton's men wave good-bye to the team of five as they head out to sea to seek help.

Vocabulary: Multiple-Meaning Words

A **multiple-meaning word** is a word with more than one definition or use. Usually, a multiple-meaning word can be used as different parts of speech. For example, the word *row* (pronounced ROH) is a noun that means "a line or sequence." *Row* is also a verb that means "using oars to propel a boat over water." And in British English, the noun *row* (pronounced ROW) means "an argument." When you encounter a multiple-meaning word and are not sure of how it is used or what it means, see how the author uses it in the sentence and look for context clues that hint at the meaning. If you still need help, check a dictionary to find the definition that best fits the context.

Try It The table below lists some multiple-meaning words from the selection.

Word	Part of Speech/Meaning in Selection	Another Meaning (and Part of Speech, If Changed)
1. **formation,** p. 104		
2. **vessel,** p. 104		
3. **engaged,** p. 104		
4. **expedition,** p. 105		
5. **rival,** p. 106		

> **Discuss** **Complete the table by writing the word's part of speech and its meaning as it is used in the selection. Then, use what you already know or a dictionary to identify another meaning of the word.**

Below are other multiple-meaning words from the text. Write each word's part of speech, and define how it is used in the selection. Then provide one alternate meaning. Look up the word in a dictionary if necessary.

1. **buckle,** p. 107 ____________________

2. **outfit,** p. 108 ____________________

Practice the Skill

When you are an active reader, you **ask and answer questions** as you read. Experienced readers ask questions before, during, and after reading. You might wonder: "Who is the author talking about?" "What does that word mean?" "Is that fact true?" or "Why did the author present information in a certain way?" It sounds simple, but it can be tricky to get yourself to stop and think about your questions—even write them down—and then figure out the answers.

Authors might not always directly reveal all the information you're looking for or wondering about. Sometimes the answers are right in the text. But other times you must reread or read further to find them. Reading thoughtfully and carefully will give you the most rewarding reading experiences.

Try It   Read the following paragraph.

Stories about the "eccentric" American poet Emily Dickinson (1830–1886) have been circulating for more than a century. While it is true that she rarely left the house in which she grew up, the idea that she was meek as a mouse is completely contradicted by her writing, which suggests that she instead had a lion's heart. She published only a handful of her thousand or so poems during her lifetime. People who read her poetry today are often amazed by its wild energy, vivid imagery, and original ideas about life and death. Letters to her publisher reveal wit and intelligence. Diaries kept by family members describe her playfulness. Some critics have suggested that Dickinson purposely did not publish her writing because she did not think the world would be able to handle it.

Discuss   **You might have asked yourself, "What does the author mean by saying that Dickinson's writing suggested she had a 'lion's heart'?" Double underline details in the paragraph that answer the question.**

As you read, record your answers on the Close Reading Worksheet on page 275.

Practice the Skill

A **primary source** is firsthand information about an event, person, time, or place. Letters, diaries, autobiographies, memoirs, speeches, interviews, blogs, and other forms of social media are types of primary sources. Primary sources are written by the people who witnessed or participated in the event described. Writers create primary sources by recording their experiences—what they did, saw, thought, said, or hoped for—during a particular point in time. Primary sources capture one person's experience for you to read that day, the next week, or years in the future.

Try It Read the following paragraph.

> It's late July, and summer is getting old. I don't have a summer job this year, so I spend my afternoons at the community pool, where I lie on a faded beach towel and stare at the sky. Yesterday I saw a tiny sliver of the moon in the afternoon sky. I never knew the moon came out during the day. Dad says it's up there all the time, we just don't notice it. He was very excited about the latest moon launch—Apollo 15. Me? I didn't care. How many times can we send men to the moon? But it was a big deal around here. Dad stayed home this morning to watch the launch on TV. He was wearing his shabby old bathrobe and hadn't shaved, but his face lit up when huge white clouds started billowing from the rocket's engines. A monotone voice began the countdown: "Ten … nine … eight …" We counted down with it: "Three … two … one—liftoff!" When the rocket soared into the sky, everybody cheered, including me.

Discuss **What kind of writing is this primary source? When was it written? Who is the writer? Box words and phrases that give clues to answer these questions. How well does the writer convey feelings and capture a specific point in time?**

As you read, complete the Analyzing Primary Sources Organizer on page 276.

from Escape from the Antarctic

by Ernest Shackleton

This excerpt from Ernest Shackleton's memoir tells how he and two crewmembers crossed the mountains of South Georgia Island that stood between them and rescue for the entire Endurance *crew.*

Why was it so difficult for the men to cross the mountains? Double underline the details that answer the question.

What details from the selection help you identify the selection as a primary source? Write your answer in the **Analyzing Primary Sources Organizer**.

1   Cautiously we started down the slope that led to warmth and comfort. The last lap of the journey proved extraordinarily difficult. Vainly we searched for a safe, or a reasonably safe, way down the steep ice-clad mountain-side. The sole possible pathway seemed to be a channel cut by water running from the upland. Down through icy water we followed the course of this stream. We were wet to the waist, shivering, cold, and tired. Presently our ears detected an unwelcome sound that might have been musical under other conditions. It was the splashing of a waterfall, and we were at the wrong end. When we reached the top of this fall we peered over cautiously and discovered that there was a drop of 25 or 30 feet, with impassable ice-cliffs on both sides. To go up again was scarcely thinkable in our utterly wearied condition. The way down was through the waterfall itself. We made fast one end of our rope to a boulder with some difficulty, due to the fact that the rocks had been worn smooth by the running water. Then Worsley and I lowered Crean, who was the heaviest man. He disappeared altogether in the falling water and came out gasping at the bottom.

2   I went next, sliding down the rope, and Worsley, who was the lightest and most nimble member of the party, came last. At the bottom of the fall we were able to stand again on dry land. The rope could not be recovered. We had flung down the adze[1] from the top of the fall and also the logbook and the cooker wrapped in one of our blouses. That was all, except our wet clothes, that we brought out of the Antarctic, which we had entered a year and a half before with well-found ship, full equipment, and high hopes. That was all of tangible things; but in memories we were rich. . . .

3   Shivering with cold, yet with hearts light and happy, we set off towards the whaling-station, now not more than a mile and a half distant. The difficulties of the journey lay behind us. We tried to straighten ourselves up a bit, for the thought that there might be women at the station made us painfully conscious of our **uncivilized** appearance. Our beards were long and our hair was matted. We were unwashed and the garments that we had worn for nearly a year without a change were tattered and stained. Three more **unpleasant**-looking ruffians could hardly have been imagined. Worsley produced several safety-pins from some corner of his garments and effected some temporary repairs that really emphasized his general **disrepair**. Down we hurried, and when quite close to the station we met two small boys ten or twelve years of age. I asked these lads where the manager's house was situated. They did not answer. They gave us one look—a comprehensive look that did not need to be repeated.

[1]**adze** an axe with a curved blade

Shackleton and Worsley lower Crean down what is now called Shackleton Falls.

4   Then they ran from us as fast as their legs would carry them. We reached the outskirts of the station and passed through the "digesting-house," which was dark inside. Emerging at the other end, we met an old man, who started as if he had seen the Devil himself and gave us no time to ask any question. He hurried away. This greeting was not friendly. Then we came to the wharf, where the man in charge stuck to his station. I asked him if Mr. Sorlle (the manager) was in the house.

5   "Yes," he said as he stared at us.

6   "We would like to see him," said I.

7   "Who are you?" he asked.

8   "We have lost our ship and come over the island," I replied.

9   "You have come over the island?" he said in a tone of entire disbelief.

10   The man went towards the manager's house and we followed him. I learned afterwards that he said to Mr. Sorlle: "There are three funny-looking men outside, who say they have come over the island and they know you. I have left them outside." A very necessary precaution from his point of view.

11   Mr. Sorlle came out to the door and said, "Well?"

12   "Don't you know me?" I said.

13   "I know your voice," he replied doubtfully. "You're the mate of the *Daisy*."

14   "My name is Shackleton," I said.

15   Immediately he put out his hand and said, "Come in. Come in."

16   "Tell me, when was the war over?" I asked.

17   "The war is not over," he answered. "Millions are being killed. Europe is mad. The world is mad."

18   Mr. Sorlle's hospitality had no bounds. He would scarcely let us wait to remove our freezing boots before he took us into his house and gave us seats in a warm and comfortable room. We were in no condition to sit in anybody's house until we had washed and got into clean clothes, but the kindness of the station-manager was proof even against the unpleasantness of being in a room with us. He gave us coffee and cakes in the Norwegian fashion, and then showed us upstairs to the bathroom, where we shed our rags and scrubbed ourselves luxuriously.

19   Mr. Sorlle's kindness did not end with his personal care for the three wayfarers who had come to his door. While we were washing he gave orders for one of the whaling-vessels to be prepared at once in order that it might leave that night for the other side of the island and pick up the three men there. The whalers knew King Haakon Bay, though they never worked on that side of the island. Soon we were clean again. Then we put on delightful new clothes supplied from the station stores and got rid of our **superfluous** hair. Within an hour or two we had ceased to be savages and had become civilized men again. Then came a splendid meal, while Mr. Sorlle told us of the arrangements he had made and we discussed plans for the rescue of the main party on Elephant Island.

20   I arranged that Worsley should go with the relief ship to show the exact spot where the carpenter and his two **companions** were camped, while I started to prepare for the relief of the party on Elephant Island. The whaling-vessel that was going round to King Haakon Bay was expected back on the Monday morning, and was to call at Grytviken Harbour, the port from which we had sailed in December 1914, in order that the magistrate resident there might be informed of the fate of the *Endurance*.

21   It was possible that letters were awaiting us there. Worsley went aboard the whaler at ten o'clock that night and turned in. The next day the relief ship entered King Haakon Bay and he reached Peggotty Camp in a boat.

Why didn't Shackleton help rescue the men he left on the other side of South Georgia Island?

Box details that tell you something about the time and place in which this primary source was written.

Look at the details you boxed. What do the details tell you about the time and place in which this primary source was written?

What question or questions do you still have that the author has left unanswered?

Why did Shackleton end this section of his memoir with a personal reflection? Write your answer on the **Analyzing Primary Sources Organizer**.

Analyze

Based on this primary source, what kind of person do you think Shackleton was?

22 The three men were delighted beyond measure to know that we had made the crossing in safety and that their wait under the upturned *James Caird* was ended. Curiously enough, they did not recognize Worsley, who had left them a hairy, dirty ruffian and had returned his spruce and shaven self. They thought he was one of the whalers. When one of them asked why no member of the party had come round with the relief, Worsley said, "What do you mean?" "We thought the Boss or one of the others would come round," they explained. "What's the matter with you?" said Worsley. Then it suddenly dawned upon them that they were talking to the man who had been their close companion for a year and a half. Within a few minutes the whalers had moved our bits of gear into their boat. They towed off the *James Caird* and hoisted her to the deck of their ship. Then they started on the return voyage. Just at dusk on Monday afternoon they entered Stromness Bay, where the men of the whaling-station mustered on the beach to receive the rescued party and to examine with professional interest the boat we had navigated across 800 miles of the stormy ocean they knew so well.

23 When I look back at those days I have no doubt that Providence[2] guided us, not only across those snowfields, but across the storm-white sea that separated Elephant Island from our landing-place on South Georgia. I know that during that long and racking march of thirty-six hours over the unnamed mountains and glaciers of South Georgia it seemed to me often that we were four, not three. I said nothing to my companions on the point, but afterwards Worsley said to me, "Boss, I had a curious feeling on the march that there was another person with us." Crean confessed to the same idea. One feels "the dearth[3] of human words, the roughness of mortal speech" in trying to describe things intangible, but a record of our journeys would be incomplete without a reference to a subject very near to our hearts.

[2]**Providence** God
[3]**dearth** scarce supply, lack

Vocabulary: Latin Prefixes

A **prefix** is a word part added to the beginning of a root to create a new word. Once you learn the meanings of common prefixes, such as those in the table below, you can apply that knowledge to figure out the meanings of unfamiliar words.

Common Latin Prefixes		
Prefix	**Meaning**	**Example Words**
com-	with, together	communicate, community
dif-, dis-	away, off, opposing	dissent, different
super-	above, extra	superhuman, superlative
un-	not	unable, uncommunicative

Try It Read this excerpt from Shackleton's memoir *Escape from the Antarctic*.

Three more **unpleasant**-looking ruffians could hardly have been imagined. Worsley produced several safety-pins . . . and effected some temporary repairs that really emphasized his general **disrepair**.

Discuss **How can your knowledge of the meanings of the prefixes *un-* and *dis-* help you figure out the meanings of *unpleasant* and *disrepair*?**

The following words from *Escape from the Antarctic* contain Latin prefixes. Read the sentences from the selection that contain the words. Then write their meanings on the lines below.

1. **uncivilized,** p. 113 ______________________________

____

2. **superfluous,** p. 115 ______________________________

____

3. **companion,** p. 115 ______________________________

____

Respond to Text: Primary and Secondary Sources

"Shackleton: An Enduring Leader" and *Escape from the Antarctic* are two kinds of literary nonfiction.

- "Shackleton: An Enduring Leader": article; secondary source
- *Escape from the Antarctic*: memoir; primary source

Try It Think about how readers get similar and different information from primary and secondary sources that cover the same topic.

Discuss **How did the source of each text influence how you understood and thought about Shackleton's experience?**

On Your Own Write a paragraph about the similarities and differences in "Shackleton: An Enduring Leader" and the excerpt from *Escape from the Antarctic*. Think about the information you got from each selection, why their authors wrote them, and who the intended audience is. Use your discussion to draw a conclusion about how primary and secondary sources on the same topic are similar and different. Give examples from the texts to support your ideas. Use the guide on the next page to organize your response. Then write your paragraph on a separate sheet of paper.

Checklist for a Good Response

A good paragraph

- ✔ describes the source of the two texts.
- ✔ identifies two or three points of comparison or similarity.
- ✔ discusses similarities, using examples.
- ✔ discusses differences, using examples.
- ✔ includes a topic sentence, supporting ideas, and a concluding statement.

How Primary and Secondary Sources Affected My Reading

1. **Topic Sentence** Include this information in your topic sentence:

   "Shackleton: An Enduring Leader" is a ________________ source, while *Escape*

   from the Antarctic is a ________________ source.

2. **Detail Sentences** Write how the different perspectives affected the selections and your understanding of them. Use the chart to organize the similarities and differences.

Primary Source	Both	Secondary Source

3. **Concluding Sentence** Your concluding sentence should restate your idea about how the different sources affected your understanding of the topic.

On a separate sheet of paper, write your paragraph.

How Not to Go Camping

Ask and Answer Questions The name of the writer who wrote inspiring nature essays has been <u>underlined</u> for you. Now <u>double underline</u> details in the selection that tell you more about him.

Primary Sources Think about the author and his or her attitude toward nature. Box the details that reveal information about the author. The first detail has been boxed for you.

1   As a lifelong city dweller, I've had little interaction with nature. I prefer the orderly arrangement of city streets to a nature trail. I also prefer to be warm and dry. Years ago, I went to a nature preserve for a school trip. It was rainy and cold, so I spent the day in a corner of the nature center reading a science fiction novel. While my classmates wandered around staring through binoculars at birds, I sat contentedly under a poster of those same animals and read about robots excavating the red sands of Mars.

2   I paid a price for ignoring nature that day. My teacher told me to read one of <u>Henry David Thoreau's</u> essays. Thoreau was a writer who lived in Massachusetts in the mid-1800s. He was famous for living in a hut in the woods and then writing about the experience. I dreaded the assignment, but one of Thoreau's ideas stuck with me: "Hope and future for me are not in lawns and cultivated fields, not in towns

Walden Pond, where
Henry David Thoreau lived

and cities, but in the impervious and quaking swamps." For Thoreau, civilization and technology were not signs of progress. Instead, he looked to the wilderness because it was wild and messy and beautiful.

3 Years later, those words inspired me to attempt camping. It was summer and the state park I chose had lean-to shelters, so I wouldn't need to build a fire for warmth or pitch a tent. I filled a backpack with water and sandwiches and treats for my dog, Mouse. Then I put on old sneakers, clipped on Mouse's leash, and drove to the state park.

4 The ranger there told me where the shelters were located and to keep Mouse on his leash. Then he wished me luck. As it turned out, I would need that luck and also several other things I didn't have: a rain jacket, a flashlight, dry socks, extra food, and hiking boots. Walking in the woods is *not* a walk in the park. The ground is rocky and uneven, and the weather is unpredictable. The exertion of walking uphill will make you hungry enough to eat all your food, and if you let your dog off his leash, he will disappear into the underbrush. Within hours, my tennis shoes were soaked, I was freezing, and my food was gone. When Mouse reappeared, we had **covered** about a mile, but then the sun started going down. We had no choice but to turn back, or we'd have to spend the night on the trail without food or shelter. Wet, filthy, and hungry, we stumbled back to the parking lot. Then we drove past the empty ranger's booth and headed back to civilization.

Camping on the Wild Side

1 According to the United Nations, more than half the world's population lives in cities and towns. So, where do people go when they want to escape urban life? Many go camping. The United States National Park Service Web site states that nearly twelve million people visit U.S. national parks each year. Not all were camping, but the numbers are staggering. Even state and local parks are overcrowded. Many campers have stories of settling into their sleeping bags only to have the sounds of crickets drowned out by a neighboring camper's music player or television. Overcrowded campgrounds are one reason many are turning to extreme camping. By visiting specialized camps, people can camp in trees or off the sides of mountains or even in igloos. Campers get to experience nature in a unique way.

Henry David Thoreau

Central Idea and Supporting Details
Think about the main point the author of "How Not to Go Camping" is trying to make. Underline the sentence that states it.

Central Idea and Supporting Details
Think about the central idea of "Camping on the Wild Side." Underline the sentence that expresses it. Look for details that support it.

Secondary Sources
Think about how the author of "Camping on the Wild Side" uses primary sources. Also think about how the information supports the selection's central idea.

2   At one camp in Germany, guests can experience a bird's-eye view of the world. They can sleep in treetop tents or on platforms suspended from steep mountain cliffs. Treetop camping involves spending the night in a tent suspended from the branches of trees. The tents look like giant tea bags with flat bottoms. Campers climb up to and descend from the tent by ropes. At night, they dangle in the air, enjoying cool breezes and night sounds. Those who prefer the mountains can sleep on platforms attached to the cliffs. These platforms are the same devices that serious mountain climbers use on overnight expeditions. They are not for campers who sleepwalk—the narrow platforms are suspended between three hundred and six thousand feet in the air! Campers must take a rope-climbing class and lessons in hiking and rock climbing before they can settle in for the night. Extreme campers say the exertion (and risk) required to get into their beds is completely erased by the spectacular views they awake to in the morning.

3   For those who prefer even more extreme conditions, winter guests at the camp can sleep in igloos. Igloos are structures formed from blocks of hard-packed snow. They are warmer than you might expect. Temperatures inside the igloos hover in the upper 30s Fahrenheit. So, campers still need to wear warm socks. The morning view may not be as breathtaking as from a treetop tent, but igloo campers can claim they have experienced conditions like those experienced by the great polar explorers Scott and Shackleton.

An extreme camper settles into bed on the side of a mountain cliff.

1. Identify the central idea expressed by the author of "How Not to Go Camping." What details does he or she include to support that idea?

2. What do the details in "How Not to Go Camping" reveal about the person who wrote it? What words might you use to describe the author?

3. Which information in "Camping on the Wild Side" comes from primary sources? What idea does the author use the information to support?

4. Why does the second author include the detail about making special preparations for camping in the treetops or off the sides of mountain cliffs?

5. Compare and contrast the two authors' attitudes toward nature. How would you characterize their attitudes?

6. Read this sentence from "How Not to Go Camping."

> **When Mouse reappeared, we had covered about a mile, but then the sun started going down.**

Write the meaning of the word *covered* as it is used in this sentence. Then, write two more meanings that the word has.

7. Read this sentence from "How Not to Go Camping." Circle the words that contain Latin prefixes. Then, use a dictionary to answer the questions.

> **While my classmates wandered around staring through binoculars at birds, I sat contentedly under a poster of those same animals and read about robots excavating the red sands of Mars.**

Which word uses the prefix *bi-*? Write the word's meaning.

Which word uses the prefix *ex-*? Write the word's meaning.

Historical Texts

Historical texts are a form of nonfiction. Fact-filled articles, firsthand accounts, and letters about real events, people, and places are all examples of historical texts. Historical texts can describe why people behaved a certain way and what life was like during a certain period. Some historical texts are written by the people who lived through the events being written about. Others are written by people who did not live through the events but perform research to learn more about them. Look at this photograph. What is its historical setting? What sort of text would you expect to accompany it?

Skills Focus

When in Rome . . . or Brazil

Summarize   **Chronology and Sequence**

Restoring a Classic

Identify Steps in a Process

Integrate Visual Information

Practice the Skill

A **summary** is a short retelling of the big ideas in a selection in your own words. Your summary should accurately describe what you read, and it should not include your opinions or personal thoughts.

You need to read the entire selection before you can write a complete summary. When you're done reading, think about the important information you've read and what the main point or idea is. Look for the details that best support that idea. Then think about how you would tell someone what the selection is mostly about. That's your summary.

Try It Read these paragraphs.

Scientists believe that climate change may have played a part in the rise and fall of the Roman Empire. Every growing season, a tree adds a new layer of wood to its trunk. Scientists know that when trees are able to get a lot of water and nutrients, they grow more and form thicker rings. During periods of drought, the growth rings are thinner. By studying the width of tree rings found in wood used to make artifacts and buildings, scientists established that when the summers were wet and warm, the Roman Empire thrived.

Later, the climate dried, and the Roman Empire faced many challenges. Barbarians invaded. There were years of fighting, and the empire finally fell in 476 CE. Scientists don't maintain that climate change was solely responsible for the empire's downfall, but they have drawn the conclusion that it may have added to the empire's other problems.

Discuss What is the big idea of these paragraphs? Underline the details that support this big idea. How you would summarize the two paragraphs?

As you read, record your answers to questions about summarizing on the Close Reading Worksheet on page 277. 

Practice the Skill

When you read historical texts, it's important to be aware of dates and other information that tell you the order of events in a text. Recognizing the chronological order in which things happen will help you better understand historic events or the cultural era that the text describes. Watch for phrases like these as you read: *early in the twentieth century*, *in 1939*, *in March of 1965*, *later that year*, *the following year*.

In addition to dates and other time-related information, look for words that tell about the sequence, or order, of events. They include the words *first*, *next*, *then*, *last*, *before*, *after*, and *finally*.

Try It   Read these paragraphs.

Restorers need to have a delicate touch when handling art and artifacts that are thousands of years old. Restorers work to bring these objects back to their original condition. First, they look closely at the objects under special lights. Then, they rearrange any broken pieces. Finally, they use glue to put them back together again.

Elizabeth Gonzalez was given the pieces of a Mayan pot to restore in February 2006. She did three months of research before she even touched them. She called experts on Mayan pottery and sent them pictures of the potsherds. Then, she looked up information on the Internet and in books. By May 2006, she was ready to begin her work. It took two long years, but in 2008, the pot was fully restored.

Discuss   **Circle the words that indicate a sequence of events.**

As you read, complete the Sequence Chart on page 278.

When in Rome ... or Brazil

What is the big idea of this page? Write a sentence that summarizes the main idea of what you've read.

From the information on this page, do you think the Romans were known as great navigators?

1   Almost two thousand years ago, the Roman Empire stretched from England to Africa and claimed most of the coast of the Mediterranean Sea. However, the Romans were not known to have ventured across the Atlantic Ocean. So when a treasure hunter named Robert Marx found ancient Roman artifacts in a bay near Brazil—thousands of miles from Rome—people wondered how they got there?

2   Many factors made an ocean crossing highly unlikely. An explorer's ship would have had to spend months crossing thousands of miles of dangerous ocean waters to reach Brazil. Such a voyage would have involved many life-threatening situations, from storms and wild winds to dead calms where the ship would drift aimlessly for days as supplies ran low. Furthermore, presumably no one in those days knew that there even was a Brazil to sail to. What lay beyond the ocean was an uninviting mystery.

3   Despite the dangers, it's *possible* the Romans really made it to Brazil. If so, they would have arrived thirteen centuries before the European age of exploration. It wasn't until 1500 CE that Pedro Cabral, thought to have been the first European to reach Brazil, sailed there from Portugal. So it would be an incredible historical find to learn that the Romans had arrived first. However, as the treasure hunter Marx soon found, getting to the bottom of this mystery wouldn't be easy.

Diving Deep

4   Robert Marx is not a pirate, but he often acts like one. In his work as a treasure hunter, he has hunted for shipwrecks and sunken treasure around the world. Marx is an explorer, just like the ones who sailed the ships he searches for.

5   According to Marx, he began his career as a diving **specialist** in the U.S. Marine Corps, where he located Civil War ships and artifacts off the coast of North Carolina. Later, he directed the massive excavation of the sunken city of Port Royal, Jamaica, then spent many years continuing his deep-sea explorations around the world. It was off the coast of Brazil, in 1982, that he stumbled upon the mystery of the Roman ship.

6   The harbor of Rio de Janeiro is a truly incredible natural site. It is a huge bay that reaches twenty miles inland. Fishers in the area had begun to notice that they were dragging up strange clay pieces in their nets. Marx decided to excavate part of the harbor to find out what was going on. He dove into Guanabara Bay, about fifteen miles from Rio de Janeiro. There he found a graveyard of amphorae. These tall jars were used on Roman ships as long ago as 200 BCE. Marx had made a discovery that could change the history books!

Roman amphorae

Mysterious Vessels

7   Amphorae, the plural of amphora, are large clay vessels that were used for trade and storage in ancient Greece and Rome. They were like the plastic storage containers of ancient times. They held products like grain, oil, and wine. Because amphorae were built with different types of clay and decorated in different styles depending on the place and time period in which they were made, historians can tell exactly where and when they were created.

8   Marx found hundreds of amphorae in what he believes to be an ancient Roman shipwreck. Dr. Elizabeth Will, who was an expert on Roman amphorae, thought he might be right. She said that the jars are similar in shape to ones produced by a Roman colony on the west coast of Morocco, in North Africa. The location may be noteworthy because it is the nearest point in the Roman Empire to Brazil.

9   "They look Roman to me," said Will, an associate professor of classics at the University of Massachusetts. "They look to be ancient and because of the profile, the thin-walled fabric, and the shape of the rims, I suggested they belong to the third century AD."

10   Even before finding the amphorae, Marx had maintained that other Europeans had reached the Americas before Columbus. This led some people to be critical of Marx's Brazilian find. They believed that Marx just wanted to find proof for his theories and that the whole thing was a hoax. Brazil still has strong ties to Portugal, so the suggestion that someone other than a Portuguese explorer first landed there was highly **controversial**.

11   One Brazilian businessman even said that the amphorae were his. He said that he had asked a potter in Portugal to make replicas of the ancient Roman jars. He claimed that he dropped them in the bay in 1961 to age them but then only recovered four of them.

A Major Obstacle

12   Marx remained convinced that he had made an important discovery. Marx had faced **adversity** before in his long career. He had had to make his way past sharks, treacherous storms, and even pirates! However, none of these challenges held him back as much as the Brazilian government would.

13   When Marx returned to Guanabara Bay to continue his investigation, he claims that he found the site covered with a thick layer of silt. Marx believes the Brazilian navy dumped the dirt there to cover the remains of the Roman shipwreck he had discovered. He believes they didn't want anyone changing Brazil's recorded history.

14   The Brazilian government counterattacked. First, they charged Marx with illegally taking artifacts from wrecks he had discovered in Brazil. They said they had an agreement with Marx, and he had broken that agreement. He was supposed to report anything he discovered during his searches in Brazilian waters. Government officials displayed catalogs of gold coins and other artifacts taken from shipwrecks in Brazil. These items were for sale on behalf of Marx. The Brazilian government said they had never been reported when they were found.

15   Then, the government issued an order that prohibited Marx from entering Brazil. They canceled all permits for underwater exploration and digging by *anyone*. This put a stop to any archaeological dives in Guanabara Bay. It was a blow to all undersea archaeologists. More than one hundred English, French, and Portuguese shipwrecks lie in the bay, filled with objects that could offer unique glimpses into history.

What happened after the Brazilian government charged Marx with illegally taking artifacts? Record two events on the **Sequence Chart.**

Why does the canceling of underwater permits matter so much?

An Unsolved Mystery

16   Marx continued his deep-sea explorations in other places and uncovered more than five thousand shipwrecks around the world. The Spanish government granted him knighthood for his reenactment of Columbus's voyage to the Americas. He wrote nearly sixty books and produced fifty-five documentary films about history, archaeology, and exploration.

17   Marx speaks out on the importance of protecting historic discoveries. "The concept of 'finders keepers' should never apply to shipwrecks or anything old which one might find under the sea. It has always been my belief that shipwrecks and other underwater finds belong to all of mankind," Marx told the U.S. congressional subcommittee on **oceanography**.

18   Marx has never been allowed to return to the Brazilian shipwreck that may have been his greatest discovery. Since he is no longer able to dive because of health problems, he never will. But the question of whether the Romans sailed across the Atlantic Ocean before Columbus has yet to be resolved.

19   Other archaeological finds have been made that some say are proof that Marx's theory is correct. A small terra-cotta head was found in Mexico. Scientists who analyzed it believe it is from ancient Rome. No one can prove exactly how the head got to Mexico, however. It may have been left in Mexico by ancient Romans, or it could have been brought there in more recent times.

20   Until someone like Marx discovers more evidence from sites like the shipwreck in Guanabara Bay, we may *never* know the truth.

A reproduction of a Spanish caravel like the one Marx used for his reenactment of Columbus's voyage to the Americas

Vocabulary: Common Latin and Greek Suffixes

Many of the words and word parts we use are derived from Latin and Greek. A **suffix** is a word part that is added to the end of a word to create a new word. Look at the word *consideration*. The suffix *-ation* is added to the word *consider*. This Latin suffix means "an action or process" or "a state or quality." Knowing that, what do you think the word *consideration* means? Can you think of other words you know that end with the suffix *-ation*?

Suffix	Language of Origin	Definition
-ist	Greek	one who . . .
-graphy	Greek	a field of study
-ial	Latin	relating to; characterized by
-ity	Latin	a state or condition

Try It The words below can all be broken into smaller parts. Double underline the suffix in each word. Then, based on your understanding of the suffix, write a definition for the word.

Word	Definition
1. **specialist,** p. 129	
2. **controversial,** p. 130	
3. **adversity,** p. 131	
4. **oceanography,** p. 132	

Discuss Look for other words with these suffixes in the selection. Discuss what they might mean and why you think so.

Practice the Skill

 Identify Steps in a Process

A process is a series of actions that have to happen in order for something to get done. Historical texts sometimes describe a process, such as the steps that people took to migrate from one place to another. Sometimes steps in a process are easy to spot in the text, especially when the author provides clue words such as *first*, *next*, and *last*. Other times, the steps might be more difficult to identify. In that case, it is useful to try to visualize the process being described. As you read, try to imagine the steps being followed in a process.

Try It Read these paragraphs.

In 1776, the Continental Congress met in Philadelphia, ready to vote for independence from England. A committee was selected to draft the document that would declare independence. John Adams, Benjamin Franklin, Thomas Jefferson, Robert R. Livingston, and Roger Sherman were on the committee.

According to Adams, the group first proposed that Thomas Jefferson and John Adams should write the draft. Adams stated that Jefferson was more popular and a better writer. Therefore, Jefferson agreed to work on the draft alone. He started on June 11 and went through several versions before he had a draft ready to present to Adams. They had a meeting, and Adams was happy with Jefferson's work. Then, they presented it to the committee, and the group approved it, with a few revisions. The draft was submitted to the Continental Congress on June 28. It was further edited and revised. Finally, it was released to the public on July 4, 1776.

Discuss Imagine you are in Philadelphia during the summer of 1776. Picture the steps that led to the creation and proclamation of the Declaration of Independence. What happened first? What happened next? What happened last?

As you read, complete the Steps in a Process Chart on page 279.

Practice the Skill

Historical texts often include **visual information**, or graphics, that provide you with additional information about the content or present facts in a different way. Common graphic features of historical texts are diagrams, time lines, and maps. Diagrams show a picture of a thing or a process and have labels and lines to indicate what the labels are describing or explaining. Time lines show the order in which historical events occurred. A map can show you what an area looks like now or looked like in the past. Maps can show geographic information like the location of rivers and mountains. They can also display political information, such as national borders and major cities. Maps have labels to show place-names, a compass rose to show direction, and a scale to indicate distances.

Try It Look at the map of modern Italy below.

Discuss Circle and discuss the compass rose, the scale, and other important parts of the map, and tell how they are used. What countries border Italy? What bodies of water surround Italy?

As you read, record your answers to questions about visual information on the Close Reading Worksheet on page 280.

Restoring a Classic

1   Battles! Sports! Wild beasts! Nearly two thousand years ago, the Colosseum in Rome was as exciting and noisy as any football stadium is today. Romans packed the arena's five sections to watch chariot races, gladiator fights, and epic mock sea battles.

2   The Colosseum was built by the emperor Vespasian, who came into power in 69 CE. Five years earlier, much of Rome had been destroyed in a horrific fire. Vespasian wanted to build a structure that would honor the people of Rome.

3   It was a **monumental** undertaking. First, architects created **intricate** plans for the building. Every detail had to be **precisely** worked out before the building started. The architectural plans included a large quantity of entrances, hallways, and staircases so that crowds could easily enter and exit the building. The building plans had to be approved by the emperor before work could begin.

4   Once the plans were finalized, it was time to get to work. The Colosseum would be built in sections. Vespasian engaged enormous numbers of skilled and unskilled laborers to do the work. A giant hole was dug in the ground to create a space for the foundation. Limestone was mined in Tivoli, a nearby city, and was used to build the main pillars, ground floor, and outer wall. The walls were held together by iron clamps.

5   Concrete, a fairly new invention, was created by mixing volcanic ash with water, rocks, and limestone. It was used to build the arches that supported the Colosseum's upper levels.

What steps were taken to build the Colosseum? As you read the whole first section, record your answers in the **Steps in a Process Chart.**

Why did the plans for the Colosseum have to be so precise? Give two reasons.

6 It took less than ten years to build the Colosseum, and Vespasian died just before it was finished. Vespasian's son Titus took over the completion of the building and opened the arena with one hundred days of games in 80 CE. Another of Vespasian's sons, Domitian, later added the top tier of the structure.

The Beauty of Engineering

7 The Colosseum was a stunning work of art, but its real beauty is found in its engineering. To build the Colosseum to its massive size required two major architectural innovations: the invention of concrete and the use of the vaulted arch.

8 Concrete was a relatively new invention at the time of the Colosseum's construction. The Romans didn't even know if it would last very long, but they had little reason to worry! Concrete is a mixture of sand, crushed stone, lime, and a volcanic material called *pozzolana*. When water is added, this mixture can be formed into any shape. Once it hardens, concrete is an incredibly strong material that we still use to build giant buildings—and most of our sidewalks—today.

9 A vaulted arch is an archway that often makes use of concrete. The amazing thing about these arches is that even though they're mostly made up of empty space, they can support very heavy loads. Because of the empty space, arches are lighter than solid walls, so buildings can be built higher without collapsing. The architects of the Colosseum included eighty entrance arches and many more on the two levels above them.

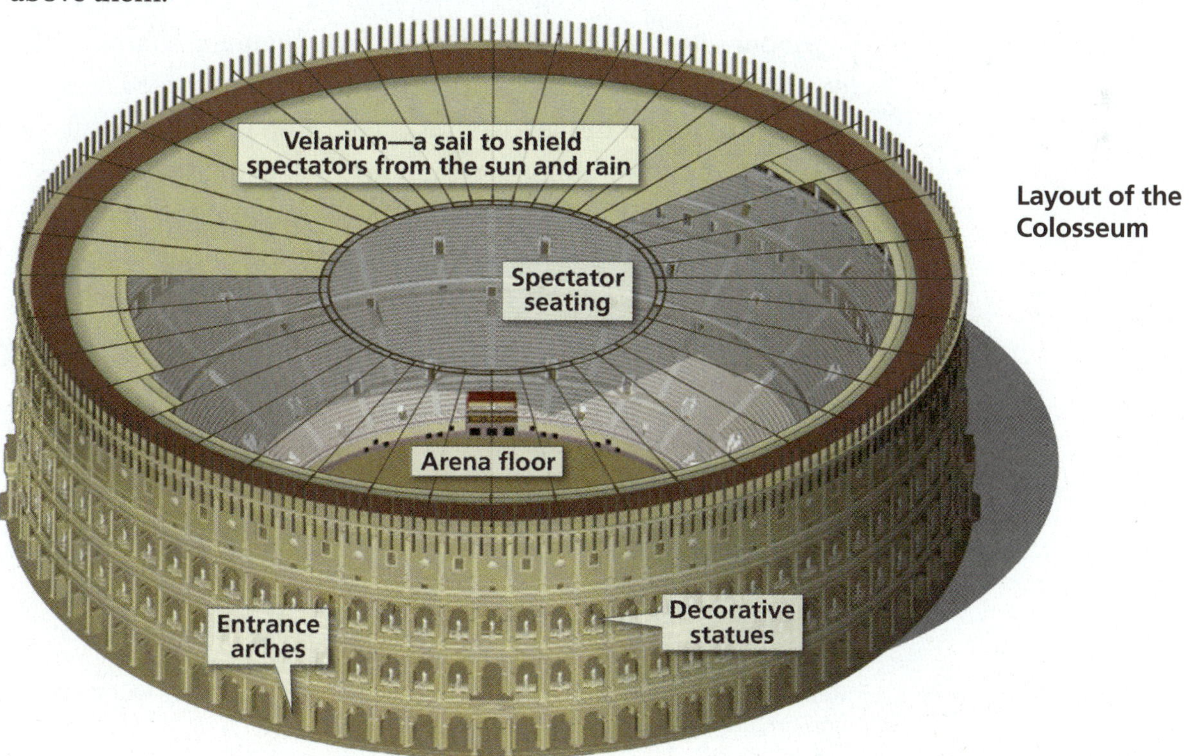

Layout of the Colosseum

Roman Colosseum through the Ages

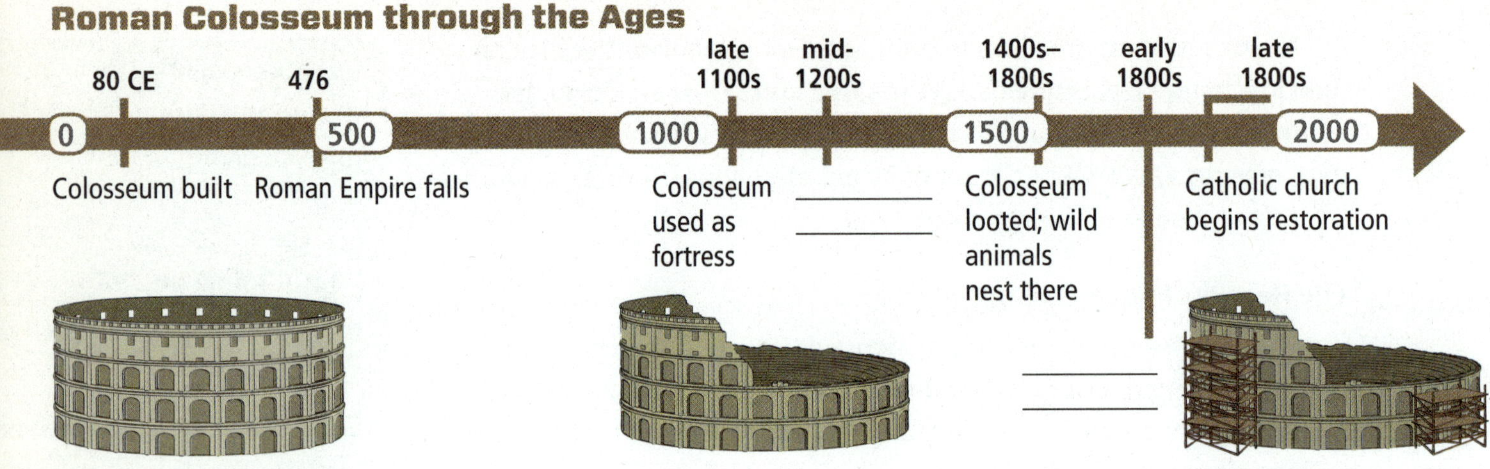

10 These architects wanted to create an impressive structure for Rome. Without concrete and the vaulted arch, it never could have happened. Not only did these inventions help make the Colosseum visually appealing, but also they made it incredibly long lasting.

Falling to Ruins

11 The Colosseum took some harmful hits during the Roman Empire. It was damaged during a fire in 217 and in an earthquake. It was repaired both times. Because of the exorbitant costs of producing events there, however, over time it was used less frequently.

12 The Roman Empire fell in 476, and by the end of the sixth century, the Colosseum had been almost completely abandoned. Over time, craftsmen rented space in the building, and the arena floor became a cemetery.

13 About seven hundred years later, the Frangipani, a family with roots in ancient Rome, took over the Colosseum and used it as a fortress. They built tunnels to connect the arena to other family homes in the area, but they didn't control it for long. In the 1200s, it was used as a quarry by the Catholic church. The Colosseum sustained much damage during this period, as the arena's stones and other materials were reused by the church for other building projects. Stones were even used to make the steps of St. Peter's Basilica, one of Rome's most famous churches.

14 During the Renaissance,[1] the Colosseum was frequently looted. All the marble seats and decorative materials vanished as people took them to use in their homes. Neglected for a long period of time, the Colosseum became overrun with plants, weeds, and trees, and wolves and other wild animals made their homes in it.

[1]**Renaissance** a period between medieval and modern times when art and architecture flourished

15   The French emperor Napoleon supervised the cleaning of the Colosseum in the early 1800s. Later in that century, the Catholic church continued to restore the structure. Even so, the once-glorious structure had lost much of its magnificence.

A Comeback for the Ages

16   Today, the Colosseum might be in worse shape than ever. That's because it's sinking! Experts have discovered that the stadium is more than a foot lower on its south side than on its north. They think that vibrations caused by cars on busy roads and subways running underground near the Colosseum may be a factor.

Some of the Colosseum's stones were taken to build St. Peter's Basilica. Look at the map scale. About how far did the Romans have to carry those stones?

How have the features of modern cities affected the Colosseum? <u>Underline</u> details in the text that tell you.

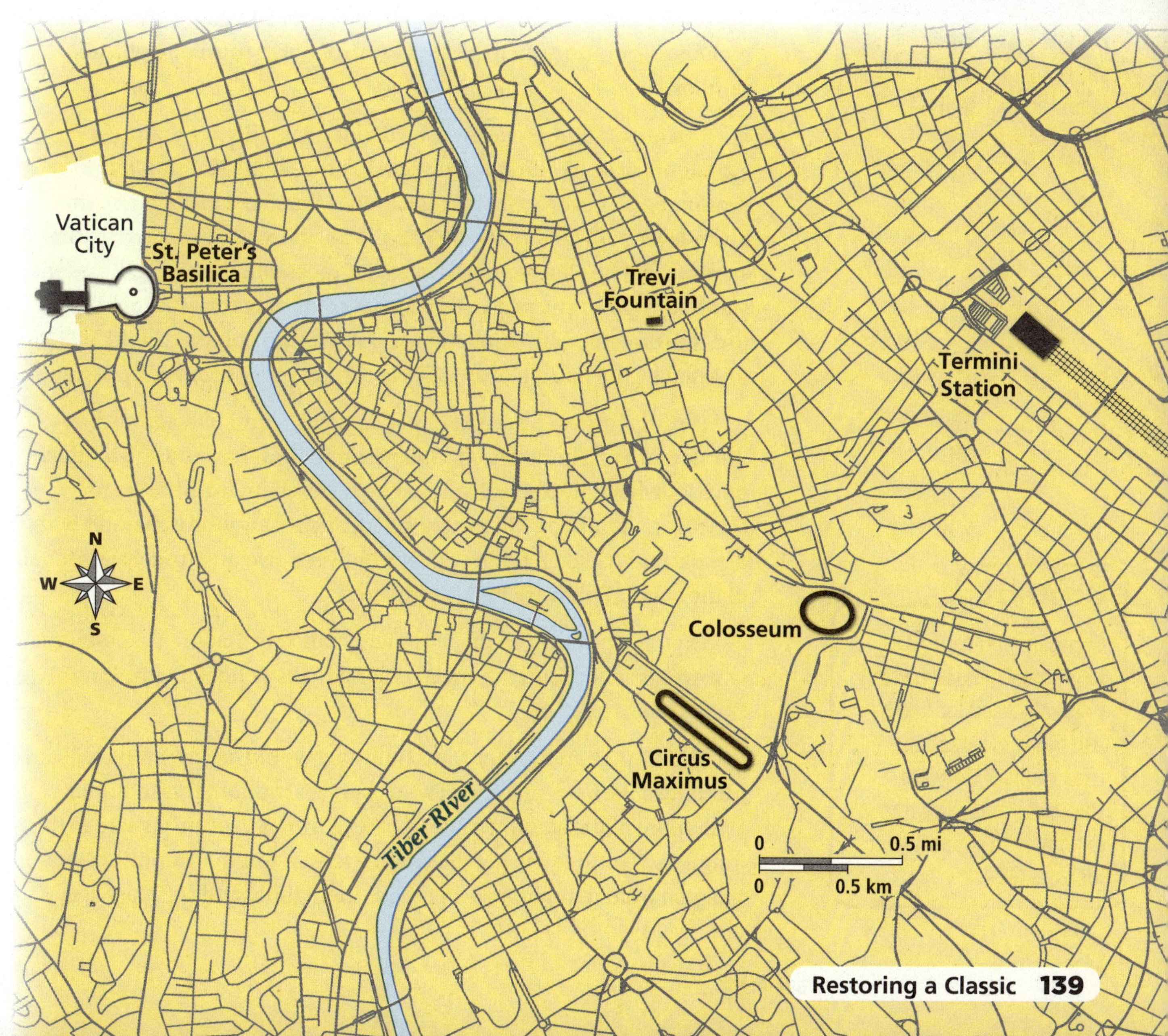

17   A multimillion-dollar restoration project is scheduled to begin in 2013. An Italian company that makes luxury goods is sponsoring the project. The company's founder, Diego Della Valle, said that the company is proud to help preserve one of Italy's most recognizable symbols.

18   The restoration project will be divided into different phases. First, four floors of scaffolding will be put up around the exterior of the monument. The temporary metal arches that were installed on the lower levels will be replaced. Then the façade, or outside part, of the stadium will be cleaned and restored. Cracks will be repaired, and the stadium will be returned to its original color, according to Rossella Rea, the director of the Colosseum site. This first phase of work will be finished by the middle of 2015 if everything goes according to schedule.

19   During the next phase, tunnels, walkways, and passageways in the stadium will be repaired. Galleries and underground spaces that have long been neglected will also be restored. In the final stages, services and utilities will be upgraded, and a new visitor's center with a bookshop will be built. It will take between two and three years for all of the restoration work to be completed.

20   Even with all the repairs, it is highly unlikely that the Colosseum will ever be filled with the spectacular crowds or host the thrilling events that it once did.

21   "No Roman monument was built so it would last for eternity," said Mariarosa Barbera, an official who oversees monuments in Rome. With more of the stadium open for view, though, future visitors to this long-lived wonder will get the chance to stand in the amphitheater and imagine what it might have been like there thousands of years ago.

Contrast

Vocabulary: Maintain a Consistent Tone

Tone is the attitude a writer takes toward his or her subject. The tone can be informative, playful, respectful, or sarcastic. In a historical text, the tone is most likely serious or scholarly. If the author were writing a comic book instead, his or her tone would have to change—a lot!

Writers carefully choose words to establish and maintain their tone. For example, if a writer had a negative attitude about a sporting event, he or she might use words like *sulked*, *depressed*, and *dragged* to describe the players. The tone a writer conveys should be consistent throughout the writing.

Try It Read this excerpt from "Restoring a Classic."

> It was a **monumental** undertaking. First, architects created **intricate** plans for the building. Every detail had to be **precisely** worked out before the building started. The architectural plans included a large quantity of entrances, hallways, and staircases so that crowds could easily enter and exit the building.

Discuss **What tone does the writer convey in this paragraph? How do the vocabulary words help to convey the author's tone?**

Each vocabulary word below is followed by a synonym. Substitute the synonym in the sentence above, and explain how it changes the tone of the sentence.

1. **monumental—massive,** p. 136 _______________________________

   ____

2. **intricate—complicated,** p. 136 _______________________________

   ____

3. **precisely—clearly,** p. 136 _______________________________

   ____

Respond to Text: Writing a Summary

Earlier in this lesson, you learned about and practiced the skill of summarizing. Now you can put that knowledge to work by writing a summary of one of the selections you have read.

Try It Think about the two selections you just read, "When in Rome . . . or Brazil" and "Restoring a Classic." If your friend asked you what each was about, could you give him or her a summary?

 Discuss **Imagine that you are a writer who is trying to sell one of these selections to a Web site or a magazine. What could you say to describe the content of each selection that would both be brief and help to make the sale?**

On Your Own Choose one of the selections you read in this lesson. Write a summary of the selection. Your summary should include the main idea of the selection and the details that support the idea. Remember, a summary isn't a detailed account of everything you read. A summary also does not include your own opinions or ideas, though it does use your own words. Use the guide on the next page to help you organize your summary. Then write your paragraph on a separate sheet of paper.

Checklist for a Good Response

A good summary

- makes notes of all the most important points.

- leaves out information that isn't important.

- arranges and organizes the important points.

- restates the important points using your own words.

- includes an introductory sentence, detail paragraphs, and a concluding sentence.

My Summary

1. **Topic Sentence** In your own words, tell about the main idea of the selection.

   ____

   ____ .

2. **Detail Sentences** Add some sentences that contain details from the selection you choose that support its big idea, again using your own words to restate them. Use this chart to organize your ideas.

Title:	
Important Detail 1:	
Important Detail 2:	
Important Detail 3:	

3. **Concluding Sentence** Your concluding sentence should include any important information that you haven't stated yet.

   ____

   ____

On a separate sheet of paper, write your summary.

Chronology and Sequence How did North and South America get their names? What was a positive result of the map, despite the mistake? Underline the sentences that tell you. The first answer has been underlined for you.

The Evolution of Maps

1   Some people might think maps are boring. One map created five hundred years ago, though, tells the fascinating story of how two continents got their names. It was all a big mistake!

2   Researchers at a university library in Germany discovered a print of a sixteenth-century map that was created by two German cartographers. The mapmakers had included a landmass far to the west of Europe and Africa. They called the landmass "America." Why? They incorrectly believed that Amerigo Vespucci had discovered the New World.

3   Two different versions of their map were made back then. One was a large map that could be hung on walls. The other, smaller version could be folded onto a small globe. Only five copies of the maps were known to exist. Four of the smaller maps are held in museum or private collections, but no one knew what had become of the fifth.

4   Imagine the researchers' surprise when they found the fifth version hidden in between two other texts from the same time period in which the map was created. The texts had been bound together in the 1800s, and somehow the map had gotten sandwiched in between.

5   Five hundred years ago, maps were printed using engraved copper plates. The mapmakers used compasses and other tools to create navigation charts of the coastlines and other landforms. Of course, they didn't know exactly what the whole world looked like yet—they had to rely on reports from explorers and use educated guesses to design their navigation charts. The mapmakers who created the map of America may have mistakenly named the landmass, but they were the first to create a true world map.

A Changing World, A Changing Map

6   Today's maps are very different from that first world map. In the 1970s and 1980s, mapmakers began to use geographic information systems (GIS). The systems are made up of computers, software, digital data, people, organizations, and institutions. All the parts of the systems help to collect, store, analyze, and display information about Earth's surface.

7   It's a lot easier to get that information when you can get an overhead view. The first world explorers couldn't do that, since they were using boats to travel around. Today, we don't even have to send people in the air to take the pictures. Satellites do it for us!

8   How does that work? Satellites orbit Earth, sending back pictures and other data to the surface. Airplanes are also used to collect pictures and data. Then people use computers to analyze it all. Then they combine it into a big picture—a map is born.

9   That's just the start, though. Today's maps provide many more details than ever before. Anyone who uses a mapping program on a computer can find information about nearly every spot on the globe. Type any city, address, or landmark into the search feature, and it will show you the pinpoint on the map. Then you can zoom out or in to see what it would look like from space or if you were standing across the street.

10   Every time you open a mapping program, you are automatically connected to its servers. These give you access to all kinds of information, from the landforms of a region to the population of the area to the roads and rivers that run through it.

A mapmaker must make precise measurements.

A History of Mapmaking

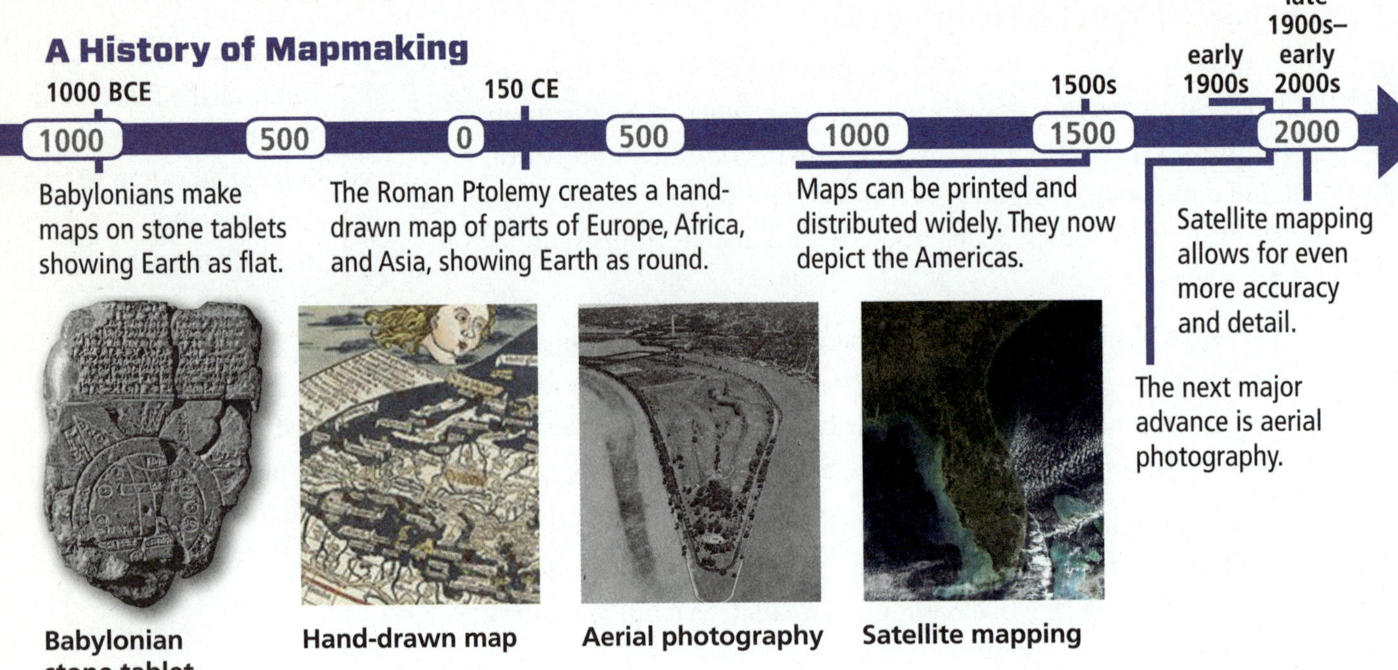

The Human Element

11   A mapping program might pull data from over one thousand sources. The data has to be merged into the map you see on your computer screen. First, it is entered into a program that turns the data into layers. Then, the layers can be dropped on top of what will later be a completed map.

12   Data is information, but it's not always accurate. One tiny mistake on a map could get someone lost. That's why teams of people take the sources of map data and put them to a real-world test. They compare the data to photos and satellite images and update the images regularly to make sure they're on top of any changes. If a street is changed from one way to two way, they'll know it, and they will adjust the data.

13   The process of mapping continues to improve every day. Not so long ago, it could take over a year to map a city in the United States. Now, it can be done in hours. The next digital mapping trend is indoor maps. In the near future, your mapping program won't just be able to tell you the directions to the aquarium, it will show you all the walking paths and spots *inside* of the attraction. Want to get a close look at the shark tank? Just check your mapping program. It will tell you where the snacks are, too, just in case you get hungry during your visit.

14   Be sure to pay attention to where you're going, though. A mapping program can tell you about stationary objects, but it won't let you know if someone is about to get in your way—at least, not yet.

Identify Steps in a Process How is data used to make maps? Why are people an important part of that process? Draw a box around the sentences that tell you.

Integrate Visual Information What can you learn from the time line shown above that is not in the selection text?

✔ Comprehension Check

1. In two or three sentences, write a summary of the selection.

____

____

____

2. Even though the German mapmakers made a mistake, why is the map they created five hundred years ago important?

____

____

____

3. Look at the pictures that accompany the time line on page 146. How do they show you the way that the accuracy of maps has changed?

____

____

____

4. What is the last step of the process involved in making a mapping program? Why are people an important part of that step?

____

____

____

5. List in chronological order the ways in which gathering data for mapmaking has changed over the years.

____

____

____

6. Why must mapmakers and computer mapping programs rely on multiple sources of information to create reliable maps?

____

____

____

7. Read this sentence from the selection. One of the words has a Latin or Greek suffix. Circle the suffix. Then write a definition for the word.

In the 1970s and 1980s, mapmakers began to use geographic information systems (GIS).

____

____

____

8. What is the author's tone in this selection? Which words does the author use that help you identify the tone?

____

____

____

Scientific Texts

Scientific texts

provide factual information about topics that are related to science. Scientific texts can appear in magazines, newspapers, books, encyclopedias, or on Web sites. You might read a scientific article to research a school project or because you are interested in learning more about a subject. If you were going to read a scientific text on the island shown in the picture, what kinds of factual information would you expect to learn from it?

Skills Focus

Opals: Rainbows in Stone
Text Structure: Cause and Effect
Scientific Texts

Rapa Nui: Island of Mystery
Draw and Support Inferences
Integrate Visual Information

Practice the Skill

Cause and effect is a relationship between ideas or events. A **cause** tells why something happens. An **effect** tells what happens as a result of a cause.

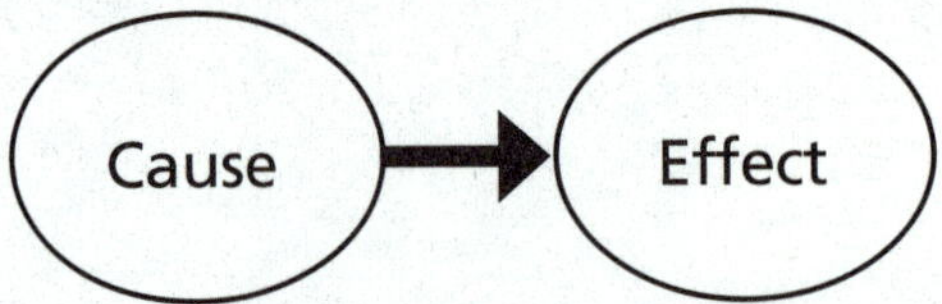

An effect can, in turn, cause something else to occur. In this way, causes and effects can sometimes lead to a series of events. Science writers often use cause-and-effect text structure to express their ideas. This text structure provides an accurate way of describing the relationships of ideas and events in many scientific processes.

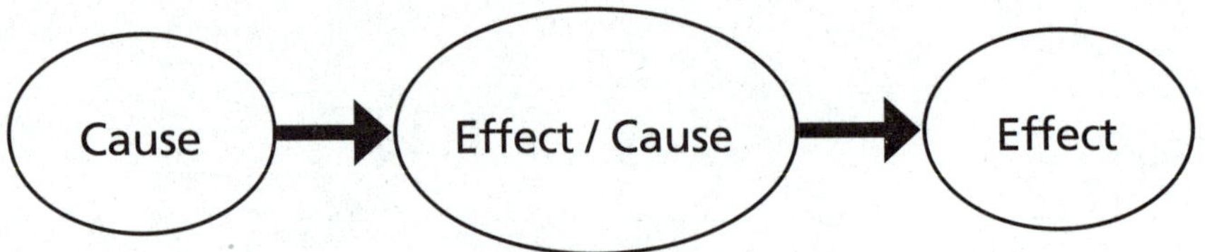

A cause-and-effect chain

Try It As you read the paragraph below, think about the causes and effects in this series of events.

Severe forest fires destroy forests, denuding the land of trees and shade and leaving a residue of ash. The land is then more exposed to sunlight, and the nutrient-rich ash mixes with the soil to support new growth. New plants and trees begin to grow where the forests used to be.

Discuss To find the effect, ask "What happens?" To find the cause, ask "Why does it happen?" In the paragraph above, underline the original cause. Then circle events that are both effects and causes. Finally, draw a box around the final effect.

As you read, complete the Cause-and-Effect Chart on page 281.

Practice the Skill

Scientific texts provide you with factual information on a topic. They introduce a topic, expand on it by giving factual details, and often present graphic information in the form of diagrams, graphs, and charts to help communicate or clarify ideas. Because they are conveying so many facts, writers of scientific texts often break up the material they are presenting into sections by adding descriptive headings.

Try It As you read the following paragraphs, look for precise factual information about *how*, *when*, and *where*.

Hawaii: Hot Spot

There are eight main islands in the state of Hawaii. Each of the islands has at least one primary volcano, and there are thirteen volcanoes in all on the eight islands. Five of the volcanoes are active, which means they emit lava, ash, and gases.

How Is a Volcanic Island Formed?

The islands that make up the state of Hawaii sit over a volcanic hot spot, a place where magma pushes through the earth's crust. Magma, which is rock that is so superheated that it becomes liquid, is found beneath the earth's surface. At hot spots, magma builds up pressure and eventually breaks through the crust, causing a volcanic eruption. When magma reaches the surface of the earth and comes out of a volcano, it becomes lava, which cools and hardens. Often these eruptions occur on the ocean floor. Lava from underwater volcanoes builds up slowly, layer after layer, until the mass of hardened rock reaches the surface of the ocean, and an island is formed.

Discuss What are some signs volcanologists would look for that indicate an active volcano? Circle scientific terms that are defined in the passage, and underline their definitions. How do the headings help you understand the text?

As you read, record your answers to questions about scientific texts on the Close Reading Worksheet on page 282.

Opals: Rainbows in Stone

Circle the scientific terms in paragraphs 2 and 3. Restate the scientific process described in paragraph 3 in your own words.

1   A gemstone, or gem, is a precious or semiprecious object that is made of minerals or fossilized materials and is usually a **vibrant** color. Gemstones can be cut and polished and used for jewelry. The value of a gemstone depends on its perceived beauty and rarity. Since Roman times, opals have been considered one of the most precious gemstones. They come in all sizes and shapes, from tiny flakes to spheres the size of bowling balls. The main appeal of opals, though, is their **brilliant** colors. These gems can flash any color of the rainbow. These flashes of color result from the way opals refract light. The most beautiful ones appear to glow, and, in fact, some of the most valuable opals are called fire opals.

Chemical Structure

2   Gemologists—scientists who study gemstones—rate the hardness of precious and semiprecious stones on a ten-point system called the Mohs scale. Diamonds are the hardest of gems, rating a 10 out of 10. Rubies are next, rating 9. By contrast, opals are 5.0 to 6.5, which means they are relatively delicate and can be damaged easily.

3   The reason opals are so soft is that they are comprised of a gel of water and silica, similar to quartz. Between 6 and 10 percent of the stones' weight is water. Their chemical formula is written as $SiO_2 \cdot nH_2O$. *Si* stands for silicon, *H* stands for hydrogen, and *O* stands for oxygen. H_2O is the formula for water. Opals form when a mixture of silica and water seeps into cracks and fissures in the ground and slowly dries and hardens.

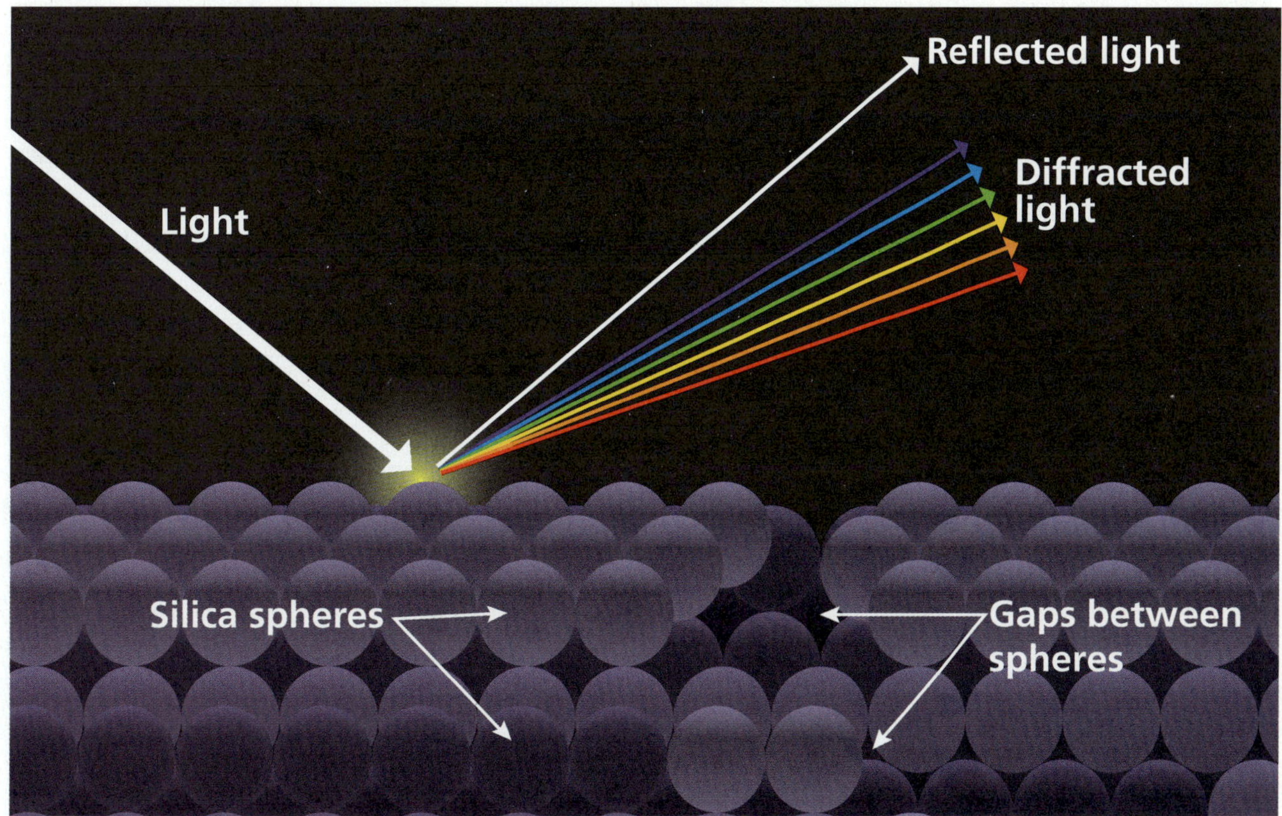

The color of an opal depends on the size of its silica spheres and the size of the gaps between the spheres.

4   The colors of a specific opal depend on its composition. When the silica in opals hardens, it forms tiny spheres. These spheres are so tiny that there are millions of them in a single millimeter. When these spheres are packed together in a tight pattern, the space between them diffracts light. This process is similar to the way a **prism refracts** light by separating it into the colors of the spectrum. The size of the silica spheres—and the size of the gaps between the spheres—determine the opal's color. Larger spheres diffract red and orange, while smaller spheres diffract blue and green. A single opal can be composed of differently sized silica spheres and thus reflect many different colors.

5   Not all **opals** flash colors. When the silica spheres aren't organized into a tight enough pattern, they don't diffract light. So while these stones have the same chemical composition as gem opals, they aren't considered valuable. These colorless opals are called **potch**. About 90 percent of the opals found in Australia are potch opals.

6   Scientists have been able to create synthetic opals in the laboratory with silica and water. However, the spheres in these opals display a regular pattern that doesn't exist in natural stones. The patches of color also tend to be very regular. Gemologists can differentiate between synthetic and natural opals using an electron microscope.

What causes the different colors in an opal? Write down the causes and effects in your **Cause-and-Effect Chart.**

What value do potch opals have? Why?

Fluoresce and Phosphoresce

7   Another way to tell the difference between a natural and a synthetic opal is to use an ultraviolet, or UV, light. UV light isn't visible to the human eye. When UV light hits the silica spheres in a natural opal, it causes the stone to fluoresce, or glow. The light hits the electrons in the silica and causes them to vibrate. This vibrating changes the wavelength of the light, which in turn causes the color to change. Natural opals can also phosphoresce. This means that the opal continues to glow with color even after the UV light source is removed.

8   Manufactured opals have the same chemical composition as natural opals but not the same structure. Because of the structure of the silica spheres in manufactured opals, they do not fluoresce in the presence of UV light.

Silica sphere arrangement in a natural opal at 4000X magnification

9   Just as opals can display every color in the rainbow, they also take many shapes and forms. A solid opal is one that formed in a large crack or fracture in the host rock—the larger rock inside of which an opal forms. Solid opals are a pure silica mixture and don't contain any impurities. They are the most valuable opals.

10   A boulder opal is one that formed on the surface of ironstone. It is also a type of solid opal. Boulder opals display streaks of color mixed with streaks of the host rock. These opals are often cut and polished for jewelry so that the streaks are visible. Another type of opal is a matrix opal. Matrix opals are a type of boulder opal in which the opal is randomly combined with the host rock, which causes flashes of color when light hits the stone.

Opal Formation

11   Opals have been found all around the world. They are in the United States, Mexico, Eastern Europe, and South Africa. More than 90 percent of the world's opals, though, come from Australia. The majority of Australian opals come from a small town in the outback called Coober Pedy.

12   The outback of Australia is a vast desert landscape in the center of the continent. It used to be an inland sea. During Earth's Tertiary period, 65 million to 1.6 million years ago, the outback was covered in salt water. The water slowly seeped into the underlying sandstone and leached, or drew, the silica particles out of the rock. This silica and water mixture filtered down into the fissures in host rocks. Then it slowly hardened over the millennia.

13   Coober Pedy sits on the edge of what used to be the inland sea. As a result, the ground surrounding it is filled with opals.

Mining for Opals

14   Opal mining is often done on small land claims by a small number of partners who buy the rights to mine the sites. Miners begin their search by drilling one-meter-wide holes, called boreholes, from which they remove waste material, or mullock. As they dig deeper, miners inspect the mullock for signs that they are near a vein of opal. A common sign is a layer of pinkish clay mixed with sandstone. Boreholes can range between one and thirty meters deep.

Opal miners use special equipment to remove dirt and waste material from boreholes.

15   Once the miners see signs that opals might be present, they descend into the borehole with hand tools. They carefully pick at the rocks. When they hit a vein of opal, they dig out sideways from the main shaft to follow it. Because opals are so fragile, it is easy to damage or destroy them in the mining process.

16   To separate opals from the host sediment, the miners dump the dirt they've taken out of a hole into machines called agitators. Agitators are like big washing machines that slosh the rocks around in water. They wash off the dirt and finer silt and leave larger rocks behind. Once the rocks have been cleaned, they are shaken through sieves, or fine metal screens, to sort them by size. At that stage, the miners carefully look through the rocks for gemstones.

17   Some large mining companies have started doing open-cut mining, which involves using large excavation machines to scoop out layers of sandstone. Once miners reach an opal layer, they switch to smaller tools. While miners can process the dirt more quickly using open-cut mining, they also face an increased risk of damaging precious stones.

Opals in Space

18   Opals have been found in locations all over Earth, and now they've been found on another planet. In 2008, NASA announced that the Mars Reconnaissance Orbiter had identified opals on the surface of the planet Mars. Because opals are formed of silica and water, this find means that the planet probably once had water. Evidence of water on Mars is further proof that there may once have been life on Mars.

19   Perhaps one day, miners will prospect for opals on Mars.

Vocabulary: Word Relationships

When you encounter an unfamiliar word, you can often figure out its meaning by looking at its relationship to other words around it. Understanding the relationship between words helps you learn the meaning of an unfamiliar word, but it can also deepen your knowledge of a word you already know. Some word relationships you might see are

- **synonyms:** words that have the same meanings (*big* and *large*)

- **antonyms:** words that have opposite meanings (*hot* and *cold*)

- **item and action:** one word that describes what the other does (*stove* and *heats*)

- **cause and effect:** one word leads to another (*sunlight* and *tan*)

- **item and category:** one word is a subset of another (*cheddar* and *cheese*)

Try It Read the sentence below. Use word relationships to define the boldface word.

By using the **desalination** process, it is possible to turn seawater into drinking water.

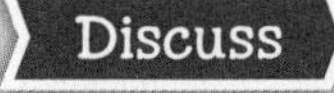 **Discuss** **What word relationship in the sentence gives you a clue to the meaning of *desalination*?**

The following related words are in the passage you just read. Reread the sentences that contain the words. Then tell what relationship the words have to each other.

1. **vibrant/brilliant,** p. 152 ____

2. **prism/refracts,** p. 153 ____

3. **potch/opals,** p. 153 ____

Practice the Skill

When you draw an **inference**, you use clues in the text along with what you already know to understand something that is not directly stated in the text. You sometimes have to draw inferences about information in a scientific text. When this happens, you must use relevant facts, details, clues, and evidence in the text to support your inferences.

Try It Read the paragraphs below.

Archaeologists are now deploying new tools in their search for ancient settlements: satellite photos. They are using infrared photographs taken from space to identify new sites for excavation. In Egypt alone, researchers have identified possible locations for more than one thousand tombs and three thousand residences from photos snapped by satellites orbiting Earth.

The process relies on the fact that humans leave a mark on the earth. Mud and brick, commonly used as building materials by ancient civilizations, are more dense than the soil surrounding them. Infrared cameras can pick up the outlines of homes, temples, tombs, and palaces.

In several test excavations, archaeologists have found structures that exactly match the outlines seen in satellite photos. By studying the infrared photos, archaeologists can pinpoint where they want their next dig to be.

> **Discuss** **Archaeologists are finding structures by analyzing infrared photographs taken from space. What can you infer about where the structures are in relation to the surface of Earth? What is the evidence in the text that supports your inference? Underline the clues in the text that lead you to your inference.**

As you read, record your answers to questions about drawing and supporting inferences on the Close Reading Worksheet on page 283.

Practice the Skill

Many nonfiction writers use visual, or graphic, information to make information clearer and easier to understand. Scientific texts frequently contain graphics of various kinds to explain a concept or to help communicate a complex idea. Sometimes using a picture or a diagram is a better way to explain some concepts than using words. Graphics include charts, diagrams, graphs, maps, time lines, and photographs with their captions.

Charts represent data in rows and columns or with symbols, such as bars in a bar chart or slices in a pie chart.

Diagrams are two-dimensional symbolic representations of information. They can take on many forms, from flowcharts to models. A **model** is typically a drawing of something with **labels** identifying different parts. **Lead lines** connect the labels and the particular part of the model they refer to.

Try It   Look at the model below. Pay attention to the labels and lead lines.

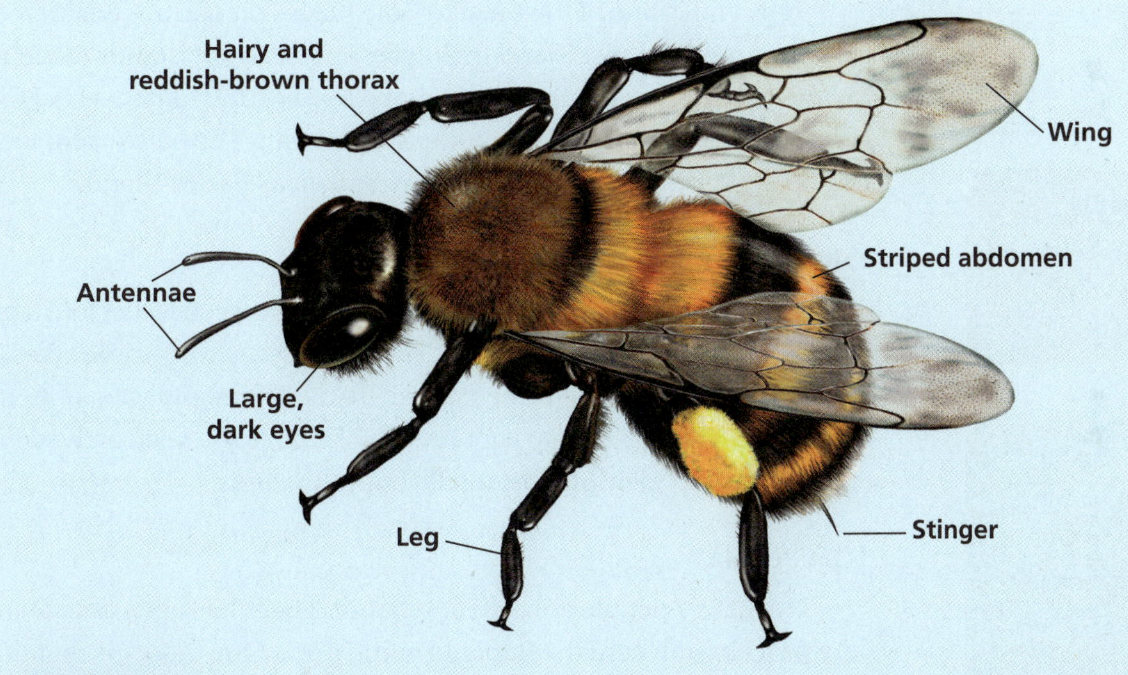

> **Discuss**   What information is this model displaying? Circle the body parts the labels identify.

As you read, complete the Visual Information Chart on page 284.

Rapa Nui:
Island of Mystery

1   Rapa Nui is one of the most remote places on Earth. Considered to be the easternmost island in Polynesia, a string of islands reaching across the western Pacific Ocean, Rapa Nui is 2,150 miles west of Chile and more than 4,600 miles southeast of Hawaii. The native people call it Rapa Nui, but it is more commonly known as Easter Island.

The Island

Why is there debate about where the Rapanui were from originally?

2   In addition to being remote, the island is small. It is just fourteen miles wide and seven miles long. The land area is sixty-three acres, or about the size of eighty-three football fields. The island was spotted by Europeans in 1722. A ship captained by Jacob Roggeveen arrived on Easter Sunday, giving the island its English name.

The People

Read paragraph 3 and look at the map on the next page. Why do you think scientists theorized that the Rapanui came from Chile? Record your answer in the **Visual Information Chart**.

3   The native people are called Rapanui. There has been debate in the past about where the Rapanui come from. One theory is that they sailed east from Polynesia. Other researchers believe that they sailed west from Chile. Recent DNA sequencing of island skeletons shows that the first settlers most likely came from Polynesia.

4   The Rapanui most likely arrived in open canoes, using stars, ocean currents, and wind patterns to find their way. There are no written records of the routes Polynesian sailors used. Instead, the science of navigation was passed from one generation to the next through oral history.

When Did They Arrive?

5   By digging through the layers of sediment in a dig site, archaeologists can learn a lot about when a civilization existed, how the people lived, and what kinds of food they ate. Soil samples can also reveal the kinds of plants that grew there at the time.

6   To find out how old organic materials are, researchers use a process called radiocarbon dating. All living organisms contain carbon-14 levels that match those in the atmosphere. When an organism dies, the carbon decays at a very specific rate, and scientists can use this decay rate to tell how old something is. This process helps archaeologists determine the age of civilizations and their artifacts.

7   On Easter Island, archaeologists have done radiocarbon dating of wood charcoal samples from the oldest known archaeological site on the island. Measurements indicate that the first sign of human inhabitants dates to about 1200 CE.

8   Soil samples show that when the first humans arrived, Rapa Nui was covered with forests of giant palm trees and more than twenty species of trees and bushes. There were six species of land birds. But when the Europeans arrived, they found the island largely barren. All the tree species and the land birds had become extinct.

9   From the soil samples, researchers know that the early Rapanui cleared forests to plant crops of bananas, taro, and sugarcane, none of which are native to the island. The island is also populated with Polynesian rats. Scientists theorize that the Rapanui cleared too much of the forests too quickly, so the trees didn't have a chance to **regenerate**. Then the destruction of their habitat, combined with rat **predation**, decimated the native land birds.

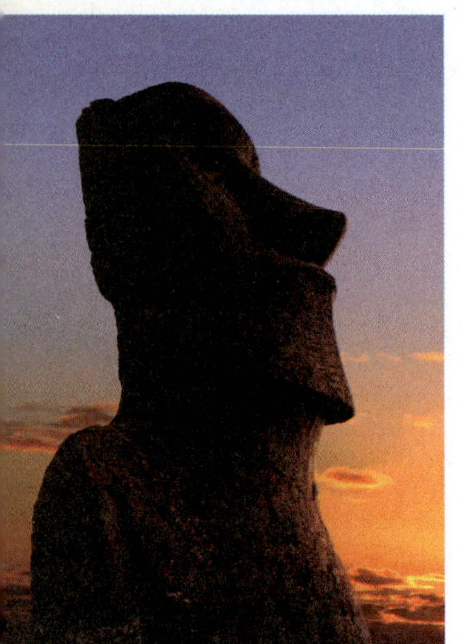

The Statues

10   When they arrived, the Europeans were surprised to find an isolated and primitive culture that had had no contact with the outside world. The Rapanui didn't have horses or cows or even wheeled carts. But the Europeans found something that amazed them even more. Scattered around the island were giant sculptures of heads called *moai* (moh-EYE). The heads measure up to thirty feet tall and weigh more than twenty tons. When they were first seen by Europeans, most were toppled over. The ones still upright stood on platforms called *ahu*, with their backs to the ocean.

11   The statues have mystified visitors to Easter Island ever since.

12   The *moai* have a distinct look, with large heads and jutting eyebrows. They are often referred to as Easter Island heads because for most statues, that's all you can see.

13   Researchers know that the Rapanui carved the figures with stone tools in a quarry[1] on the island. They also know that the statues represent spirits of Rapanui ancestors. What they don't know is how the islanders moved these giant statues from the quarry to their final locations. Some *moai* were moved more than eleven miles.

14   Not all *moai* were moved successfully. The road leading out of the quarry is lined with fallen and broken statues that did not survive transport. The quarry also contains unfinished *moai*, abandoned where they were carved.

15   No *moai* were carved after the Europeans arrived on Easter Sunday in 1722. By the nineteenth century, all of the statues had been knocked over, most onto their faces. Researchers think that the Rapanui knocked them over during fights between different tribes that lived on the island.

16   When researchers started studying the *moai*, there were no living Rapanui who had participated in the carving, moving, or toppling of the statues. Island elders told stories and legends about the statues, but there were no written records or firsthand accounts that detailed their creation.

[1]**quarry** a pit from which builders get stone

Moving the Statues

17   There are many theories on how the Rapanui moved the giant statues to their final resting places. The islanders didn't have wheels or animals such as oxen or horses to work with. While no one may ever know for sure how the figures were transported, researchers have performed experiments to determine some methods that might have been used, moving copies of the statues with just human labor.

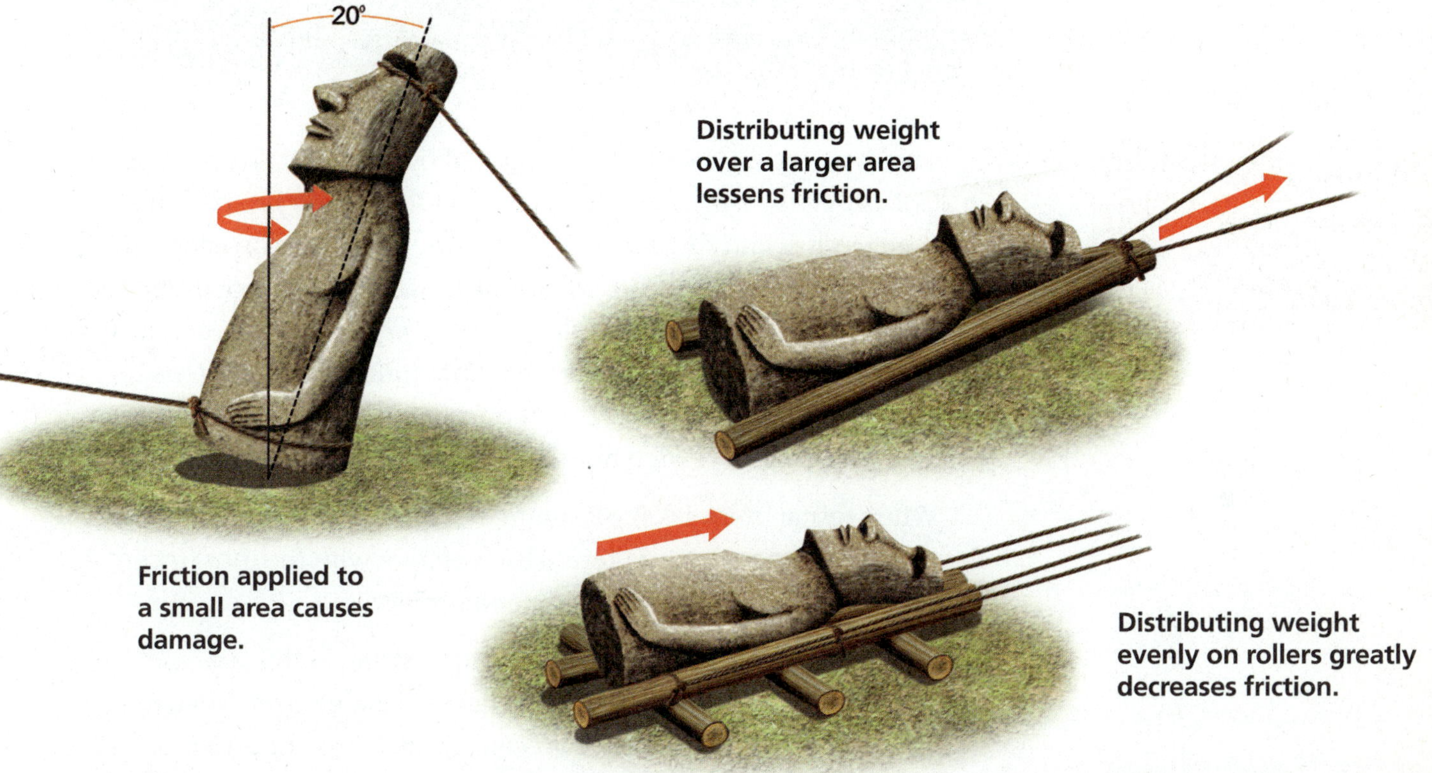

18   The Norwegian adventurer Thor Heyerdahl had teams move statues by using ropes to twist the statues from side to side, using **torque**. The friction of being twisted into the soil over long distances, however, damaged the *moai* stone bases.

19   Other researchers think that the Rapanui dragged the *moai* with ropes. They could have placed a statue on a V-shaped wooden sledge to drag it. Or they could have dragged a statue on its belly. The **friction** that results from dragging heavy stones across dirt makes this method extremely difficult.

20   Another idea is that the Rapanui placed the statues on wooden carts and then rolled the carts over logs. This would have required a lot of people to push and pull the *moai* and move the roller logs. It would have also required a lot of trees. Some researchers believe this construction method is why the Rapanui cut down so many trees.

Based on the diagram and the text on this page, which method of moving the *moai* do you think was most effective? Explain why on the **Visual Information Chart**.

Why would people spend so much time doing experiments to figure out how the *moai* were moved?

In 2012, teams of workers "walked" a statue using ropes.

21   The most recent theory, demonstrated by a team of archaeologists in 2012, is that the islanders walked the statues to their final locations with three ropes and three teams of workers. The teams on each side pulled the statue from side to side, while the team in back of the statue held it steady. The statues' rounded bottoms and low center of gravity made walking easier than some of the other methods. During the demonstration, a total of eighteen people working in three teams easily walked a small *moai* several hundred yards.

22   When researchers ask the Rapanui how the *moai* got to their *ahu*, they say the statues walked there. This would fit with the most recent theory of walking *moai* while they stood upright.

23   In addition to researching how the Rapanui moved the *moai*, archaeologists are excavating statues that have fallen over and been buried by soil over the centuries. Recent excavations show that some *moai* have arms and bodies, not just heads. Others show traces of coral and pigments that were used to decorate the statues' faces.

The Island Today

24   Easter Island was designated a World Heritage site in 1995, and 40 percent of the island is protected parkland. In 2012, seventy thousand tourists visited the island, which has a population of about five thousand. The island economy depends largely on tourism.

25   Tourists are not allowed to touch the *moai*, whose faces are disintegrating. The volcanic **tuff** they are carved from is soft. Wind and rain also contribute to their erosion.

26   While air travel has made the island more accessible to visitors, the Rapanui are working hard to preserve their culture and artwork. With the help of researchers and archaeologists, they hope to ensure that their ancient statues are around for a long time.

Describe

Describe three ways scientists have studied Easter Island.

Vocabulary: Science Terms and Symbols

When reading scientific texts, you will encounter words and symbols that are familiar. For instance, if you read about climate change and temperatures are discussed in *degrees* using the symbol °, you would most likely understand what that means. However, as you read "Rapa Nui: Island of Mystery," you may have been tripped up by the word *torque*. Just imagine if the writer had used only the symbol τ! Sometimes you can figure out science terms and symbols in context, but often they are so specialized that, unless they are defined on the page by the author, you will have to look them up in a glossary or dictionary.

Try It Read these sentences from the selection.

> Scientists theorize that the Rapanui cleared too much of the forests too quickly, so the trees didn't have a chance to **regenerate**. Then the destruction of their habitat, combined with rat **predation**, decimated the native land birds.

Discuss **What do you think *regenerate* means? Underline the context clues that helped you figure out the meaning. Is there context for *predation*, or would you look up that word?**

Below are more scientific words from the selection. Reread each word in context in the selection, and then write a definition for the word. If there aren't enough context clues, use a dictionary.

1. **torque**, p. 163 ______________________________________

____

2. **friction**, p. 163 ______________________________________

____

3. **tuff**, p. 164 ______________________________________

____

Respond to Text: Understanding Visual Information

The passage "Rapa Nui: Island of Mystery" contains several different types of visuals, including a map, photographs, and a diagram.

On Your Own Prepare to write about the visuals in "Rapa Nui: Island of Mystery." Think about the information presented in the visuals. Describe how **one or more** of the visuals affected your reading experience. Give examples from the text, and tell how the visuals helped you understand the content better or enjoy the article more. Cite details from the visuals to support your thoughts. Write a conclusion that sums up how the visuals were or were not effective. Use the guide on the next page to help you organize your response. Then write your paragraph on a separate sheet of paper.

Checklist for a Good Response

A good paragraph

✔ gives a brief description of the visual or visuals being discussed.

✔ gives specific examples of how the visuals did or did not add to your understanding.

✔ gives specific examples of how the visuals did or did not add to your enjoyment.

✔ clearly states how the visuals affected your reading experience.

✔ includes a topic sentence, supporting ideas, and a concluding statement.

How Visuals Affected My Reading

1. **Topic Sentence** Include this information in your topic sentence.

   The visuals in "Rapa Nui: Island of Mystery" are _______________________

   ____ .

2. **Detail Sentences** Choose one or two visuals and tell how they affected
   your experience of reading the passage. Add sentences to supply
   supporting details. Use this chart to organize your ideas.

Visual	How It Affected My Reading
map	
photo of *moai*	
diagram of three methods of moving *moai*	
illustration of scientists walking *moai*	

3. **Concluding Sentence:** Your concluding sentence should restate and sum up
   in a fresh way how the visuals affected your reading experience.

   ____

   ____

   ____

On a separate sheet of paper, write your paragraph.

Subways under the Sea

Text Structure: Cause and Effect How did fishers attract more fish? Underline the cause in the text.

Draw and Support Inferences Why is it important for objects in artificial reefs to last a long time?

Scientific Texts Think about what kind of information you expect to learn from this scientific text.

1   Up and down the East Coast of the United States, there are more than one thousand New York City subway cars on the bottom of the ocean. The cars aren't there because the city sprawled out onto the ocean floor. They aren't the result of some environmental disaster. Rather, they are part of a massive project to create artificial reefs for marine life.

2   The floor of the ocean off New England is rocky, with lots of places for sea life to grow. But much of the seafloor off the Middle Atlantic states, from New York south to Georgia, is sand. Marine animals such as oysters, **barnacles**, and mussels need hard surfaces to attach to. If the bottom of the ocean is mostly sand, there is no place for them to live.

3   Fishers have been creating artificial reefs in the Atlantic Ocean since 1830. They noticed that areas where there were shipwrecks had larger fish populations. They decided to encourage the growth of marine life by sinking old ships and other large items, which in turn attracted more fish.

4   Through the years, people have experimented to see what worked best. They sunk different items. Old tugboats, ships, and army tanks were the most popular. They are large enough to stay stable after sinking. In addition, they offer plenty of room for different species of fish. Old ships and tanks also last a long time.

5   Other items that have been tried include shopping carts, refrigerators, and washing machines. These items made less-successful artificial reefs. First, they didn't provide enough shelter for marine life. Second, they deteriorated quickly. They broke apart in just a few years.

6   State wildlife and fisheries departments were looking for just the right thing to sink. Then the New York City Metropolitan Transportation Authority (MTA) announced it was trying to get rid of its old subway cars, some built as far back as 1964. The MTA had more than one thousand cars from the "Redbird" fleet, which was so named because the cars were painted a deep red color to combat graffiti. Best of all, the MTA was offering them to other states for free!

7   The Delaware Department of Natural Resources was the first to create reefs using subway cars. More than six hundred cars were sunk during the first reef creation. Delaware's largest artificial reef, Redbird Reef, is named for the subway fleet. Other states watched Delaware's progress. Then they asked for cars of their own. Six states now have subway car reefs.

8   Before the MTA ships out the cars, they are stripped of anything that could pollute the ocean. All doors, windows, handrails, signs, wheels, seats, and engines are removed. The trains are also steam cleaned to remove any harmful oil or grease.

9   It costs the MTA about $8,000 to get each car ready for sinking. This is half of what it would cost to bury a car on land.

10   The reefs have been called "fish condominiums" by wildlife experts. They provide an excellent habitat for a wide range of species. Each stainless steel subway car weighs nineteen tons and measures fifty-one feet by nine feet. Their structure includes the openings for doors and windows that have been removed. These openings allow for good water circulation while providing lots of **nooks** and **crannies** for fish and other marine wildlife to live.

11   Because the cars are so heavy, they don't shift once they are on the bottom of the ocean. Wildlife departments carry the cars to their new home on huge barges, forty cars at a time. They then use global positioning system (GPS) devices to map the exact location where they leave the cars.

Draw and Support Inferences <u>Underline</u> text that supports the inference that states will continue to create artificial reefs.

Integrate Visual Information What does the diagram of the artificial reef show about how the reef interacts with the environment?

Critical Thinking Think about whether environmentalists should be concerned about artificial reefs made from subway cars.

12   After one big Atlantic storm, officials went out to several reef sites to check on the reefs. Using GPS and **sonar**, they found that the cars were right where they had been deposited.

13   Not everyone likes the reefs. Some environmental groups worry that materials in the cars can pollute the ocean and harm the marine life. Their main concern is asbestos, which is used for insulation and as a fire retardant. It was used in the subway cars in glue for the floors and in insulation. When inhaled by humans, asbestos fibers can cause severe lung damage. The environmental groups are concerned that as the subway cars deteriorate, they will release asbestos. That could damage marine life and pose a danger to humans.

14   Environmental agency officials, however, are confident that the asbestos poses no risk. Studies of the water around the subway car reefs have not shown asbestos levels higher than those occurring in nature. In addition, for asbestos to harm humans, it needs to be airborne. Asbestos in water can't be inhaled and isn't considered harmful to humans.

15   The reefs have been very successful at attracting marine life. First, mussels, barnacles, oysters, crabs, and plants take up residence on the surfaces of the cars. Once they have established a presence, larger fish such as sea bass and flounder move in. Finally, large game fish such as tuna and sharks show up. Scientists have found more than 150 species of fish living in and around the reefs.

16   Sport and commercial fishers have benefited from the increased marine populations. Visiting fishers and divers boost the economies of the coastal communities. State game and wildlife officials are keeping an eye on the reefs to help them thrive.

✅ Comprehension Check

1. What did you expect the passage to be about when you read the title "Subways under the Sea"?

2. Why were items like shopping carts, refrigerators, and washing machines not effective in creating artificial reefs?

3. Define the following scientific terms from the passage. Explain how you determined the meanings, whether from context clues, using a dictionary, or both.

   barnacle, p. 168

   sonar, p. 170

4. How do the labels on the diagram of an artificial reef help you understand the text?

5. How do artificial reefs help local economies?

____

____

6. Why do you think wildlife officials call the subway cars "fish condominiums"? Use details from the text to support your ideas.

____

____

____

7. What is one effect of having larger populations of fish like sea bass and flounder?

____

____

8. Read these sentences from the selection.

Their structure includes the openings for doors and windows that have been removed. These openings allow for good water circulation while providing lots of nooks and crannies for fish and other marine wildlife to live.

What clues in the selection help you understand the meanings of the words *nooks* and *crannies*? What is the relationship between the two words?

____

____

Technical Texts

Technical texts provide true information about scientific topics or mechanical processes. You can find this kind of writing in magazine or newspaper articles, textbooks, encyclopedia entries, or on Web sites. Suppose you read a technical text about satellite dishes. What kinds of information would you expect to learn from it? What questions might get answered?

Skills Focus

How to Move a Lighthouse

Text Structure: Problem/Solution

Technical Texts

Taking to the Air: The Technology of Flight

Skim and Scan

Integrate Visual Information

Practice the Skill

First Read   **Text Structure: Problem/Solution**

Problem and solution is a way writers can organize information in texts. In this text structure, a problem is presented, and then one or more possible solutions are examined. Technical texts often contain examples of problems and solutions. Read this sentence: *If your basement floods regularly, you need to install a sump pump.* To find the problem, ask "What is happening?" *The basement floods regularly.* To find the solution, ask "How can the problem be solved?" *Install a sump pump.*

In technical writing that discusses problems and solutions, the first paragraph or paragraphs might introduce the problem and analyze it. The next few paragraphs might describe solutions that were tried but failed. Finally, the last paragraphs could show the solution that fixed the problem.

Writers make their problem and solution texts clear by using connecting words and phrases, such as *because, if, so, therefore, finally,* and *as a result.*

Try It   Read the following text.

> In remote areas, TV reception may be poor. Cable TV might not exist, and mountains can cause signal interference. So, many people find that a satellite dish is the proper approach for good TV reception.

Discuss   **Underline the problem, and double underline the solution. Draw a circle around the connecting word or phrase.**

Read on to find another example of problems and solutions.

> Wireless Internet reception can be difficult to find in rural areas because signals are weaker when farther from their source. Technicians sometimes solve the problem in an unusual way. First, they place a special antenna called a router on a tall tree. The router transfers a signal to a modem. As a result, the modem can send a wireless signal to a computer.

Discuss   **What is the problem? What is the solution? Underline the problem, and double underline the solution. Circle any connecting words.**

As you read, complete the Problem/Solution Chart on page 285.

Practice the Skill

Technical texts contain many facts. They may include **technical terms**, or words that are specific to the topic. Writers usually explain any technical terms they use when they are first mentioned. Technical terms are also often included in a glossary.

To make information easier to find, technical texts are often divided into sections with descriptive headings. Sometimes, the information is organized in a step-by-step sequence, with **diagrams** illustrating each of the steps. For example, a technical text on Egyptian pyramids might show labeled diagrams that illustrate the construction techniques used at each step of the building process.

Try It Read the following paragraph and study the diagram.

A satellite dish is a special kind of antenna that can be used to pick up a TV signal from a satellite in space. The receiving dish picks up an incoming microwave signal and focuses the signal into a narrow beam. The feed horn then transmits the signal to the TV.

Discuss What is this paragraph about? Box the technical terms the writer uses.

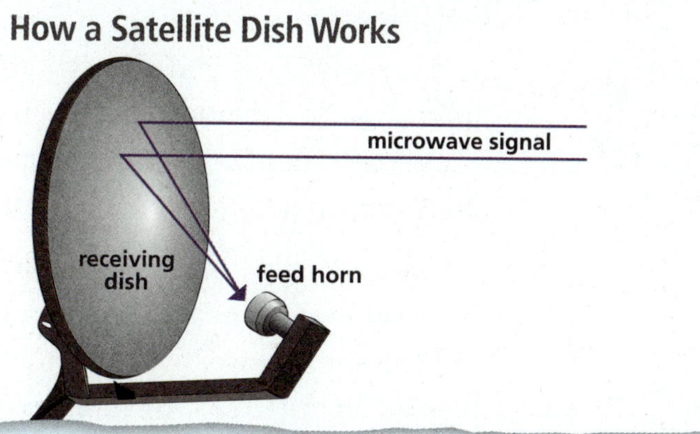

Discuss How does this diagram help you understand the technical text? Which part is the feed horn? Box the part that tells you.

As you read, record your answers to questions about technical texts on the Close Reading Worksheet on page 286.

How to Move a Lighthouse →

1   On an island off the coast of North Carolina, sparkling white sand stretches for mile after mile. Seabirds soar and glide in a blue sky, while a gentle breeze blows from the ocean. This is Hatteras Island, one of many barrier islands found thirty miles off the mainland.

2   Although they have some of the most beautiful beaches in the world, these barrier islands are dangerous. These bits of land have been called the graveyard of the Atlantic. The Gulf Stream, a swift ocean current, is close by and affects both the weather and the water. It pulls tropical storms inland, while deep water beyond the continental shelf causes **turbulent** seas. Currents pull in opposite directions, causing dense fog. In addition, hidden sandbars sometimes cause shipwrecks.

3   In 1803, a lighthouse was built at Hatteras Island's southern end to warn ships of the nearby dangers. It was replaced by a bigger lighthouse in 1870, with a tower over two hundred feet tall. Its powerful lantern pierced far out to sea, keeping sailors safe in storms and dense fog.

4   The Cape Hatteras Lighthouse was first built 1,500 feet away from the ocean. At the time, that seemed like a safe distance. But beaches are **dynamic**, which means they are constantly changing. Waves and winds pound the shore, moving sand from one place to another in a natural process called erosion. Erosion can happen relatively quickly on flat, sandy beaches like those on Hatteras Island. Year by year, the sands were pulled away by erosion, and the ocean crept closer. By 1970, it was only 120 feet away from the lighthouse.

5   The lighthouse's foundation of pine timbers sat on hard, compacted sand. As saltwater wore away at the sand, the foundation became less and less secure. Before long, the timbers would rot, and the 4,400-ton tower would fall. Something had to be done to save the lighthouse—and fast!

An Unusual Suggestion

6   Scientists and engineers began to study the erosion problem in the 1930s. At first, the Coast Guard tried building low metal walls, called *groins*, to keep the sand in place. Unfortunately, these **perpendicular** beams, set at right angles to the shore, were strong, but not strong enough to prevent continued erosion. The lighthouse tower was simply too close to the ocean, and the wind and waves were too powerful. So, the Coast Guard shut down the old building and moved its light to a temporary steel tower while they continued to study the problem.

7   It was time to find a permanent solution. Engineers suggested building a strong concrete and metal seawall all around the lighthouse station, which included the lighthouse and six other buildings. However, this idea was dismissed as too expensive. Plus, a seawall could not prevent erosion entirely. As the coastline continued to erode up to the seawall, the lighthouse station would have become a tiny island. The circle of the seawall would serve as its own coastline. Furthermore, as the sea continued to eat away at the sand beneath the seawall over time, it would eventually collapse.

The ocean came dangerously close to the lighthouse.

8   Then in 1988, a group of scientists and engineers proposed an unusual solution. Why not relocate the lighthouse to a safe place farther away from the ocean? The suggestion was fiercely debated for years. No one had ever attempted to move such a tall building. Did the technology exist for such a massive undertaking? Could the money be raised? By 1999, the answer to both questions was yes.

9   In 1999, plans were put into action. The lighthouse would be moved to a new location 2,900 feet southwest of its original location. Six other buildings that were part of the lighthouse station would also move.

The Challenge

10   Moving the lighthouse involved many challenging steps. The most difficult problem for the project's engineers was to lift the 4,400-ton tower from its foundation. The tower was more than one hundred years old, assembled from more than a million red bricks. The lighthouse would have to remain absolutely plumb, exactly vertical. Not a single brick could be allowed to fall.

One Step at a Time

11   The process began with the removal of eight hundred tons of granite from the original foundation. The granite was replaced with a network of temporary posts and supports.

12   Next, one hundred steel support beams were inserted under the temporary posts. Each steel beam contained a powerful lifting tool called a hydraulic jack, operated by hydraulic pressure.[1] As the steel beams were set into place, the temporary posts were removed. The beams crisscrossed one another, forming a strong mat of steel under the tower.

[1]**hydraulic pressure** hydraulic systems use pressurized liquids to create force; hydraulic pressure can be used to lift extremely heavy objects

Workers used machinery to replace the granite foundation with steel beams.

13   When all the beams were in place, the hydraulic jacks raised the tower six feet. All one hundred jacks had to lift at exactly the same time in order for the tower to stay plumb. The jacks had to support the lighthouse throughout the move.

14   After the tower had been lifted, steel *track beams* were put in place under the tower. As their name suggests, these track beams acted like the rails on a train track. Rollers were placed on the track beams, under the steel beam support mat. These rollers worked like the wheels on a train that grip the track, allowing the whole structure to slide along the track.

15   Once all the track beams and rollers were in place, hydraulic push jacks were added to push the lighthouse along the track beams, slowly and steadily. At last, the tower was ready to begin its 2,900-foot journey to the new site.

Why does the author include the diagram on this page?

What might have happened if all one hundred jacks did not lift at the same time and keep the lighthouse plumb?

A Light for the Future

16   On June 17, 1999, the lighthouse began to move. It was a slow crawl, just a few feet per hour, for an average of 130 feet a day. To keep from having to lay track beams the entire length of the route from the old to new location, the steel track beams in the rear were **dismantled** and reassembled at the front as the lighthouse inched forward.

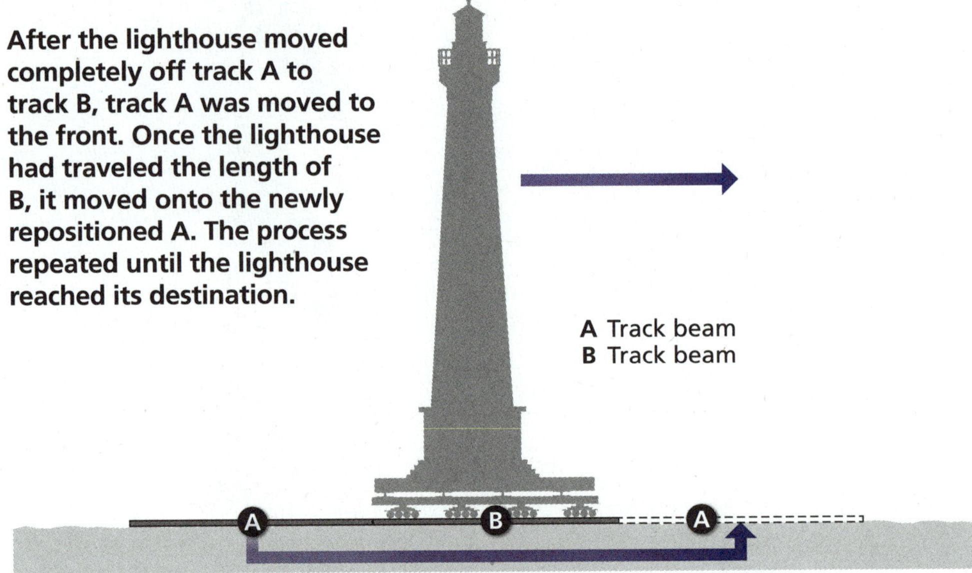

17   Fortunately, the weather stayed relatively calm. Weather monitors at the top of the tower measured wind speed and temperature. Wind gusts were recorded at twenty miles per hour on June 30, but the hydraulic jacks kept the tower on a perfect vertical axis.

18   It took twenty-three days to move the lighthouse. The move was completed on July 9, three weeks sooner than expected. Slowly and carefully, the historic tower was placed on its new foundation. The six other station buildings were placed nearby, exactly as they had been in their original location. The total cost of the move was $12 million.

19   Today, the lighthouse is a national historic site, a proud part of the Cape Hatteras National Seashore. The tallest brick lighthouse in North America, its famous black-and-white candy-stripe tower is frequently the subject of artwork, and its powerful searchlight continues to warn ships away from hidden dangers.

20   Meanwhile, water levels along the East Coast are rising year after year. Erosion continues to do its work, eating away at the shore. In one hundred years—if not sooner—the Cape Hatteras Lighthouse may have to move again.

Vocabulary: Academic Vocabulary

Academic vocabulary words are the kinds of words you use in school. You read them in textbooks, on quizzes and tests, on educational Web sites and hear them in classroom discussions. For example, in science, math, and English classes, you use words like *analyze*, *calculate*, and *synonym*. You might also see these words in technical writing, since those texts often relate to subjects you study in school. If you come across an unfamiliar academic vocabulary word, you may find that the author has defined or restated the word for you. At other times, you can figure out the word's meaning by using context clues, or a dictionary or glossary.

Try It Read this excerpt from "How to Move a Lighthouse."

> At first, the Coast Guard tried building low metal walls, called *groins*, to keep the sand in place. Unfortunately, these **perpendicular** beams, set at right angles to the shore, were strong, but not strong enough . . .

Discuss **What words help you understand the meaning of *perpendicular*?**

The following academic vocabulary is found in "How to Move a Lighthouse." Find each term in the selection. Then, write a definition of the term, and use it in a sentence.

1. **turbulent,** p. 176 _______________________________

____

2. **dynamic,** p. 176 _______________________________

____

3. **dismantled,** p. 180 _______________________________

____

Practice the Skill

 Skim and Scan

Technical texts are often loaded with information. It can be difficult to locate specific ideas or details unless you **skim and scan** for them. You **skim** a text by reading it quickly, looking for the big ideas. Notice text features such as the title, headings, photos, captions, numbered lists or steps in a process, and diagrams. Pay attention to boldface, italic, or highlighted words.

When you are looking for specific information, such as an important date or a definition, **scan** the text. This is quickly looking for what you want to know about. You do not read every word but instead search for important words or phrases.

Try It Skim the following text.

How a Lock Works

Boats travel up or down rivers that rise or descend in elevation by using *locks*. A lock is a mechanical device that raises and lowers boats by raising or lowering the water level between two gates. Here's how the process works going downriver:

1. The upper gate is opened.
2. The boat enters the lock.
3. The upper gate is closed.
4. Valves are opened downstream to let water out of the lock.
5. The boat is lowered as water drains and the water level goes down between the gates.
6. The lower gate is opened when the water level in the lock matches the water level downstream.
7. The boat exits the lock.

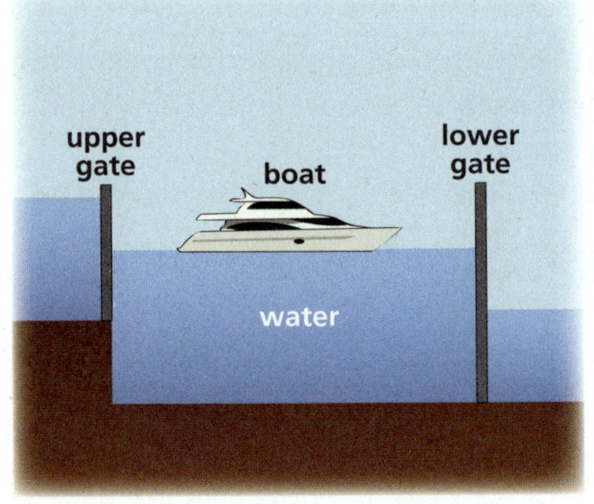

A boat using a lock to go downriver.

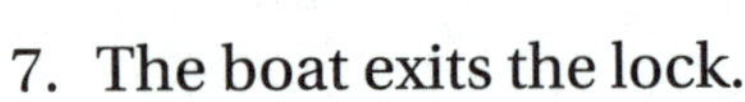

Discuss What is the main idea of the text? Underline the sentence that tells you. Now, scan the text to find out what a lock is.

As you read, complete the Skim and Scan Organizer on page 287.

Practice the Skill

Second Read **Integrate Visual Information**

Technical texts often involve complex and unfamiliar objects and processes. You might be confused about what something looks like or how it works if the writer were to describe it with words alone. **Visual information**, such as pictures and diagrams, are essential when words aren't enough. For example, camera manuals include graphics that help explain how the camera works or how to troubleshoot if there is a problem. If a process is best explained in a number of steps, a **flowchart** is often the best graphic to use.

Try It Read the instructions and the flowchart.

If your digital camera isn't working, here are some steps you can take. First, check to see if it is turned on. If not, turn the camera on. This may solve your problem. If it is turned on, check to see that the battery is fully charged. If not, charge the battery. If the battery is charged and the camera still does not work, you may need to take it to a repair shop.

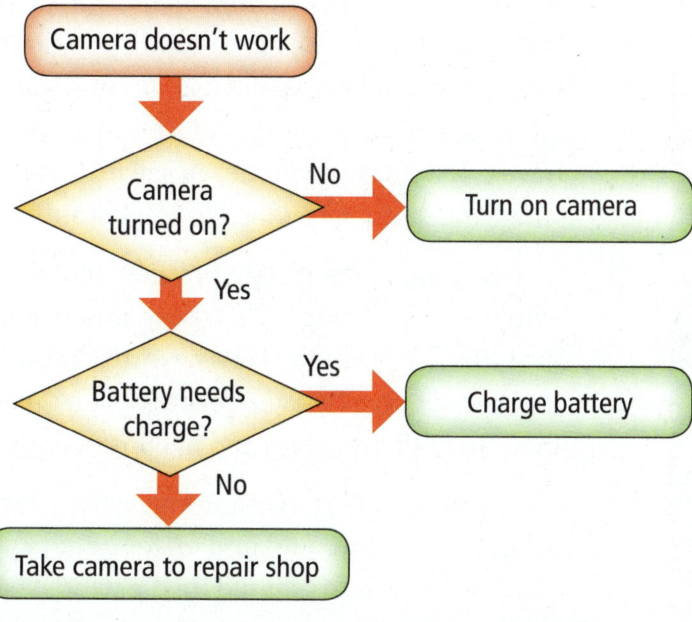

Discuss **How does this flowchart add to your understanding of the instructions? Which format is easier to follow?**

As you read, record your answers to questions about visual information on the Close Reading Worksheet on page 288.

Taking to the Air: The Technology of Flight

Skim the title and headings of this selection. What will you learn from the selection? Record your answer on the **Skim and Scan Organizer.**

What was the major difference between the Wright brothers' first flight at Kitty Hawk and the September 1904 flight? Why was this difference important?

1   On a September morning in 1904, in a field in Ohio, a strange wooden **contraption** with wings moved across the grass. It gathered speed and took to the air. Guided by a pilot lying on one wing, the flying machine circled above the field for one minute and thirty-six seconds and returned to its starting place. An excited onlooker, who had traveled two hundred miles to see the demonstration, described the "huge machine" as being like "a locomotive that has left its track."

2   Once again the Wright brothers had made history. This time it was with the first circling flight by a manned airplane. Their very first flight the year before at Kitty Hawk, North Carolina, was a straight flight that had lasted only fifty-nine seconds. The dream of sending a heavier-than-air craft into flight had become a reality.

3   For several years, Orville and Wilbur Wright had studied all the information they could find on *aeronautics*, the science of flight. They observed how birds soared on the wind, changing the shape and position of their wings slightly to **maneuver** in the sky. They applied their observations to hundreds of experiments with unmanned gliders and kites. Many of their early experiments failed, but Orville's boundless enthusiasm kept them going. Wilbur took careful notes on what worked and what didn't so they wouldn't repeat the same mistakes. Together they tested over two hundred designs for wings, recording which designs offered the least wind **resistance**. They designed a propeller to control their gliders' motions. The next step was to add enough power to get the gliders into the air.

Flyer II, the Wright brothers' second airplane, taking flight near Dayton, Ohio, 1904

4   By the time the Wright brothers came along, scientists had already learned a lot about the basic principles of *aerodynamics*, or the study of moving air. They knew, for example, that a powered flying machine needed a certain amount of *thrust*, or force pushing it forward, to move it into the air. The internal combustion engine[1] had been invented about forty years earlier, so it was available as a power source for the Wright brothers. They built their own four-cylinder combustion engine, which weighed 750 pounds and could **propel** a vehicle 31 miles per hour.

Flying Today

5   Leap forward in time to the present day. Whether you've traveled on an airplane or have only watched a flight on TV or in a movie, you are probably familiar with the very basics: The plane zooms down the runway and takes flight. After flying a certain distance, the plane descends and lands. This simple description could describe the Wright brothers' first flights. Modern flight does indeed share the same basic principles with flight one hundred years ago, but beyond the basics, the technology today is vastly different. Let's take a quick flight to see how this technology really works.

Before Flight: The Takeoff

6   As you taxi from the terminal to the runway, you might notice that there are several different runways, each running in different directions. Which one will your pilot pick, and why?

[1]**internal combustion engine** an engine that burns fuel inside the engine instead of using an outside furnace

7   The answer is simple. Airplanes require airspeed to take off. *Airspeed* is the measure of how fast air flows over the airplane, not how fast the airplane is traveling. Airspeed is increased if the airplane is traveling into a *headwind*, which is wind blowing in the direction opposite the direction in which the airplane is moving. This is why most airplanes take off into the wind. Your pilot has been assigned a specific runway for takeoff. It's the one that will provide the airplane with the best headwinds.

8   Now your plane is on the correct runway. If you look out your window at this point, you will likely notice that the pilot has lowered the flaps on the wings. *Flaps* are moveable surfaces toward the rear, or *trailing edge*, of the wing. Lowering the flaps slows the speed of the air passing under the wing while increasing the speed of the air over the wing. This helps create more *lift*, the upward force acting on the plane, at lower airspeeds. The plane needs this additional lift to get into the air.

9   Suddenly you hear the engines revving up. They do this while the brakes are engaged to build up to the desired force without wasting runway. When the brakes are released, the airplane builds speed quickly as it moves down the runway. The engines are steadily pushed to full power for takeoff.

10   When the airplane reaches the correct takeoff speed, its nose begins to lift off the ground. As the nose of the airplane rises, the whole plane tilts upward. This means the wings also tilt upward, creating even more lift. When the airspeed over the wings becomes great enough, the plane lifts off the ground.

11   Now that the airplane is off the ground, the flaps are no longer needed to create lift. In fact, at this point they begin to create *drag* and slow down the airplane. So, the pilot retracts the flaps, or draws them back to their original position. Another thing the pilot retracts to limit drag is the *landing gear*, which is the wheels and other equipment that support the airplane when it is on the ground.

12   You can review the takeoff procedure in this flowchart.

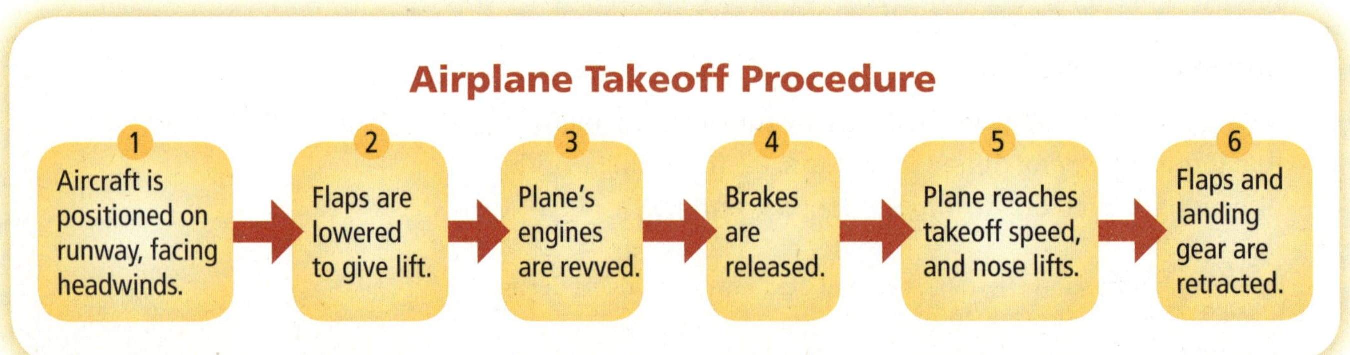

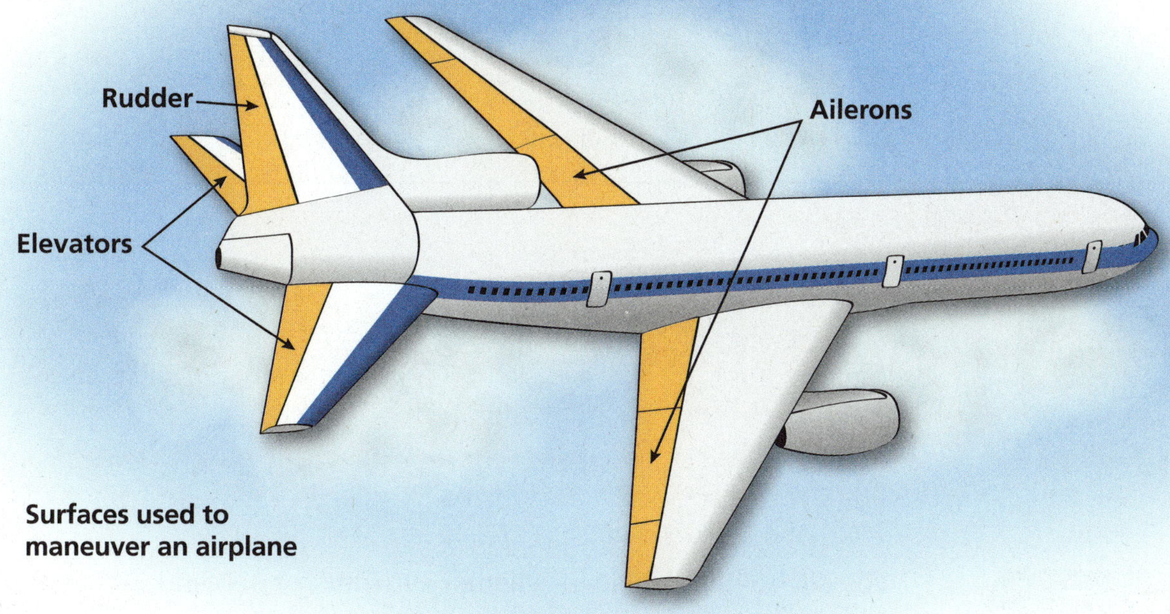

**Surfaces used to
maneuver an airplane**

During Flight: Maneuvering the Airplane

13   Once the airplane is off the ground, the pilot must control where it is going. When the Wright brothers steered their first powered flying machine in a circular path above a farmer's field in Ohio, they steered with a simple pulley system that operated wing flaps. Modern airplanes use the same basic concepts but take them further with **ailerons**, a rudder, and elevators.

14   You've already seen how wing flaps help create lift when the plane takes off. Modern planes also have a second set of outer wing flaps, called *ailerons.* By raising and lowering the ailerons, the pilot causes the airplane to roll to the left or to the right.

15   The ailerons are only part of what is needed to turn a plane. In addition, the rudder on the tail operates like the rudder on a boat. If the pilot turns the rudder to the right, the airplane will turn right, with the help of the ailerons also rolling the plane to the right. Similarly, the pilot goes left by turning the rudder left and adjusting the roll to the left using ailerons. This makes a big difference between whether you turn north to Alaska or south to Hawaii!

16   As the flight progresses, the captain may use the intercom to let you know of an approaching weather disturbance. To avoid it, the pilot has decided to raise the airplane. *Elevators*, flaps on the plane's tail, control

How does the diagram help you skim and scan the selection? Record your answer in the **Skim and Scan Organizer.**

Why does a plane's tail rudder have the same name as a boat's rudder?

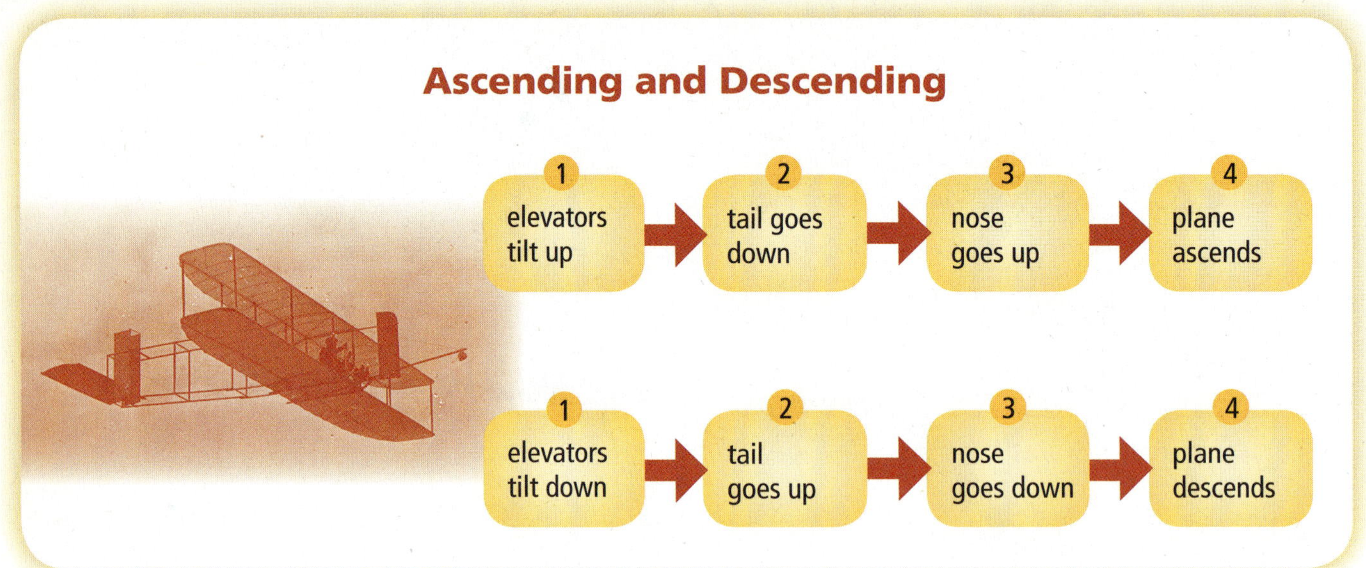

the *pitch* of the airplane—whether it ascends or descends. When the elevators tilt up, the tail goes down. This causes the nose to go up and the plane to rise. The opposite happens when the pilot wishes the aircraft to descend.

Enjoying the Flight

17   Most of us are passengers, not engineers and inventors like the Wright brothers or pilots like those that fly today. However, as we carry our backpacks on board the plane, store them overhead, and settle in our seats, it's reassuring to know some basics about aerodynamics. The first moments of takeoff, when a heavy plane leaves the ground and becomes airborne, will always be a thrill. But with a bit of knowledge, those moments will be a little less of a mystery.

Vocabulary: Using a Dictionary

When you come across a difficult word in a technical text, you should first try to make sense of it in context, or by looking at the words and sentences around it. If that doesn't work, you should look the word up in a dictionary. Not all dictionaries list the same information in their entries, but most include the word's pronunciation, part of speech, and one or more definitions.

ma•neu•ver (mə-ˈnü-vər) *noun.*
1: a planned movement of troops;
2: a skillful change in movement or direction; *verb.* **3:** to change the position of troops; **4:** to skillfully move or change direction

Try It Read this sentence from "Taking to the Air: The Technology of Flight."

They observed how birds soared on the wind, changing the shape and position of their wings slightly to **maneuver** in the sky.

Discuss **Use the dictionary entry above for the word *maneuver*. How is the word pronounced? Is it used as a noun or verb in this sentence? Which meaning is used in the sentence?**

The following words appear in "Taking to the Air: The Technology of Flight." Find the words in the selection. Use a dictionary to check their meanings, and determine pronunciations and parts of speech. Then write the pronunciation, part of speech, and definition on the lines.

1. **contraption,** p. 184 ____

2. **resistance,** p. 184 ____

3. **propel,** p. 185 ____

4. **ailerons,** p. 187 ____

Respond to Text: Compare Text Structures

The two selections you have just read are organized using different text structures. "How to Move a Lighthouse" has a problem/solution structure, and "Taking to the Air: The Technology of Flight" uses a sequential structure, showing steps in a process.

 Try It Think about how the ideas are organized in each selection and how the text structures affected your reading.

 **Discuss** **How did the text structure of each selection affect your understanding of the technical information? Would you have understood either selection better if it had been arranged differently?**

On Your Own Write about the text structure of each selection. Explain how it affected your understanding of the technical ideas in each selection. Include details from the texts to support your response. Use the guide on the next page to help you plan your response. Then write your paragraph on a separate sheet of paper.

Checklist for a Good Response

A good paragraph

✔ describes the text structure of each selection.

✔ shows an understanding of the technical information presented in each selection.

✔ explains how the arrangement of ideas influences how well you understand them.

✔ includes a topic sentence, supporting ideas, and a concluding statement.

How Text Structure Affected My Reading

1. **Topic Sentence** Include this information in your topic sentence:

    The text structure of "How to Move a Lighthouse" is ___________________

    and "Taking to the Air" presents information ___________________.

2. **Detail Sentences** Tell how the text structure of each selection affected your understanding and experience reading it. Give details that support your ideas. Use this chart to organize your ideas.

	"How to Move a Lighthouse"	**"Taking to the Air"**
How did the text structure and the content of the selection work together?		
How did the text structure help me understand the technical information?		
How did the text structure help me enjoy the selection?		

3. **Concluding Sentence** Your final sentence should restate in a fresh way how text structure added to your understanding.

____

On a separate sheet of paper, write your paragraph.

The Technology of Ski Design

Skim and Scan What is the main topic of the selection? How do you know? Underline two places where you found that information. The first has been done for you.

Text Structure: Problem/Solution Think about the problem skis were created to solve.

1   Like a shot, the racer leaves the starting gate. Weaving in tight loops between the poles, the skier flies quickly down the mountain. She is a colorful blur of spandex against a white landscape. With each turn, the skis carve into the hill, sending up small sprays of snow. In a few short minutes, the skier is at the bottom of the hill, checking her time. How good was the run? Fast enough for a medal or to set a new record?

2   As the racer heads for the ski lodge, she removes her helmet and skis. Let's take a look at those skis. They are without a doubt "shaped" skis. They have curved sides for carving short, neat turns. The edges are made of steel to cut into the snow. Today's skis reflect state-of-the-art sports technology and design that have resulted from many years of development.

Skis of the Past

3   The skis used by racers today would look very strange to skiers of the past. Human beings first strapped on skis in the northern European country of Norway about four thousand years ago. The first skis were made of animal bone and looked more like snowshoes than like today's skis.

4   During the Middle Ages, skis were made of wood instead of bone. They were about seven feet long, two inches thick, and five inches wide. They attached to the toe of a boot with a leather strap. The skis looked like what we call Nordic, or cross-country, skis today. In snowy countries, skis were necessary for doctors, midwives, clergy, traveling salespeople—for everyone who had to get around in deep snow. No one at the time thought about using skis for sports racing.

5   In the nineteenth century, skiing gradually developed into a sport. Skiers learned new methods of turning and stopping. By the twentieth century, alpine, or downhill, skiing had spread from Norway and Sweden to the rest of Europe and the United States. Settlers of Norwegian ancestry established some of the first ski contests in Michigan and Minnesota.

6   The Winter Olympics in France in 1924 gave the world its first close look at cross-country skiing and ski jumping, while alpine skiing made its debut at the 1936 Winter Olympics in Germany. Then, after World War II, downhill skiing took off as a serious sport in North America. Millions of people learned to ski, and ski resorts opened in Canada, New England, and western states.

7   While alpine skiing was becoming popular, the skis themselves did not change much. They were still made of light wood such as hickory and were about seven to eight feet long. However, ski technology was about to change.

New Materials

8   The first changes in ski technology were in materials. Metal edges were added that made skis grip hard-packed snow better. Designers first tried making skis of wood and aluminum, gluing the aluminum to a wood core. They discovered that the aluminum froze too easily. Then an American skier invented a light plastic ski with steel edges. The design was quickly favored by both weekend skiers and professionals. Factories began to make skis out of steel and fiberglass, using molds. The skis were still almost as long as they were in the old days, when skiers carved them by hand. The basic shape also had not changed.

Carving a Breakthrough

9   As downhill skiing grew more competitive and popular, champion skiers became athletic superstars. However, beginners struggled, sometimes tripping over the long six- and seven-foot skis. So, by popular demand, skis got shorter. By 1965, skis for beginners shrank to five feet or less. The short ski was described as "ten times the fun for one-tenth the effort."

10   Skiers also wanted skis that made tighter turns. So ski designers experimented by making *side cuts* in skis. They pinched in the *waist* of the ski by about ten millimeters. The waist is the narrowest part of the ski, the point where the ski boot is mounted. This pinch made the skis much wider at the tip and tail than at the waist. Deeper side cuts meant that the ski could turn on a tighter, smaller radius—meaning skiers could now make sharper turns. Fiberglass skis with deeper side cuts allowed for more control on the slopes for both beginners and experts.

The parts of a shaped ski

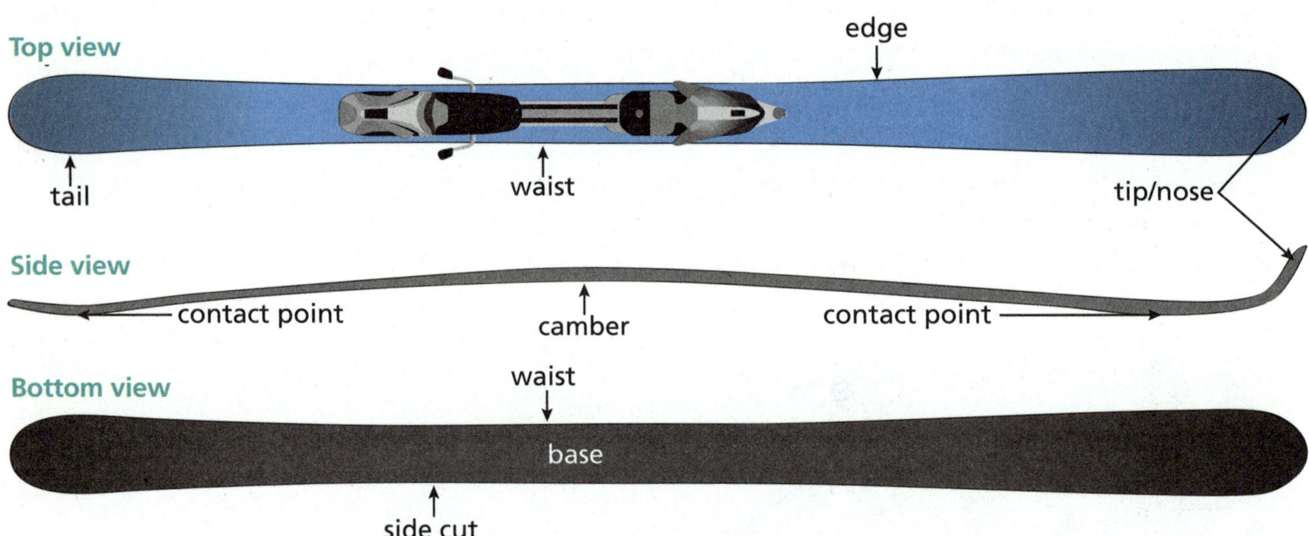

11   People called the new skis *shaped* or *carved* because they carved a tighter circle in the snow. They also called them ***parabolic*** skis because of the bend of the ski, called the *camber*. This bend was curved in the shape of a parabola, or bowl shape.

12   In race after race, competitors using shaped skis ruled the mountains. Within a decade, shaped skis became the new standard for all skis.

Extreme Side Cuts

13   Designers continued to experiment with shaped skis. If side cuts were good, would deeper side cuts be better? In the winter of 1993 to 1994, one company introduced a ski with an extreme side cut and a very skinny waist. These skis proved to be especially good for slalom skiing. In slalom skiing, competitors race downhill while following a winding course marked by flag-topped poles placed close together. The extreme side cuts allow the skier to carve into the snow to make the necessary turns without losing **velocity**.

A slalom skier must make sharp turns without losing speed.

Making the Modern Ski

14   As ski designs changed over time, manufacturers responded to satisfy buyers' demands for new shaped skis. They experimented with materials, coming up with several different models. Laminated[1] skis are the most common variety of skis today. The process for making them allows the greatest variety of models and materials. In a laminated ski, materials such as plastic, fiberglass, wood, steel, and aluminum are layered above and below the ski's wood core. All these materials are sealed by heat. The process involves six steps. The steps are best shown on a flowchart.

The Future

15   The process of making laminated skis takes several days. It involves many technically skilled workers. To save time and cost, manufacturers are likely to make more single-shell skis in the future. In single-shell skis, a core of wood or other durable material is enclosed in a single fiberglass or plastic shell. This kind of ski is faster to produce and requires fewer chemicals. As technology develops, robots may take over some steps in the future manufacturing process. This will likely make skis less expensive. And as costs go down, the popular winter sport of alpine skiing may become even more popular!

[1]**laminated** produced by placing layer on layer

✔ Comprehension Check

1. How did ski designers solve the problem of skis that did not turn tightly enough?

2. Are paint and logos applied to the skis before or after they are sanded and polished? How do you know?

3. Under which heading in the selection would you look to find information about the earliest skis?

4. Explain what *slalom skiing* is. What words in the selection help you understand the meaning of the term?

5. Why does the manufacturing process for laminated skis take several days?

____

____

____

6. Synthesize the text and the visual information in the section "Making the Modern Ski" to briefly summarize how skis are manufactured today.

____

____

____

7. Read these sentences from the selection.

> **They also called them *parabolic* skis because of the bend of the ski, called the *camber*. This bend was curved in the shape of a parabola, or bowl shape.**

Circle the words that help you understand the meaning of *parabolic*.

8. Read this sentence from the selection.

> **The extreme side cuts allow the skier to carve into the snow to make the necessary turns without losing velocity.**

Use a dictionary to find the pronunciation and part of speech of the word *velocity* as it is used in the sentence.

Part of speech: ____

Velocity is pronounced: ____

Persuasive Nonfiction

Persuasive nonfiction is about presenting clear, strong arguments. The author wants you to do something or agree with his or her opinion on an issue. The author's argument, or main idea, has to contain evidence that convinces you to agree with that argument. What issue is represented by the image on this page? What persuasive argument might an author make concerning this issue?

Skills Focus

Technology Is Killing My Movies!

Author's Point of View and Purpose

Author's Argument

Thank You, Technology!

Denotation and Connotation

Evaluate Author's Claims

Practice the Skill

Every author has a **purpose**, or reason, for writing. When a comic book author puts a joke into a character's speech balloon, her purpose is to entertain. She wants to make the reader laugh. Another author might write an editorial for a political Web site, sharing his opinion about an upcoming election. His purpose is to persuade the reader why it is best to vote for a particular candidate.

Whether an author is writing to **entertain, inform,** or **persuade** will affect the author's point of view. The **point of view** is an author's opinion about the topic. Author's purpose and point of view go hand in hand. The author wants you to see the topic through his or her eyes. In persuasive nonfiction, it should be very clear that the author is for or against something. Authors will stress certain facts about a topic and leave out other facts altogether in order to press their viewpoints. Keep an eye out for particularly negative or positive words and phrases an author uses to influence his or her audience. This is called **loaded language**.

Another thing to keep in mind as you read persuasive nonfiction is that you don't have to agree with an author's point of view.

Try It Read the following paragraph.

It's time for pet owners to stop posting their pets' pictures all over the Internet. I smiled like everyone else when I first saw a picture of a puppy poking its head out of the laundry basket or a kitten wrapped up in a tangle of yarn. But recently it feels as if a cute pet invasion has taken over my computer. I'm happy that you love your adorable pet. You can hang pictures of your lop-eared bunny all over your walls at home. I just don't want to see him every time I open an e-mail. Even worse, sometimes they're tricks. Last week, I clicked on a pygmy hedgehog picture, and I got a computer virus! These pet pictures are a menace that needs to end now.

> **Discuss** What is the topic of this paragraph? Underline the sentence that states the author's point of view. Double underline any loaded language you find.

As you read, record your answers about the author's point of view and purpose on the Close Reading Worksheet on page 289.

Practice the Skill

An author's **argument** is the opinion that he or she wants you to agree with. Usually, the author directly states his or her **claim**, or main idea about the issue, to make sure you understand it. The author then gives you **reasons** *why* you should agree with the claim. However, reasons are not enough. A good argument uses evidence to support its reasons. Supporting **evidence** can include research findings, personal experience, facts, and advice from experts.

An author should also acknowledge and argue against any **counterarguments**— the reasons why someone might disagree with his or her position.

Try It Read the following paragraph.

It's time to put more money into the space program. This year, the United States will invest nearly twenty billion dollars in NASA. That amount could seem extreme, especially when the national debt is already trillions of dollars. However, every penny spent for NASA is a penny spent on our future. Many advances in technology come directly from the space program. We wouldn't have computers, cell phones, or the World Wide Web without it.

Discuss **Draw a box around the author's claim. What reasons and evidence does the author give? Circle details that support the claim.**

Read on and compare the following argument to the previous one.

The United States needs to cut NASA's budget. Did you know that the government will spend nearly twenty billion dollars on the program this year? Tons of people are struggling to put food on the table! Everyone knows this money would be better spent fighting hunger and homelessness or curing diseases.

Discuss **Draw a box around this author's claim. Circle the reasons and evidence. Which author makes a better argument? Why?**

As you read, complete the Claims and Supporting Evidence Chart on page 290.

Technology Is Killing My Movies!

Underline the sentences that state the author's point of view. What is the author's purpose?

Draw a box around the paragraph that presents a counterargument.

Is the author a fan of the *Jetmorphs* series? Why or why not?

1   A deep cobalt-blue sky fills the screen. The camera zooms out to show a boy with eyes that match the sky exactly and hair as golden as the wheat field in which he sits. The boy gasps as fighter jets tear across the sky over his head. Two of the jets spiral down and engage in a battle right above him. Just when it looks like the boy is doomed, another jet zooms in, transforms into a robot, and swats the two planes out of the picture frame. As the boy grins, an enormous explosion offscreen showers the field with metallic **debris**. Then the robot winks and scoops the boy into its mechanical hand.

2   This sounds like a pretty cool opening scene for a movie, right? If only the rest of the movie had lived up to it. Sure, *Jetmorphs Return IV* is filled with amazing effects and stunning action scenes. Fans of the series will probably **flock** to the theaters, just as they've done for the last three *Jetmorphs* movies. Yet it seems the stories have been getting dumber and dumber with each sequel, and the acting is as flat as a pancake. But *Jetmorphs Return IV* is not just a bad movie. It is proof that technology is ruining the film industry.

3   Some will argue that technology is the best thing that ever happened to the moviemaking **industry**. Filmmakers can use computers to create new worlds that look nearly as believable as the one we live in. Last year's *Apotheosis*, with its wildly colorful alien species, set on a planet with landscapes more lush than any on Earth, was a landmark in moviemaking.

4   In *Apotheosis*, computer artists created every **petal** of every flower and every bubble that rises from a babbling brook. It was a stunning accomplishment by the creative team that made the film, but special effects alone do not make a great movie. *Apotheosis* also had a well-crafted plot.

5   Unfortunately, movies like *Apotheosis* are the exception these days. Too often filmmakers put so much effort and money into the movie's computer-generated imagery (CGI) that the other filmmaking aspects suffer. In the early days of film, special effects had little to do with a movie's success. Some black-and-white movies were filmed on sets composed of little more than cardboard props and costumes gathered from a thrift shop. Those classics can still move an audience, however, because of their powerful plots, excellent writing, and skilled acting.

6   Another problem with CGI is that it fixes too many mistakes. The real world isn't perfect, and the images that we see on our screens don't have to be either. Jeremy McKay, the child star of the *Jetmorphs* series, is adorable. However, his eyes are slate gray, not cobalt blue, and his hair is more brown than golden. Every strand of it probably doesn't flutter prettily in the wind the way it does when the jets race over him in *Jetmorphs Return IV*. These artificial images create a distance between the film and the viewer's real-life experience. The robotic jets aren't the only things that look unreal in *Jetmorphs*. The people do, too, and it is distracting.

7   One of the things everyone enjoys about old films is the chance to see the **flaws** in an actor's appearance. The cracked lines of worry and regret in the sheriff's face and the gap between the beautiful star's teeth that makes her smile delightfully imperfect are assets, not mistakes to be fixed. Filmmakers need to embrace the blemishes, not erase them.

8   This leads to another area in which technology is ruining movies, the triumph of digital video over film. In recent times, manufacturers of digital projectors forced theaters to remove their old film projectors before the new digital equipment could be installed. Now there are few movie theaters in the country that can project a 35-millimeter film, a format that has been around since 1895. The rise of digital video means that movies can be made more easily and for less money than they were before, which is a great thing. Digital video has made incredible advancements in the past twenty years. Most viewers today can't tell the difference between the two. However, a true film lover knows that the whites are brighter, the blacks are deeper, and the color is richer in 35-millimeter film.

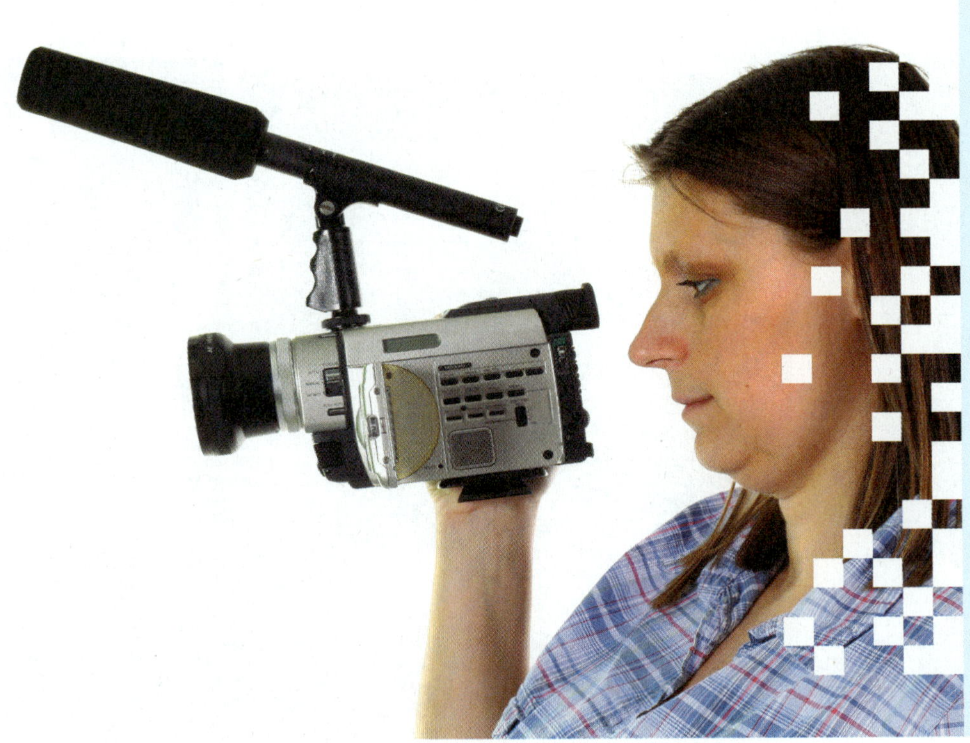

Light, handheld digital cameras like this one are rapidly replacing the much larger and more awkward film cameras of the past.

9   Also, what will happen to digital files over time? While reels of old film can break down over time, they are physical things that can be touched. They can be inventoried, stored, taken out, cleaned, and replayed. Digital files can vanish with the click of the mouse. Of course, they can also be protected and saved in different places, but you can't put your hands on them. It seems like their existence is more fragile and less real than that of film. Anything can happen to digital files.

10   An even bigger problem with digital video, though, is that it has led to the downfall of the theater-going experience. I'll admit, it is a luxury on a bitterly cold winter night to cuddle up with a quilt on the couch and watch a movie that looks just as good on your high-definition television as it does in the theater. It's just that watching movies at home has become the **norm**, rather than the exception. And it seems like a trend that will continue to grow in the future.

11   That makes me sad. In 1948, ninety million Americans went to the movie theater each week. Today, less than a third of that number can be found in theaters. Watching movies has become more convenient but less of a social experience. Back in the 1940s, every kid from the neighborhood waited in line outside the theater. They cheered, and gasped, and booed together. When it was over, they got back on the line and watched the film again . . . and again . . . and again.

12   Until recently, film fans couldn't click a button to get a movie on demand. They couldn't watch the movie at home whenever they wanted, and they couldn't watch movies on a phone in the car. When a movie left the theater, they weren't able to see it again for a long, long time. It made going to the theater to see a single movie a **precious**, shared experience to be treasured.

13   Even though kids in the 1940s weren't able to watch a movie over and over every day after it left the theater, the movie would stay with them. They played at being their big-screen heroes—brave police officers, hard-boiled detectives, daring musketeers, and fearless knights—with their friends, fighting over who would be the good guys and who would be the bad.

14   One movie, and the fact that we all saw it together, transformed our childhoods. Technology has robbed us of that. Sure, kids still watch the same movies and talk about them with their friends, but there's just not always the thrill of waiting for the movie to come to your theater or the shared cheers and tears that were once a guaranteed part of the theater-going experience.

15 I realize that there's no stopping technology now. Advances in technology have brought new ideas and methods to the movie industry that have changed it in some positive ways for which I'm grateful. I'm sure that in ten years, or even five, the way that movies are created and the way that the audience views them will change even more. We're living in an age where every day seems to bring a new technological advancement.

16 However, I would like to say one thing to all the filmmakers out there: Use technology; don't let technology use you. The qualities that made movies great fifty years ago are the same qualities that make them great now. Start with a great writer and a great story, and then add a director with a vision, and cast a team of talented actors. Then let the artists create. If you do that, you can throw in any number of CGI explosions and brave new worlds, and I won't complain. I'll just head to the theater, grab my popcorn, and sit back and enjoy it all.

Vocabulary: Word Relationships

When you encounter an unfamiliar word, look for the relationship between it and the words that surround it to help you understand its meaning. Sometimes the relationships are easy to see, like *happy* and *glad*. These words have similar meanings, or are **synonyms**. The words *happy* and *sad* have an opposite relationship, or are **antonyms**.

Sometimes you have to look at the words more closely to figure out their relationship. How is *thirst* related to *drink*? Thirst causes someone to take a drink. These words have a **cause-and-effect** relationship.

Words can also be related as **part to whole**, where one word is part of another; for example, *finger* and *hand*. Similarly, words can have an **item and category** relationship, where one word is a subset of another; for example, *oak* and *tree*.

Try It Look at these word pairs from "Technology Is Killing My Movies!"

Word 1	Word 2	Relationship	Definition
explosion	**debris**		
petal	flower		
crack/gap	**flaws**		

> **Discuss** Write the relationship for each pair above. Then write a definition for the boldfaced word to complete the chart.

Complete the chart below with these additional word pairs from the selection.

Word 1	Word 2	Relationship	Definition
fans	**flock**		
filmmakers	**industry**		
norm	exception		
precious	treasured		

Practice the Skill

Often words that mean the same thing can have shades of differences between them. Take *cheap* and *economical*, for example. They have similar **denotations**, or meanings that you find in a dictionary. *Cheap* is an adjective that describes things that don't cost a lot of money. *Economical* describes things that are not expensive to own and use. Though the words' denotations are similar, their **connotations**, or the emotions and associations connected to them, differ. *Cheap* has a negative connotation, meaning something that doesn't cost a lot and isn't worth a lot, either. *Economical*, on the other hand, has a more positive connotation, suggesting something that has value even though it is not expensive. Now consider the word *inexpensive*. It inspires neither positive nor negative feelings. *Inexpensive* has a neutral connotation.

Try It   Read the following paragraph.

It's time for professional sports players to earn their million-dollar salaries, not on the playing fields of their sports but on the playing field of life. I remember a time when players were **confident** but didn't **show off**. I'm tired of watching ballplayers do their **ridiculous** dances whenever they make a successful play. It's their job! A doctor doesn't do a dance when he cures a **patient**. Coaches should **demand** that players take a course in sportsmanship at training camp every year.

Discuss   Look at each boldface word in the selection. Write each word in the correct connotation column below. Then write each word's dictionary definition. The first word has been done for you.

positive	negative	neutral	definition
confident			sure of oneself

As you read, complete the Connotations Chart on page 291.

Practice the Skill

In persuasive nonfiction, authors base their arguments on **facts** and opinions. Facts are pieces of information that can be proven true. For example, "Dogs are mammals" is a fact. **Opinions**, on the other hand, express personal beliefs and feelings and can't be proved true or false. "Dogs are better pets than cats" is an opinion because it can't be proved true or false. It's fine to express an opinion in persuasive writing, but an opinion must never be presented solely as fact. When writers do that, it weakens their arguments.

A good persuasive argument makes **reasoned judgments**. The author logically supports every **claim**, or main idea about an issue, with factual evidence. If facts are missing or weak, the author is not presenting a reasoned judgment. In these cases, the author may rely on opinions to appeal to your emotions.

You should approach an author's argument the same way a juror looks at arguments in a trial. Try to separate fact from opinion to decide whether the argument is sound.

Try It Read the following paragraph.

> Playgrounds can be fun and enjoyable places, but they can also be dangerous. The playground in Middletown Park is too dangerous to keep open. It should be closed for repairs immediately. Last year in the United States, 220,000 children under the age of fourteen were treated in emergency rooms for injuries that happened on playground equipment. Just last week, a four-year-old boy suffered a serious head injury when he fell off the swing at Middletown Park. Those swings are a safety hazard and should be taken down! They are not worth the risk of another child being seriously injured. They are not worth the cost, either. Playground-related injuries cost our town $140,000 in the past two years. Let's work together to build a better, safer playground for all the children of Middletown!

Discuss Box facts the author gives. Circle any opinions. Does the author make a reasoned judgment? Why or why not?

As you read, record your answers to questions about evaluating author's claims on the Close Reading Worksheet on page 292.

Thank You, Technology!

1   Technology has completely transformed our world in the past fifty years. Some people complain about newfangled gadgets and would prefer a return to simpler ways and times. These **antitechnology** people are reactionary and out of touch. Technology has had a positive impact on all of our lives, and for that I say, "Thank you, technology!"

2   Most Americans feel the same way. According to a recent poll, 86 percent of Americans surveyed agree that "science and technology are making our lives easier and more efficient." A similarly sized group thinks that "because of science and technology, there will be greater opportunities for the next generation."

3   Of course, because most people agree with a statement doesn't mean that it is correct. In this case, though, it is. Let me explain the reasons why.

Technology Makes Difficult Tasks Easier

4   You'd probably be considered lazy if you thought that getting up from the couch to change the channel was a difficult task. While the invention of the remote control in 1956 would eventually affect almost every household in our country, it alone was not a significant change. However, the ability to remotely control all of the devices in our homes is significant. Today, you can use your cell phone to operate the lights in your home, activate your home alarm system, and control your **thermostat**.

5   The "smart home" that once seemed like a fantasy is well on the way to becoming a reality, and one that will make us more efficient and better **protected**. Let's say you get stuck at a meeting to plan the next school dance. You're going to get home later than usual but before your parents get home from work. It's winter, so it will be dark in the late afternoon, and you live on a quiet street. You can use your cell phone to turn on the outside spotlight and some indoor lights. Then you won't be fumbling with your keys in the dark when you unlock the front door. And we all know that outside lighting deters crime.

Technology Connects Us to One Another

6   It's been almost 150 years since the telephone was invented. Even before it became widely used, Alexander Graham Bell saw the potential of the device he invented. He wrote, "I believe, in the future, wires will unite the head offices of telephone companies in different cities, and a man in one part of the country may communicate by word of mouth with another in a distant place."

7   Mr. Bell, you were correct, but modern advancements in technology have taken communication far beyond what even you could have imagined! Today, we are connected to one another in far more ways than ever before. We don't need wires to communicate—we can text, call, or even talk face-to-face over wireless networks. Social media platforms, such as Facebook, Twitter, and Instagram, allow us to share our thoughts, photos, and videos with large groups of people at the same time.

8   Fifty years ago, if you moved across the country, there weren't many options for regularly keeping in touch with your friends back home. You could write and send letters in the mail, but it could take a week or more for them to arrive at their destination. You could make a long-distance phone call, but those calls were **atypical** because they were expensive and had to be kept short. Today, long distances between people are no longer a communication obstacle. If you're at the mall and you bump into the lead singer from your favorite band, you can send a picture of her to all of your friends with one press of a button. Now that's progress!

Is the claim made about social media in paragraph 7 based on fact or opinion? How do you know?

Technology Makes Us Smarter

9 Technology doesn't literally make us smarter, but it gives us access to a wide world of information. Some think this is a problem, because the more easily we can access information, the less we'll store it in our brains. Throughout time, people have always been concerned that the more tools we have, the less we think. The ancient worrywart and Greek philosopher Socrates feared that the invention of writing was anti-intellectual and made people think and remember less.

10 Socrates wrote, "I cannot help feeling, Phaedrus, that writing is unfortunately like painting; for the creations of the painter have the attitude of life, and yet if you ask them a question they preserve a solemn silence." He believed that once ideas were written down, the writer was left with little more to say.

11 IQ scores would indicate that Socrates was mistaken. Over the past hundred years, IQs in the United States have risen steadily, about three points every ten years. We're not alone, either. Scores in many other countries around the world, including Japan, Canada, and Israel, have also increased in that time period.

12 Many of today's educators disagree with Socrates, as well. When surveyed, 85 percent of them said classroom computers improved student performance. Three-fourths said computers improve students' attention in class. Technology is becoming a bigger and bigger part of the classroom experience every day, as teachers move away from chalkboards and use interactive whiteboards.

13 In the past, students had to sit at their desks and copy pages and pages of notes about the Civil War that their teacher wrote on the board. Today, teachers can show a video of a Civil War reenactment, then display an image of a letter written by a Union soldier, and then have students click through an interactive time line. It's clear to see which approach the students would find more interesting. If they're more interested, they'll learn more.

Technology Makes Us Healthier

14 Technology has also brought about great strides in the health-care industry. It has changed the way we detect and treat all kinds of health problems, from minor colds to life-threatening illnesses.

15 The Internet is now a wonderful source of medical information. People are able to look up their symptoms and read what professionals have to say about them. They then make more empowered decisions about their next steps, which usually involve seeing their doctor.

16   If you have a few itchy bumps on your leg, you can compare them to pictures on health-related sites to see whether they might be bug bites or something else. A bug bite is probably not a big problem, and you might just be able to deal with the itchiness. Bumps that are the sign of an illness or a rash would be a good reason to get to the doctor, though.

17   New technology has made possible new equipment, medicines, and treatments that improve the quality of our lives. It can save them, too. A person who suffers from a chronic heart problem can now be checked at home so that a doctor can remotely monitor whether there is a serious problem. Similar **paramedical** technology also helps emergency responders. Paramedics can send critical patient information to hospital emergency rooms as the ambulance rushes to the hospital.

18   Technology has also made it easier for health-care professionals to work together. Results of lab tests, X-rays, and other medical history are now stored in databases. If a patient was treated for an infection in a hospital in Wisconsin, his doctor back home in Florida can access that information and find out what medicine was given to help in his treatment. In the past, it could have taken days or even weeks for that information to be shared.

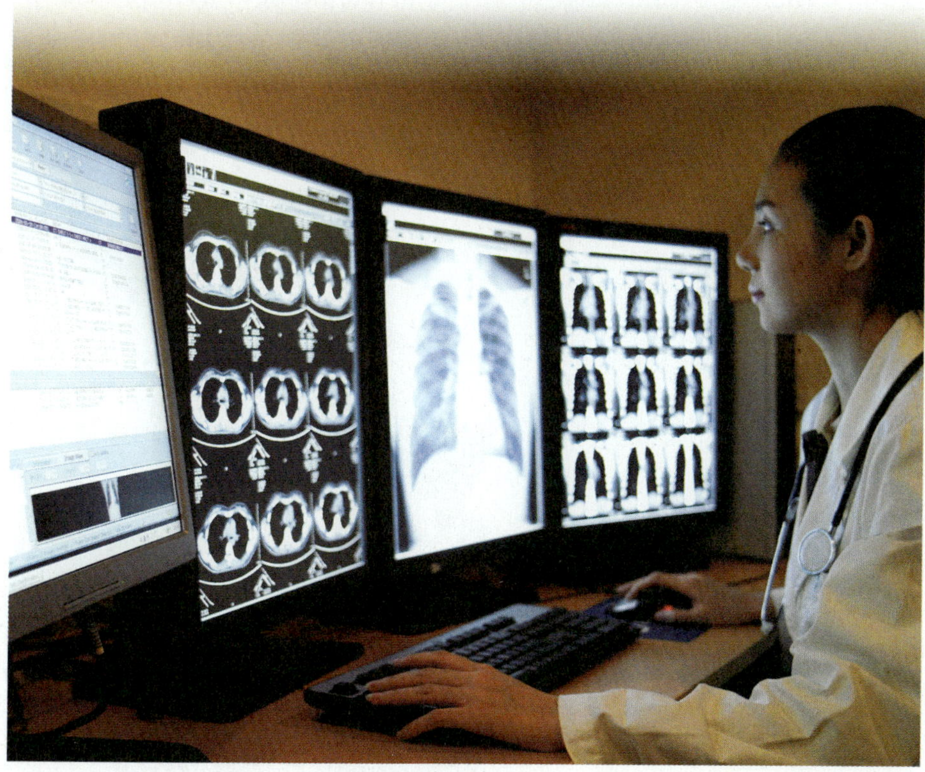

Technology Entertains Us

19   You don't have to look any further than your living room to see how much entertainment technology has brought to our lives. You can watch a television show, or stream a movie, or view a video clip on a Web site, all on a high-definition television. Vast libraries of music can be accessed on a tiny digital device. With the mere touch of a button, you can record the TV show or sporting event that you may not have time to watch and then enjoy it whenever you want.

20   But let's get back to basics: writing a story. Although times have changed, you still don't need a lot of complicated equipment to write a story; just a pen and paper will be enough if you don't have anything else. Of course, writing a story will take you a lot less time if you have a computer. The editing and revision process will be easier, too. Writing on a computer will also result in a digital file for your story.

21   It was once possible to distribute that story only by printing copies of it. Now, the digital file can be shared in many ways. You can submit your story to a publisher, but if you want, you can publish your story online or print and distribute copies on your own. Technology means that the people who create art—books, music, movies—also have the power to distribute it. Since this is a relatively recent development, no one can say exactly how this will change the entertainment industry, only that it will be changed.

22   There is a wide range of ways that technology has improved our lives, making difficult tasks simpler and communication easier. Technology has made us smarter, healthier, and thoroughly entertained. It's difficult to see why anyone would want to live without it! Would you?

Vocabulary: Greek Prefixes

Prefixes are word parts that attach to the beginning of a word to form a new one. Many prefixes are drawn from other languages. Knowing Greek prefixes can give you a clue to the meaning of an unfamiliar word. Look at the word *provision*. It begins with the prefix *pro-*, which means "before, in front of." The prefix gives you a clue that *provision* means "looking ahead, preparing." Here are some other common Greek prefixes and their meanings.

Prefix	Meaning	Prefix	Meaning
a-, an-	no, without, not	*para-*	beside, alongside of
anti-	opposite, against	*pro-*	before, in front of
geo-	earth	*therm-*	warm

Try It Look at these words from the selection that have Greek prefixes.

Word	Prefix	Definition
antitechnology, p. 210		
paramedical, p. 213		

Discuss Write each word's prefix in the table. Using information from the chart above, write a definition for each word.

The three words below are from the selection. Find each word's prefix in the chart above, then write a definition for the word.

1. thermostat, p. 210 ____

2. protected, p. 211 ____

3. atypical, p. 211 ____

Respond to Text: Compare and Contrast Methods of Argument

"Technology Is Killing My Movies!" and "Thank You, Technology!" present arguments against and for technology. In addition to their different points of view, each author uses different methods to build the argument.

Try It Think about how the authors of the selections used facts and opinions to support arguments and how persuasive his or her arguments were.

Discuss Which author made a more persuasive argument? How did each author's use of facts and opinions influence how you felt about his or her claims about technology?

On Your Own Compare and contrast the two selections you read in this lesson. Write about the claims each author made and include examples of evidence he or she used to support those claims. Which author was more successful at making reasoned judgments? Use the guide on the next page to help you write your response. Then write your paragraph on a separate sheet of paper.

Checklist for a Good Response

A good comparison and contrast paragraph

✔ identifies claims each author uses to support his or her argument.

✔ discusses the facts and opinions used to support the claim.

✔ explains whether the claim is based on reasoned judgment.

✔ includes a topic sentence, supporting ideas, and a concluding statement.

Which Argument Has Better Support?

1. **Topic Sentence** State which selection provides the more persuasive

   argument. Of the two selections, ________________________ gives a better

   persuasive argument because ____.

2. **Detail Sentences** Tell how each author supports his or her claims. If the
   author has not included supporting evidence, say so, and tell how he or
   she might have done a better job. Use the following chart.

Selection	Claim	Support
"Technology Is Killing My Movies!"		
"Thank You, Technology!"		

3. **Concluding Sentence** Your concluding sentence restates which author
   gives a more persuasive argument and why.

   ____

   ____

On a separate sheet of paper, write your paragraph.

Bring Back the Band

Author's Point of View and Purpose Think about the topic of this selection. Underline details that show whether the author is for or against it. Details in paragraph 2 have been underlined for you.

Evaluate Author's Claims Think about whether the author presents strong or weak evidence to support the claim that music helps students in other subjects.

1   You're never going to be a violinist. The time you spend learning to play the tuba could be better spent doing other things. You're embarrassed to sing in front of an audience, and it makes you uncomfortable. Schools should focus on the fundamentals.

2   You might think some or all of those statements are true, but you would be wrong. Research has proven that school music programs have benefits for all students, not just the musically inclined. When you pick up an instrument, you won't only be learning a new skill, either. Chances are you'll improve your performance in your other classes as well.

3   A study done in 2005 compared students who were in a music program to those who were not. When students who were struggling in reading and math learned and practiced music, their reading and math scores improved.

4   The connection between music instruction and other subject areas has been studied many times. Students who studied music improved their SAT math scores by more than forty points.

5   What is the connection? Researchers at Northwestern University in Illinois believe that taking music lessons during childhood leads to changes in the brain. They found that students who took music lessons were better able to identify different musical elements, like pitch, than those who hadn't. This might help with learning language and reading.

6   Other researchers have studied the connection between music and memory. They found that music can trigger memory. Have you ever heard a song that immediately made you think about the day at the beach with your best friend? Music tickled your memory!

7   You probably don't need a researcher to tell you that it's easier to memorize lyrics to a song than it is to remember the words of a poem. There are studies to prove it, though. In 2008, several classes of students were taught songs to help them learn curriculum content. Then, they were interviewed and tested on the subject matter. At the same time, a control group—classes who were taught the content through reading and discussion alone—was compared to the classes that used music. The researchers found that students not only preferred to learn through music, but the use of music helped them recall the information later during tests or when asked a question by a teacher.

8   The ancient Greeks believed that music had the power to shape both the individual and society. Sally Henson, director of the National Music Education Partnership, agrees. Henson wrote, "Music promotes growth in positive social skills. Students gain self-confidence and self-control when they learn music in school. Music instruction also helps develop collaboration and conflict-resolution skills."

9   It can be frustrating to hit wrong notes and make sounds that cause other people to wince. Your first song may be a real clunker! Learning to play music requires a lot of hard work. The process will test your perseverance and discipline. Once you start getting the hang of your instrument, though, you'll be one step closer to playing your first piece, and you'll be rewarded with feelings of accomplishment and pride.

10   Another **reward** will be all the time that you get to share with your **fellow** musicians. A band or orchestra needs every musician to work together during a performance. You'll be improving your ability to work on a team while you hang out with your buddies. It's a win-win situation!

11   Most important, learning music will give you another language with which to express yourself. You can use it to communicate with others, even those who don't know how to read and play music themselves. As the poet Henry Wadsworth Longfellow once wrote, "Music is the universal language of mankind."

12   A recent study shows the truth in that statement. Researchers played Western music such as jazz, rock, and pop to farmers in Cameroon, Africa. The farmers said they had never heard anything like it before. They listened and then pointed to photos of faces to say whether they thought the music expressed happiness, sadness, or fear. They were able to identify the correct emotion at least half of the time.

13   There are songs that make you smile. Others might make you cry. Imagine if you could play those songs on your own instrument and make people feel deep emotions just by listening to the notes you play. Imagine if you could write your own songs that express what you're feeling inside to others.

14   Music has also been shown to reduce stress. It can act as an antidepressant and even contribute to the physical healing process. Another recent study showed that listening to music helped heart patients deal with anxiety that increased their heart rate.

15   "We believe that music may be extremely **beneficial** for heart disease patients," says Dr. Paul Bent. "We know that music can have a **favorable** effect on our emotions, and I am looking forward to using it more with my patients."

16   Music programs are proven assets to schools that have them and to the students who choose to participate. So pick up an instrument and start practicing. Your brain—and your heart—will thank you!

✓ Comprehension Check

1. What is the author's purpose for writing this selection?

____

____

2. Read this sentence from the selection.

> **Another reward will be all the time that you get to share with your fellow musicians.**

Do *reward* and *fellow* have positive, neutral, or negative connotations? How would the sentence have been different if the words *benefit* and *other* were used instead?

____

____

3. What is the author's main argument? What reasons does he or she provide to support the argument?

____

____

____

4. What facts does the author include to support the claim that music helps people memorize things?

____

____

5. What does Longfellow mean when he says, "Music is the universal language of mankind"?

____

____

6. Why do students who learn music in school gain self-confidence and self-control?

____

____

7. Read this excerpt from the selection.

   "We believe that music may be extremely beneficial for heart disease patients," says Dr. Paul Bent. "We know that music can have a favorable effect on our emotions, and I am looking forward to using it more with my patients."

   The words *beneficial* and *favorable* are related because they

   ❏ are synonyms.

   ❏ are antonyms.

   ❏ show part to whole.

   ❏ show cause and effect.

8. Read this sentence from the selection.

   (Music) can act as an antidepressant and even contribute to the physical healing process.

   Circle the word that uses a Greek prefix. Then write a definition.

   ____

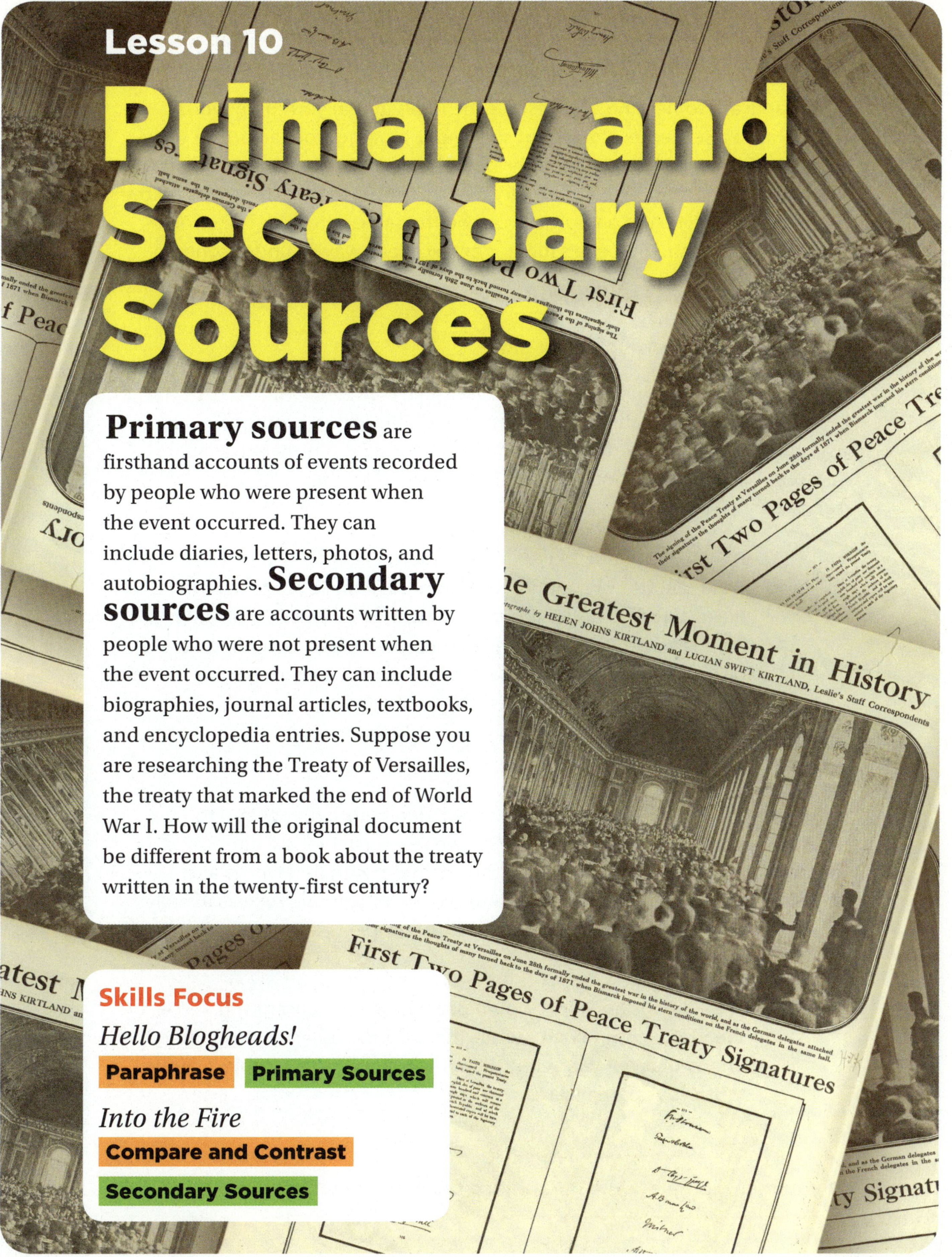

Lesson 10

Primary and Secondary Sources

Primary sources are firsthand accounts of events recorded by people who were present when the event occurred. They can include diaries, letters, photos, and autobiographies. **Secondary sources** are accounts written by people who were not present when the event occurred. They can include biographies, journal articles, textbooks, and encyclopedia entries. Suppose you are researching the Treaty of Versailles, the treaty that marked the end of World War I. How will the original document be different from a book about the treaty written in the twenty-first century?

Skills Focus

Hello Blogheads!

Paraphrase   Primary Sources

Into the Fire

Compare and Contrast

Secondary Sources

Practice the Skill

To **paraphrase** something is to restate the ideas in it in your own words. You can paraphrase a sentence, a group of sentences, a paragraph, an entire story, or the plot of a movie. You can paraphrase written material or something you hear, such as a speech. Unlike a summary, which requires you to briefly state the "big picture" of the text, a paraphrase can be the same length as the original text. Paraphrasing someone else's ideas is an excellent way of understanding and retaining those ideas.

Try It Read the following paragraph.

> In order to ensure the independence and reliability of your research, it is almost always preferable to use primary sources. If none are available, it is only with great caution that you may proceed to make use of secondary sources.

Discuss Think about how you might paraphrase these sentences. First, make sure you understand the text. Then, say it in your own words. Use these questions to help you: What two things are being compared? Circle them. Which one is better, according to the writer? Underline it. Now write a paraphrase.

Read the paragraph below.

> Primary sources—particularly those written before the twentieth century—can be difficult to analyze for two reasons: they are often fragments of larger documents, and they contain outdated words and expressions. Therefore, the interpretation of older primary texts is usually taught as part of an advanced college history course.

Discuss Think about how you would paraphrase the paragraph. Circle the words that tell you what the writer's subject is. Underline the words that tell you what the writer thinks of the subject. Now write your paraphrase.

As you read, complete the Paraphrase Chart on page 293.

Practice the Skill

Primary sources can be original documents, such as the Declaration of Independence, or firsthand accounts written by people who were eyewitnesses to events. A modern primary source is a blog, a personal journal that is posted online with a writer's reflections, photos, comments, and sometimes hyperlinks so a reader can click on text and get more information at a different Web source. Primary-source accounts are produced by people who are writing directly of their own experience—what they see, hear, think, and feel—and so they usually use the first-person pronouns *I*, *me*, *us*, *we*, and *my* and present-tense verbs.

Primary sources are organized in different ways, depending on how the writer wants to present information. Different methods of organization might include description, sequence, comparing and contrasting, cause and effect, steps in a process, or problem and solution. Here are some examples of text organization.

- a diary or journal organized as a sequence of events, in chronological order

- a log of field notes from a scientific expedition into the Amazonian rain forest organized as description

- a scientist's notes comparing and contrasting the results of different experiments

Try It Look at this excerpt from a pioneer's diary.

April 11: It rained and snowed as we started out this morning. We have a dangerous trip around the falls today. The oxen have to be coaxed every inch of the way through the mud and slush. Ben and Thomas walk with their father; I am behind them carrying Abigail in my arms. We make for a strange procession.

Discuss **What tells you this is a primary-source account? Underline parts of the text that show you. Think about what kind of organization this diary uses. How is it presented?**

As you read, record your answers to questions about primary sources on the Close Reading Worksheet on page 294.

Hello Blogheads!

posted by Casey Witkowski

Friday, September 12, 2014
6:00 P.M.

1   Hello Blogheads! As your official class blogger, it pains me to report that nothing very exciting has happened this week except that Cheryl, the class hamster, got lost, but then someone found her wandering around the resource room. You've probably all heard that story by now.

2   Wait, here's something. The TV news is on. What is all this? The anchors are acting really excited! The TV is full of banners and graphics! *America on Alert!* one banner says. Apparently a wildfire is burning somewhere.

3   At first I think it's somewhere way on the other side of the world, but then I see that it's right outside Susanville, which is near where I live. Oh my gosh! Now I'm paying attention! I run to the window, and—I'm not kidding, guys—the forest is on fire! It's on fire! And close enough that I can see smoke! This can't be happening!

4   In the distance, about five miles west on Highway 36, there's a shimmering layer of smoke just over the horizon, rising up and out, billowy white puffs turning into the thick angry smoke of a mushroom cloud against a backdrop of sky in dramatic shades of black and blue, then white and black. It looks like a painting or a video game.

7:00 P.M.

5   We've had wildfires around here before but never like this; according to Vivienne Vasquez of Channel 2 News, this could be a really serious one. It depends on which way the wind blows.

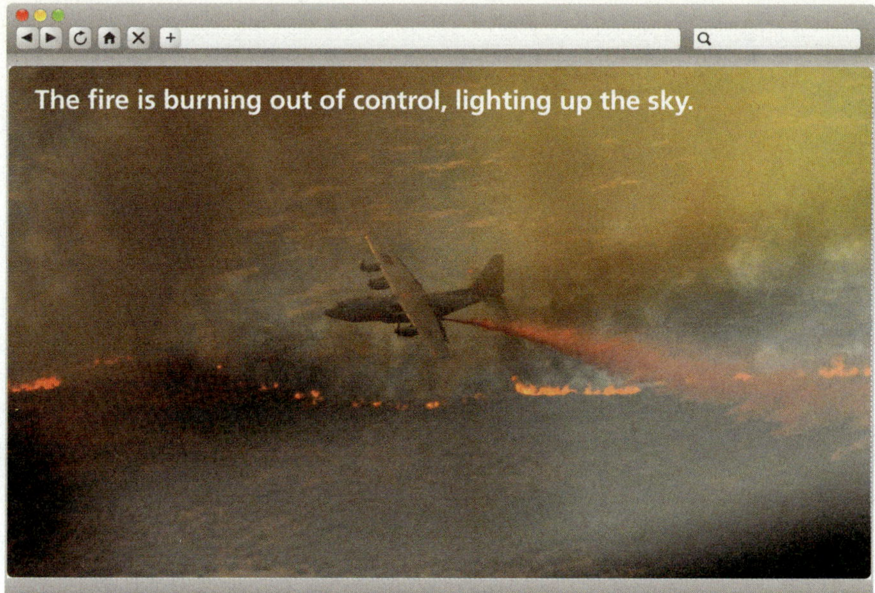

(I know that's an old expression, but in this case, it's true!) My mom says she's been expecting something like this, because of the terrible drought we've been having.

6   We don't exactly know what to do, but we're actually kind of prepared for this. We always keep the pine needles raked around the house in case there's a fire, but Dad and I go out and check on that and do some quick raking. Dad turns off the gas line to the house and then goes out to look at the van to make sure it's ready to go if we have to leave suddenly. My mom goes upstairs to call my aunt Eva. Aunt Eva is my mom's sister, and she lives just down the road from us. She and Mom are really close, and Mom wants to make sure she knows what's happening. I'm staked out here by the window, keeping watch. I keep thinking if I leave my post, the fire will somehow spread faster, so I'll keep writing for as long as I can, as a public service to my readers.

Saturday, September 13, 2014
9:00 A.M.

7   I must have fallen asleep, because at some point I wake up, fully dressed, and stagger into the kitchen. Dad is in front of the TV, and it looks like he hasn't slept much either. The fire's still raging; in fact, it's now being referred to as "out of control." I look out the window and see a spectacular sunset, only it's nine in the morning and so, therefore, not a sunset at all. The smoke column rises out of a blue-green landscape and towers above us, its lower third brown and black, its middle a marbled yellow-gray, its top a crown of sunlit silver.

8   Sparks fly from the top of the column and hit the ground while something that sounds like thunder cracks loudly, trailing off to a distant rumble. I can feel the heat, smell the burning, even from so far away.

Reread paragraph 6. Write your paraphrase on the **Paraphrase Chart.**

On this page, circle the text that indicates that the blogger is presenting information sequentially. Why does the blogger present information sequentially? Is it effective?

What could you learn about an event from reading a first-person, real-time blog account that you couldn't learn anywhere else?

Paraphrase the caption that accompanies the photograph on this page. Write it in your own words on the **Paraphrase Chart.**

Why does the blogger post the primary-source photograph of the fire?

10:00 A.M.

9   At the top of the hour, TV newscaster Vivienne Vasquez is joined by cohost Ron Tepper. Despite the awful news, Ron's voice is deep, rich, sonorous, and comforting: "There is massive devastation as Mother Nature forces residents from their homes . . ." Behind him on the screen, a wildfire blazes. It's like I'm in a movie or a bad dream.

10:30 A.M.

10   Aunt Eva is here now in the kitchen with my parents, and we're all huddling together. I'm on the floor with my laptop. Now the talk is all about evacuation, which is horrible because no one wants to leave their home. After all, who knows what will be there when they get back? Aunt Eva has lived in the same place for twenty-two years. She built the house almost entirely with her own hands. My parents have been in this house since before I was born—I've lived here my whole life.

12:00 P.M.

11   I'm looking out the window. The smoke, which had been miles away before, now fills the sky, and the fire is definitely coming closer. The sky, more black than blue, is shot through with red sparks that look like fireworks. Those poor trees! Only their charred skeletons remain. I'm posting a photo I just took with my phone. I'm afraid this forest is never coming back. It's horrible! Just horrible!

12:30 P.M.

12   My dad is tossing stuff into the back of the van—suitcases, dresses on hangers, boxes of books, photographs, important documents. Vivienne and Ron, the newscasters, are still holding down the fort, giving us up-to-the-minute information in real time, without any breaks for commercials. Having no commercials is one way to know how serious this whole thing is.

12:45 P.M.

13   They're sending in the smoke jumpers! In the distance I see a small plane darting in and out of the column of smoke, sending out streamers like in a parade. Vivienne, the Channel 2 coanchor, says that the streamers are for monitoring the wind's direction and velocity, although measuring speed this way seems strange given all the high-tech equipment they have. This is how they do it, though. As Vivienne explains it: "Before they leap from the plane, jumpers toss out bright crepe-paper streamers that serve as free-form wind socks, so they can see the wind direction and strength."

14   The older brother of one of my friends works as a smoke jumper, and I've talked to him quite a bit. Smoke jumping is a very dangerous line of work, and you have to have lots of specialized know-how, which is why they only bring those guys out if the fire is in a remote place and uncontainable by any other means. Smoke jumpers have to learn things like how to leap out of an airplane at 1,000 feet and how to hit the ground without breaking their legs.

1:15 P.M.

15   Vivienne Vasquez plays a <u>clip from last night</u>, which shows town residents evacuating their homes in the dark. "Officials say the leading edge of the fire is approaching western Stoddard and is expected to continue moving northeast . . ."

16   Then in a 1:00 P.M. newsclip, I see my old piano teacher bravely holding onto Albert, her fourteen-year-old cat. She is being interviewed by Kathy Keller, one of the Channel 2 News team. "You can rebuild a house, but you can't rebuild a memory," she is saying. Seeing her, someone I actually know, makes me think about what it must be like for people who have to flee their homes and return only to find that they have nothing left besides what they could get together before they had to evacuate. I can't even imagine what that would be like.

17   Which reminds me: <u>the Alliance for Animals Veterinary Services</u> is helping evacuees who need food and temporary shelter for their dogs, cats, horses, guinea pigs, goats, and birds.

18   The winds have picked up considerably, carrying embers from one section of forest to the other. I can see the embers literally jumping across the gravel road that we live on. The wildfire is getting really close now—areas that were just recently considered to be safe no longer are. Mom tells me it's time to go, and I get in the van. This is really it.

We're actually leaving, and at this moment we don't know when we'll be able to come back, whether our home will be here when we do or only charred remains, whether we'll lose everything, whether our lives will change forever because of this fire—we don't know any of that. How is anyone supposed to cope with that kind of uncertainty?

2:00 P.M.

19   We're in the van now, heading down the road through a haze of thick black muck, downwind of the fire. My dad is driving, focused solely on the road ahead, my mom is next to him, trying to be brave, and Aunt Eva and I are in the back. At least we're headed the right way. Dad wasn't going to listen to me at first. He was rushing to get everything loaded up, plus he was upset and really had too much to think about, but I finally got his attention and sat him down and made him look at a clip from last night's news. In it Vivienne tells us that Highway 36 is now closed and that our best bet is to go north on Eagle Lake Road before cutting across to Highway 44. Was he glad he stopped to listen to me!

20   Pretty soon I'll lose this connection, so this is going to be the last thing I'll write for a while. I trust, hope, and believe that the smoke jumpers will successfully cut off the path of this murderous fire before more families are displaced, more homes destroyed.

21   Now that we are safe, I hold on to this optimistic thought: that when we are able to return, our homes will still be there. Or better yet, I will wake up soon and this will all turn out to have been a dream. I look forward to seeing you all in school on Monday, and I hope you are safe and well. Meanwhile, tell us your stories about this fire in the comments section.

Vocabulary: Vary Sentence Patterns

To make writing more interesting and less repetitive, writers **vary sentence patterns**. Sentence pattern refers to a sentence's structure, length, and style. To vary sentence beginnings, a writer may start with an introductory adverbial clause, such as "When I left the house." Using phrases set off by parentheses or dashes is another way to vary sentence patterns, as in "I finally found some persimmons—ripe ones, that is—at the farmers market." Using a combination of both short and long sentences is a good way to make your writing more interesting. Sentences can be statements, questions, or exclamations. They can be simple, compound, or complex. You will notice in your reading that good writers make use of lots of variation in sentence patterns.

Try It Read this excerpt from "Hello Blogheads!"

Oh my gosh! Now I'm paying attention! I run to the window, and—I'm not kidding, guys—the forest is on fire! It's on fire! And close enough that I can see smoke!

Discuss **What kinds of sentence patterns do you see? Analyze the patterns in terms of length.**

The following sentences are from "Hello Blogheads!" For each one, tell which words from the following list can be used to identify the sentence pattern: question, statement, exclamation, simple sentence, complex sentence, long, short.

1. Vivienne, the Channel 2 coanchor, says that the streamers are for monitoring the wind's direction and velocity, although measuring speed this way seems strange given all the high-tech equipment they have.

2. I'm afraid this forest is never coming back. It's horrible! Just horrible!

Practice the Skill

First Read **Compare and Contrast**

To **compare** means to explain how two or more things are alike. To **contrast** means to show how two or more things are different. If you compare and contrast two things, you tell how they are alike and how they are different. Comparing and contrasting is a common text structure that is used in nonfiction writing.

Sometimes clue words tell you if things are being compared or contrasted. Examples of comparing words and phrases are *like, same as, similar, likewise, as well as, also, too,* and *just as.* Examples of contrasting words and phrases are *unlike, in contrast to, different from, less, more than, however, but, as opposed to, yet, however,* and *on the other hand.*

When you see these words in a sentence, it can be a clue that two items, people, characteristics, or ideas are being looked at side by side and compared or contrasted in some way. Comparing and contrasting is a way for writers to express complex ideas and for readers to better understand them.

Try It Read the following sentences.

1. The Mid-Atlantic Coast may get hurricanes, but New England regularly gets hammered by snowstorms.
2. The Midwest has long winters, thunderstorms, and tornadoes; on the other hand, the West Coast has earthquakes, wildfires, and mudslides.
3. The Pacific Northwest has mudslides, too, like the Southern California Coast; however, there is a lot more rain in the Northwest.
4. The South has severe thunderstorms, tornadoes, hurricanes, and ice storms in the winter, yet in the summer it is generally hot and humid.

Discuss **Think about what two things are being compared or contrasted in each sentence. Underline any clue words that signal comparing or contrasting. Identify the two things being compared or contrasted in each sentence.**

As you read, complete the Venn Diagram on page 295.

Practice the Skill

Secondary sources are accounts written by people who were not present when an event occurred. They take a much wider view of events than primary sources do because the writers have the benefit of more information. Examples of secondary sources include newspaper and encyclopedia articles, textbooks, and biographies.

Secondary sources rely on primary sources for information about some thing, person, or event and then interpret that information in a larger context. For example, an article about the importance of braille to visually impaired people might include a quotation from Helen Keller's memoir *The Story of My Life*, a primary source in which she states that she was able to learn languages and math because of it. A secondary source is also a factual account and may include statistics such as dates, percentages, and measurements. It is told in a more formal manner and uses the third-person point of view. When reading, look for these clues to see whether a document is a secondary source.

- third-person pronouns such as *he*, *she*, or *they*

- titles or names of primary sources and quotations from them

- statistics and citations from other secondary-source studies

Try It   Read the paragraph below.

In the 1800s, thousands of families made the westward trek in covered wagons. They braved scorching heat, freezing ice and snow, floods, biting insects, Indian attacks, and diseases. Many of them made it to the West Coast, yet many died along the way. This excerpt from the diary of a pioneer woman speaks to the difficulties of the journey: "I am tired and cold and numb all at once, my feet blistered and sore from so many days on the trail. There is not a dry thread on any one of us."

Discuss   **How do you know that this is a secondary source? Underline the clues. How is an article like this different from the diary of a pioneer woman?**

As you read, record your answers to questions about secondary sources on the Close Reading Worksheet on page 296.

Into the Fire

Meet the Smoke Jumpers

1   Smoke jumpers are an **elite** group of professional firefighters. They can be quickly deployed to parachute into wildfires, surrounding and attacking them. They fly in special aircraft with short takeoff and landing capabilities—they don't require long runways. They use specially designed parachutes to land in places that can't be reached by any other means.

2   Most smoke jumpers jump about sixty-five fires a year. Usually the fires are started by lightning, and smoke jumpers are often the first responders. They try to make quick work of putting out the fires, and in the process, they save lives, trees, and property.

3   Though both risk their lives to save others, conventional firefighters work mostly in urban and suburban areas. Smoke jumpers, on the other hand, fight fires in **remote** places that can't be reached by any other means than parachuting in. Most wildfires are extinguished within a few days. However, some go on for weeks. Smoke jumpers who go on these extended tours of duty have to be in excellent shape.

A Risky Business

4   The remoteness of an area is the most common reason for using smoke jumpers. This isolation adds to the risks involved with the job. Crews are often hours away from help. If the wind shifts or someone gets injured, without any backup on hand, the results can be catastrophic.

5   With smoke jumping, the ordinary risk of a parachute jump, which is dangerous in itself, is compounded by both the dangerous conditions for the jump and those already inherent in firefighting and rescue. All this gives smoke jumping a well-deserved reputation for being a very dangerous line of work.

6   However, the potential dangers of this firefighting method are offset by its efficiency and its spectacular rate of success for catching fires within twenty-four hours. The specially designed aircraft smoke jumpers use to reach fires quickly can go faster than the helicopters used for conventional fire deployments. These planes are also lighter and cheaper to operate over long distances than helicopters.

Smoke Jumper's Gear

7   As you can imagine, smoke jumping requires lots of specialized gear. Jumpers wear padded jump jackets and pants made from the material used for bulletproof vests. They wear motorcycle-style helmets with heavy, wire-mesh face masks. Each smoke jumper has a small gear bag in which he or she carries water, gloves, a hard hat, a fire shelter, and other personal belongings. Each smoke jumper also carries a "let-down" rope in the right leg pocket. This rope is used to jump from tall trees. Heavier equipment, if needed, is dropped separately.

8   Once the jumpers land safely, the plane drops them their gear: cargo boxes of shovels and chain saws used to cut containment lines. The smoke jumpers cut trees and clear brush to make a containment line, also called a firebreak, which is a bare area in the path of the fire.

Smoke jumpers cut a containment line, or firebreak.

Based on the information in paragraph 6, how is the special aircraft smoke jumpers use different from helicopters used by other firefighters? What is the same about both kinds of aircraft? Record your ideas in the **Venn Diagram**.

Is the photo on this page a primary or a secondary source? How do you know?

Why would a smoke jumper want to include a fire shelter with his or her equipment?

When the fire reaches the containment line, it is starved of fuel and cannot keep spreading. The cargo boxes also contain enough food and water to last three days. After that, new supplies must be flown in.

9   After the fire is completely out, smoke jumpers may leave by helicopter or on a four-wheel-drive fire engine. Sometimes, though, they have to **haul** all their equipment and rigging—about 125 pounds' worth per person—out on their backs. And that's after nights of little or no sleep and days of backbreaking work in the middle of nowhere.

Smoke Jumper School

10   Smoke jumper school is an intense, six-week-long program that resembles basic training in the military. It consists of rigorous physical training as well as instruction in parachuting. Getting into a smoke jumper school is not easy; the competition is intense, and few make the cut. The dropout rate is often high, mostly due to injuries or failure to keep up. By contrast, students who train to become conventional firefighters may take classes for up to fifteen months.

11   In the course of their training, smoke jumper rookies learn a host of specialized skills. They learn how to leap out of an aircraft from at least 1,000 feet. They learn how to maneuver their parachutes in shifting winds. Rookies must also practice hitting the ground safely. They learn how to cut down parachutes that get caught in trees and how to patch them up. As with conventional firefighters, smoke jumpers also need some qualities that can't necessarily be taught in school. They must be flexible and have a wide range of experience and background to deal with a variety of kinds of situations. And they must be brave.

12   As difficult, stressful, and dangerous as the job is, there are always many applicants vying to get into the smoke jumper schools. In his essay "Why I Choose Smoke Jumping," twenty-year-old Matt Blalen explains, "I thrive on danger. Not danger for danger's sake, but I like my life to be exciting. And I want to do something worthwhile. I know smoke jumpers save our forests and they save lives. I also like to be challenged, and I know this is a job that would take everything I can give—strength, stamina, mental stability. This is the job for me—I just know it."

On the Job

13   Jumps are normally from 1,500 to 3,000 feet above ground level. Jumpers go in at the safest spot that is nearby but not in the fire. For most fires, eight to ten smoke jumpers are dropped. However, additional smoke jumpers or further reinforcements are called in if necessary.

14   While leaping out of the airplane becomes fairly routine over time, experienced jumpers say the biggest challenge is hitting the "jump spot." That is the spot nearby but not in the fire. It might be a few hundred feet or a mile away from the flames. Sometimes they hit it exactly. Other times they barely make it, due to the shifting winds, tall trees, and dangerous rocks. If they totally miss it, they're in for a long hike with all their gear on their backs.

A Smoke Jumper's Toolbox

15   Because smoke jumpers are called in while fires are still small, they mostly use hand tools such as the Pulaski. The head of the Pulaski has an ax on one side. On the other side is an adze, a cutting tool with a thin arched blade normally used for shaping wood. The Pulaski is considered the greatest fire hand tool ever invented. It is a very efficient tool for constructing firebreaks because it can be used both to dig in the dirt and to chop wood.

16   Chain saws are used when needed. Sometimes backpack pumps are used, too. Smoke jumpers carry tanks of water on their backs like backpacks. Then they use a pump and sprayer connected to the tank. If there is a water source nearby, power pumps are dropped in. These pumps are usually powered by diesel fuel. They have a hose for spraying the water.

17   Cutting the containment line is job one when the smoke jumpers get on the ground. Using chain saws, shovels, Pulaskis, and other tools, they clear trees, brush, and flammable debris along the edge of the fire. Then when the fire hits that line, they hope it will stop.

A secondary-source writer consults many sources when writing an article on a broad subject. For the section "A Smoke Jumper's Toolbox," what kinds of sources do you think the writer used?

Compare the language, word choice, and tone in "Into the Fire" with that of "Hello Blogheads!"

The Pulaski, invented by Edward C. Pulaski in 1911, is an essential tool for smoke jumpers.

18   At the same time they may be using their portable backpack pumps or power pumps to put out the fire. When the fire is out or nearly out, its perimeter is sometimes secured by beating it with burlap sacks. If the sacks can be soaked with water, all the better.

19   If the smoke jumpers are going to be at the fire for a long time, they'll have to eat. So what do smoke jumpers eat on the job? Ordinarily the fare will include things like beef jerky, powdered energy drinks, canned chili, powdered soup mixes, protein bars, candy bars, small cans of meat or fish, MREs (military Meals Ready to Eat), canned fruit, nuts, freeze-dried meals, and ramen noodles. Most of the time smoke jumpers get to choose what goes into their boxes. Unlike smoke jumpers, conventional firefighters grocery shop together (because they are on call all the time) and are able to prepare and eat whatever they want with one another.

20   As you can imagine, smoke jumpers have to be in absolute tip-top shape physically. They also have to be in excellent condition mentally and emotionally to deal with the stresses of the job. Their professionalism and fast action can literally save lives—and forests.

Vocabulary: Use a Thesaurus

A **thesaurus** is a book of synonyms (words with similar meanings) and antonyms (words with opposite meanings), arranged in alphabetical order.

As a writer, you want to use words that are as descriptive and precise as possible. A thesaurus can help you find a word that better expresses what you have in mind. For example, instead of saying *glad*, you may want to use a more powerful word, such as *pleased*, *cheerful*, *delighted*, or *thankful*. Whenever you are stumped for a better word, a thesaurus will give you several choices.

Try It   Read this sentence from "Into the Fire."

> Smoke jumpers, on the other hand, fight fires in **remote** places that can't be reached by any other means than parachuting in.

Discuss   **If you look up *remote* in a thesaurus, you might find the following synonyms: *isolated*, *long-ago*, *reserved*, *faraway*. Which of these synonyms do you think would work as a replacement for *remote* in the sentence?**

The following sentences appear in "Into the Fire." Look at the word in boldface and circle the synonym choice that makes the most sense. Then write an original sentence using the synonym.

1. **Smoke jumpers are an elite (select, influential, prime) group of professional firefighters.** p. 234 __________________________

   ____

2. **Sometimes, though, they have to haul (draw, pull, lug) all their equipment and rigging—about 125 pounds' worth per person—out on their backs.** p. 236

   ____

   ____

Respond to Text: Primary and Secondary Sources

"Hello Blogheads!" is a primary source. It is a first-person eyewitness account of an event the writer witnessed and participated in as he was writing. "Into the Fire" is a secondary source. It is written from a third-person point of view and shows an outside perspective on the subject. Smoke jumpers are discussed in both selections but in different ways, and they are viewed from vastly different viewpoints.

Try It Think about what you learned about primary and secondary sources from reading the two selections.

Discuss **What are some similarities between "Hello Blogheads!" and "Into the Fire"? What are some differences? Base your answer on the information you read in the selections. Make sure your ideas are supported by sound reasoning and evidence from the texts.**

On Your Own Write your ideas about the similarities and differences between the primary source "Hello Blogheads!" and the secondary source "Into the Fire," and about how the two texts affected you differently. Include details from the texts that helped you form your thoughts. Use the next page to help you plan your response. Then write your paragraph on a separate sheet of paper.

Checklist for a Good Response

A good paragraph

✔ identifies ways that the two sources are different and ways they are the same.

✔ explains the reasoning behind your answer.

✔ includes evidence from the texts.

✔ shows your understanding of the information.

✔ includes a topic sentence, supporting ideas, and a concluding statement.

My Analysis of Primary and Secondary Sources

1. **Topic Sentence** Include this information in your first sentence:

   "Hello Blogheads!" and "Into the Fire" are sources that both address the

   topic of ____.

2. **Detail Sentences** Tell how the selections present information differently
   and how each affected you. Use this chart to organize your ideas.

Detail from Selection A	Tells me this is a _______ source because	The effect it has on me is
What is all this? The anchors are acting really excited! The TV is full of banners and graphics! *America on Alert!* one banner says. Apparently a wildfire is burning somewhere.	primary;	
Detail from Selection B	**Tells me this is a _______ source because**	**The effect it has on me is**
Using chain saws, shovels, Pulaskis, and other tools, they clear trees, brush, and flammable debris along the edge of the fire.	secondary;	

3. **Concluding Sentence** Your concluding sentence should restate
   in a fresh way how the two selections affected you as a reader.

   ____

   ____

On a separate sheet of paper, write your paragraph.

The Effects of Social Media on Today's Youth

Compare and Contrast How has the way young people communicate with one another changed over the years? Underline the words in the text that tell you. The first one has been done for you.

Paraphrase Think about how you would paraphrase paragraph 2. What is unimportant and could be left out?

1   Using social media is one of the most common activities of young people in the United States today. Social media sites, such as Facebook, MySpace, and Twitter, are popular. They provide many opportunities for daily connection with friends, classmates, and people with shared interests all over the world. Experts say that participating in social media helps young people in many ways. It strengthens their communication, social, and even technical skills.

2   Social media sites also provide a portal into a variety of entertainment and communication options. They enable young people to do online many of the things that they would otherwise do offline. Through social media, young people stay connected with friends and family. They meet new friends and exchange photos, videos, and music. They share ideas and opinions. Social media can broaden young people's views of themselves and can give them a better understanding of their communities and their world.

3   But there is a downside to social media use. Some researchers believe that today a large part of the social and emotional development of young people is occurring online rather than face-to-face.

4   Over the last five years, the number of young people using social media sites in this country has gone through the roof. A recent poll found that 22 percent of all teenagers log on to social media sites more than ten times a day. Seventy-five percent of all teenagers now own cell phones. Twenty-five percent use them for accessing social media sites.

Twenty-four percent use them for instant messaging. And a whopping 54 percent use them for texting!

5   What this means is that the social rules that govern teenage behavior have completely changed.

6   This change has led researchers to identify a new condition called "Facebook depression." They say that Facebook depression can develop when young people spend too much time on social media sites. Often they begin to show signs of classic adolescent **depression**. They may become socially isolated or develop feelings of low self-worth. They might lose the ability to take pleasure in normal activities.

7   Studies show that social media can cause teens to have heightened expectations for their lives. They might begin to want more material things like clothing, shoes, jewelry, expensive games, spending money, and travel. They may come to expect various kinds of luxury experiences such as taking a limo to the prom. When those expectations aren't met, teens can feel they are lacking or inadequate. These feelings contribute to low self-esteem. Or teens may focus on the idea that life isn't fair. Either way, the results are not good. Such feelings can affect teens' grades, their ability to make friends, and even their appetites.

8   Most experts agree that there's nothing wrong with social media. It was just never meant to replace real life.

9   Dr. Thomas Van Hoose at the University of Texas Southwestern Medical Center suggests stepping away from the computer. "As simple as it sounds," advises Dr. Van Hoose, "turn it off."

A recent poll found that 75 percent of U.S. teenagers own cell phones, and 25 percent of them use to phones to access social media sites.

10   Facebook is not the only social networking site to come under fire. It's just the most popular. MySpace, Pinterest, and Xanga are other popular sites. Users can make and keep friends, post pictures, and update their online profiles. Twitter allows users to communicate in short bursts of information, or tweets.

11   There are also Digg and Reddit. These sites allow users to post links to outside articles. Then the community "votes" on the ones they like best and want prominently displayed. There are also YouTube and Flickr. These are both media-sharing sites that allow the user to share pictures and videos. There are countless online forums in which members engage in conversations. The comments sections of blogs provide another venue for online group conversation.

12   Though there is much research suggesting that online activity is causing depression in teens, there is also evidence showing that the effects of social media may be more subtle and long-term. Social media may ultimately affect the way we function as a society. Some experts claim that extended use of these sites actually rewires the brain. People develop a need to be constantly reassured. Shorter attention spans, the need for instant gratification, and the persistent self-focus make teenagers less likely to reach outside themselves. They may fail to ask for information or context at a time when they need it most. Teenagers may focus on only their problems and find it difficult to escape from them. They may be online so much that they never get the opportunity to meditate and reflect. Or they may never just enjoy being in the moment.

13   The message from the researchers is clear: you may find comfort in having large numbers of online "friends," but authentic friendships— although they may take more work—are the ones that help you grow.

Joanne's Project

Friday, October 4

1   So today we had a long discussion in Ms. Franconi's English class about social media. Everyone agreed it had both positive and negative effects, but also that we couldn't, as a culture, do without this technology—it would be like putting the toothpaste back in the tube. Social media is an important part of contemporary life and always will be.

2   Of course I had to disagree. "I couldn't care less about social media," I announced. Everyone stared at me as if I'd just said I was going back to Alpha Centauri.

3   But I stood my ground. I couldn't care less what my friends were doing, or planning to do, or had done the day before. I had no wish to know that Yousefa was getting her braces off, or that Shawn had downloaded some music, or that Theo was getting his hair cut, or even that Marla and Renaldo had broken up—and I said as much.

4   So Ms. Franconi offered me a challenge—to conduct the experiment of staying away from Twitter, MySpace, Facebook, e-mail, and texting for the entire weekend. I had to keep a daily journal and later share my findings with the class. I would do the one thing that only the fearless would dare to contemplate: I would do without social media for one entire weekend. I don't see what the fuss is—I'm sure it will be easy.

Saturday, October 5

5   Today I took myself to the movies. My friends were just leaving as I was going in, but they didn't see me. Obviously they had left me out of their plans, since their ability to schedule events starts and stops with text messaging, and under the terms of my agreement with Ms. Franconi, I only have use of my landline. I suppose they couldn't have called even if they'd wanted to, due to the fact that they don't know that phone number and never did.

6   I'm back home now, writing this. It feels very weird to write longhand, but computers are off-limits this weekend. I'm wondering what everyone is up to right now. WHERE ARE THEY? It's Saturday night, and we usually hang out at someone's house. Whose? So maybe I'm suffering a little from the lack of social media, but it's really nothing to worry about. I'm fine, just fine.

Compare and Contrast
Underline the main difference between the journal writer and her group of friends at the movies.

Primary Sources
Circle text on this page that shows this is a primary source.

Primary Sources
What feature lets you know that this is a journal? Double underline the feature.

Sunday, October 6

7   As soon as I woke up this morning, I headed straight for my desk to get on my computer to find out what's been going on. Luckily, before I actually pressed any keys, I remembered my pledge to be "different." I'm different all right. I'm so different I feel like I can't breathe, like my air passages have shut down, like I'm suffocating. Maybe I'm having a panic attack. AAUUUGGGHH! I can't take this! Okay, calm down now. Breathe in, breathe out, breathe in, breathe out . . .

8   I admit it. I want to be plugged in. I *need* to be plugged in.

9   It would be very good for me now to do some yoga, but I can't remember which poses are good for calming you down. I know I could easily find out through YogaChat, but that's against the rules. For the time being, I'm out of the loop, with no means of accessing *information*.

Monday evening, October 7

10   I made it through the weekend, but just barely. Okay, yes, it was a LOT harder than I thought it would be. This morning I went to class armed with my journal and read it to the class. People were actually interested. Ms. Franconi is encouraging me to write up this experience and submit it to the school magazine. She thinks I'm a really good writer, or could be if I kept at it. I have to say this has been a really interesting experience. I feel that I've learned a lot about myself, about how addicted I actually am to social media, without having even realized it. Anyway, I intend to keep at my writing—in fact, I plan to do some writing tonight, right after I finish my homework. Even though I know a part of me will want to check out my friends on Facebook.

✔ Comprehension Check

1. Which of the two selections—"Joanne's Project" or "The Effects of Social Media on Today's Youth"—is the primary source and which is the secondary source? Use textual evidence from the selections to explain your answer.

2. In "Joanne's Project," find two examples of short sentences showing excitement and one example of a long, thoughtful, reflective sentence. Write the sentences on the lines that follow.

3. Read these sentences from "The Effects of Social Media on Today's Youth."

   Over the last five years, the number of young people using social media sites in this country has gone through the roof. A recent poll found that 22 percent of all teenagers log on to social media sites more than ten times a day.

   In your own words, write a paraphrase of the two sentences.

4. Read these sentences from "The Effects of Social Media on Today's Youth."

    They say that Facebook depression can develop when young people spend too much time on social media sites. Often they begin to show signs of classic adolescent depression.

    Circle the word from a thesaurus entry for *depression* that is closest in meaning to and could be used to replace *depression* as it is used in the selection: *recession, slump, melancholy, indentation.*

5. In "The Effects of Social Media on Today's Youth," the writer includes primary-source material. What is that material? What purpose does it serve?

6. In a few sentences, compare and contrast how the topic of social media is treated in the "The Effects of Social Media on Today's Youth" and "Joanne's Project."

Glossary

academic vocabulary words that are commonly used in writing and discussing school subjects; for example, *analyze* and *summarize* are words that you might hear or use in many different subjects (Lessons 3, 8)

antonyms words that have opposite meanings (Lessons 4, 7, 9)

argument the act of taking a position on something and providing reasons and evidence for others to accept the position; author's claim (Lesson 9)

ask and answer questions to actively engage with a text before, during, and after reading by asking yourself questions and then answering them (Lesson 5)

cause and effect a word relationship in which one word leads to another; for example *tornado* and *damage* (Lessons 4, 7, 9); a text structure that shows the relationship between ideas or events; *cause* tells why something happens; *effect* tells what happens as a result of the cause (Lesson 7)

central idea the most important, or main, idea that an author wants you to understand (Lesson 5)

characters the people or animals that participate in the main action of a story to advance the story's plot or theme (Lesson 1)

chart a graphic representation of data with symbols (bars or slices on a pie chart) or rows and columns (Lesson 7)

chronology the order of dates, events, and other information, often used to organize the information in historical texts (Lesson 6)

cite textual evidence to point out the specific words and details that support your ideas (Lesson 4)

claim the main idea about an issue in an argument; stated by an author of persuasive nonfiction (Lesson 9)

climax an element of plot that is the turning point of a story, often involving great suspense (Lesson 1)

compare to find the similarities between two things (Lessons 3, 10)

compare and contrast to explain how two things are alike and how they are different (Lessons 3, 10)

connotation the positive, neutral, or negative emotions or associations that a word communicates, beyond its dictionary definition (Lessons 1, 4, 9)

context the words and sentences that surround a particular piece of text (Lesson 1)

context clues the nearby words or sentences that give clues to the meaning of an unknown word (Lessons 1, 2)

contrast to find and explain the differences between two things (Lessons 3, 10)

counterargument an argument against an author's stated claim or argument; good arguments anticipate possible counterarguments (Lesson 9)

denotation the literal dictionary definition of a word (Lessons 1, 4, 9)

diagram a usually labeled illustration that makes an idea, an object, or a process easier to understand (Lessons 7, 8)

dictionary a printed or digital resource with words and their meanings listed in alphabetical order, as well as such other information as pronunciation, syllabication, and part of speech (Lessons 3, 8)

domain-specific vocabulary a word or phrase that has a specific meaning within a particular field of study or profession (Lesson 4)

drama stories that are written to be performed by actors on a stage; a drama is usually broken into acts and scenes (Lesson 2)

dramatic structure the organization of a play through the use of acts, scenes, and stage directions (Lesson 2)

draw inference to use prior knowledge and facts and details from a text to decide what an author is saying indirectly (Lessons 1, 2, 7)

entertain a purpose for writing; to please and delight readers (Lesson 9)

epic poem a long poem that tells the story of a great hero or cultural event (Lesson 3)

evidence the proof that supports an argument; usually factual information, such as research findings, firsthand experience, facts, statistics, and expert opinions (Lesson 9)

exposition an element of plot in which the characters and setting are established (Lesson 1)

facts pieces of information that can be observed or proved true (Lesson 9)

falling action an element of plot during which the main action winds down (Lesson 1)

fiction a kind of writing that is made up from an author's imagination, even though some details may be based on fact (Lesson 1)

figurative language language used in a special way to convey an idea, such as simile, metaphor, hyperbole, or personification; figurative language usually does not mean what it literally says (Lessons 2, 3)

first-person point of view the voice of the narrator, who is a character in the story, characterized by the use of words such as *I*, *me*, *my*, *we*, and *us* (Lesson 4)

flowchart a visual representation of the steps in a process, usually with symbols and labels to clarify a complex process (Lesson 8)

free verse a style of poetry that has no set form or rhyme scheme and that may have both long and short lines and a variety of stanza types or no stanzas at all (Lesson 3)

historical fiction stories and novels set in a specific time period, with historical settings and characters that may be fictional or real (Lesson 4)

historical texts nonfiction texts such as articles, firsthand accounts, and biographies about real people and events from the past (Lesson 6)

hyperbole exaggerated language used to make a point or for humorous effect (Lesson 2)

inference an educated guess that you can make based on the facts, details, or ideas in the text and your prior knowledge (Lessons 1, 2, 4, 7)

inform a purpose for writing; to provide factual information on a topic (Lesson 9)

item and action a word relationship in which one word describes what the other does; for example *stove* and *heat* (Lesson 7)

item and category a word relationship in which one word is a subset of another; for example *carrot* and *vegetable* (Lessons 4, 7, 9)

label the brief textual explanation for a part of a diagram (Lesson 7)

Latin and Greek roots basic word parts that come to us from these ancient languages (Lesson 2)

lead lines the lines that connect labels to particular parts of a diagram or model (Lesson 7)

literary nonfiction true stories told with some of the elements of fiction; for example, books and articles that have a dramatic arc, dialogue, and figurative language (Lesson 5)

loaded language particularly strong words and phrases an author of a persuasive argument uses to influence the emotions of his or her audience (Lesson 9)

make predictions to use your own prior knowledge and details from the text to guess at what might happen next in a story or how a character will behave (Lesson 4)

metaphor a direct comparison of two unlike things; saying one thing is another (Lesson 2)

model a type of diagram, usually with labels and lead lines (Lesson 7)

multiple-meaning word a word with more than one meaning or use; for example, *row* ("a line or sequence") and *row* ("to propel a boat using oars") (Lesson 5)

narrative poem a type of poem that tells a story, usually with more than one stanza (Lesson 3)

ode a kind of lyric or musical poem that expresses strong feeling toward its subject (Lesson 3)

onomatopoeia a type of figurative language in which words make the sound that is being described; for example, *buzz* and *clatter* (Lesson 3)

opinions expressions of personal beliefs and feelings that cannot be proved true or false (Lesson 9)

paraphrase to restate a text or speech in your own words; usually the retelling is the same length as the original text (Lesson 10)

part to whole a word relationship in which one word is part of another; for example, *Congress* and *government* (Lessons 4, 9)

personification a type of figurative language that gives human attributes or characteristics to something not human (Lesson 3)

persuade a purpose for writing; to argue on a course of action, an issue, or an opinion (Lesson 9)

persuasive nonfiction a type of writing that presents clear, strong arguments and reasoned judgments supported by facts on a course of action, an issue, or an opinion (Lesson 9)

plot a series of episodes that move a story from start to finish (Lesson 1)

poetic form a particular type of poem, defined by either the content or the structure (Lesson 3)

poetic structure the way in which a poem is organized, including rhythmic structure, lines, and stanzas (Lesson 3)

poetry a form of literature based on rhythmic language that may include rhyme, vivid language, and strong imagery (Lesson 3)

point of view the voice of the narrator telling the story; the narrator's perspective on the action (Lessons 4, 9)

prefix a word part added to the beginning of a root word to make a new word (Lessons 5, 9)

primary source a document, speech, image, or other piece of evidence created by someone who was present when an event occurred (Lessons 5, 10)

problem and solution a text structure that introduces a problem along with a solution; a presentation of a series of problems and solutions (Lesson 8)

purpose an author's reason for writing, such as to entertain, inform, or persuade (Lesson 9)

reasoned judgment a decision made about an idea or an argument that is based on an evaluation of reasons and evidence (Lesson 9)

reasons the statements in persuasive nonfiction used to convince you to agree with the author's argument (Lesson 9)

resolution an element of plot that occurs at the story's end; when conflicts are resolved (Lesson 1)

rising action an element of plot; the series of events that build up to the story's climax (Lesson 1)

scan to look quickly through a text for specific information, such as a date or a definition (Lesson 8)

scientific terms specialized words and symbols used in scientific texts (Lesson 7)

scientific texts nonfiction that presents factual information about topics related to science, sometimes accompanied by charts, graphs, and other forms of graphic information (Lesson 7)

secondary source a text about a real person or event written after the fact, often based in part on information from primary sources (Lessons 5, 10)

sequence the order in which things happen, often signaled by words such as *first, next, last, before,* and *after* (Lesson 6)

simile a comparison of two unlike things using the word *like* or *as* (Lesson 2)

skim to read a text quickly for an overview of the content (Lesson 8)

sonnet a kind of poem that has fourteen lines of similar length and rhythmic structure (Lesson 3)

steps in a process the series of actions that must happen in order for something to be done, sometimes indicated by the words *first*, *second*, *next*, and *last* (Lesson 6)

suffix a word part added to the end of a root word to create a new word (Lesson 6)

summarize to use your own words to briefly retell the big ideas in a selection (Lessons 2, 6)

summary a kind of writing that includes only the most important details of a story or article and briefly states what happened (Lessons 2, 6)

supporting details the facts, statistics, quotations, examples, and anecdotes an author uses to reinforce the central idea (Lesson 5)

synonyms words that have the same or similar meanings (Lessons 4, 7, 9)

technical terms words that are specific to a technical field of study or profession; usually explained in a glossary (Lesson 8)

technical texts nonfiction that provides factual information about something mechanical or specialized (Lesson 8)

textual evidence words, facts, details, and ideas in a text (Lesson 4)

theme the general idea about life an author wants to convey that is expressed through a story's characters, setting, and events; *themes* are expressed as complete sentences; *topics* are expressed as single words or short phrases (Lesson 1)

thesaurus a printed or digital resource containing words along with their synonyms (words with similar meanings) and antonyms (words with opposite meanings), listed in alphabetical order (Lesson 10)

third-person-limited point of view the voice of a narrator who tells the thoughts and feelings of only one character in the story (Lesson 4)

third-person-omniscient point of view the voice of a narrator who tells the thoughts and feelings of all the characters in the story (Lesson 4)

third-person point of view the voice
of a narrator who is not a character in the
story, characterized by the use of the words
he, *she*, *they*, *them*, and *their* (Lesson 4)

tone the way an author feels about
the subject of the text, which is often
expressed through his or her word choice
(Lessons 4, 6)

vary sentence patterns to change the
structure, length, and style of sentences
in a text in order to make the writing more
interesting and less repetitive (Lesson 10)

visual information graphic information
accompanying a nonfiction text;
for example, photos with captions,
illustrations, time lines, maps, charts,
models, and diagrams (Lessons 6, 7, 8)

visualize to picture images in your mind
about what you are reading (Lesson 3)

word relationships the way that one
word is connected to other words close
by, including synonyms, antonyms, part-
to-whole, cause-and-effect, and item-to-
category relationships (Lessons 4, 7, 9)

Acknowledgments

Photo Credits 5, 29, 32, 40, 55, 74, 64, 66 (t), 66 (b), 80, 84, 89, 121, 122, 128, 130, 136, 140, 145, 149, 152, 155, 156, 160, 162, 169, 173, 177, 188 (bg), 193, 199, 203, 206, 210, 211 (t), 211 (bg), 213, 219, 220, 223, 227, 228, 230, 235, 237, 238, 244, 245, 246 Thinkstock; 77, 105, 120, 125, 132, 146 (tl), 146 (tm), 185, 188 (t), 223 Library of Congress; 104, 108, 116, 129, 144, 178 Wikimedia; 101, 177 United States Air Force; 107, 131 NOAA; 146 (tr) NASA; 204, 243 Shutterstock; 227, 229, 234, 235, 237 Mike McMillan; 228 USDA; 238 United States Army (Mark Hughes).

Illustrations 7–12 Jamie Pogue; 17–19 Doloras Avenado; 25–26 Mike Laughead; 33–44 Q2A Media; 49–52 Stacy Budnick; 58–60 Peter Francis; 65, 113, 115 Fabio Leone; 71 Mike Laughead; 73 Ralph Voltz; 81–83 Giorgio Bacchin; 88–98 Jim Eldridge; 135–138, 146, 153–154, 175, 179–195 XNR Productions; 159, 161–164 Pete Bull; 170 Bob Kayganich.

Name: ____

✏️ Close Reading Worksheet

First Read: Draw and Support Inferences (orange boxes)

Page 8: Aaron is ____.

Page 9: With regard to his trip to Icealia, Aaron feels _________________

____.

Page 10: Aaron expected Hiz to be _____________________________,

but instead Hiz is ____.

Page 11: Hiz cries because _________________________________.

Page 12: Hiz's hug is awkward because ___________________________

____.

Third Read: Critical Thinking (blue boxes)

Page 8: Aaron kept the Icealia guide because _____________________

____.

Page 9: The author builds suspense in the story by _________________

____.

Page 10: Hiz is described as "alien in mind" because _______________

____.

Page 11: The pictures on Hiz's wall are surprising because ___________

____.

Interpret—Page 12: Companionship can make any world kinder because _________

____.

Plot Sequence Chart

Climax, p. 12

Rising Action, p. 11

Rising Action, p. 10

Falling Action, p. 12

Rising Action, p. 9

Resolution, p. 12

Exposition, p. 8

Name: ____

✏️ Close Reading Worksheet

First Read: Theme (orange boxes)

Page 16: I think the story will develop the theme that ___________________

____.

Page 18: The characters handle their good fortune by ___________________

____.

The life lesson their reactions reveal is that __________________________

____.

Page 19: The theme about families is that ___________________________

____.

Third Read: Critical Thinking (blue boxes)

Page 16: An unstated reason why Tía Olga may be moving is ______________

____.

Page 17: The narrator feels that she has to comfort her father because ___________

____.

Page 19: The pumpkin festival (will / will not) be a success because ______________

____

____.

Judge—Page 20: It was (right / wrong) for Tía Olga not to tell her family because

____

____.

Character Webs

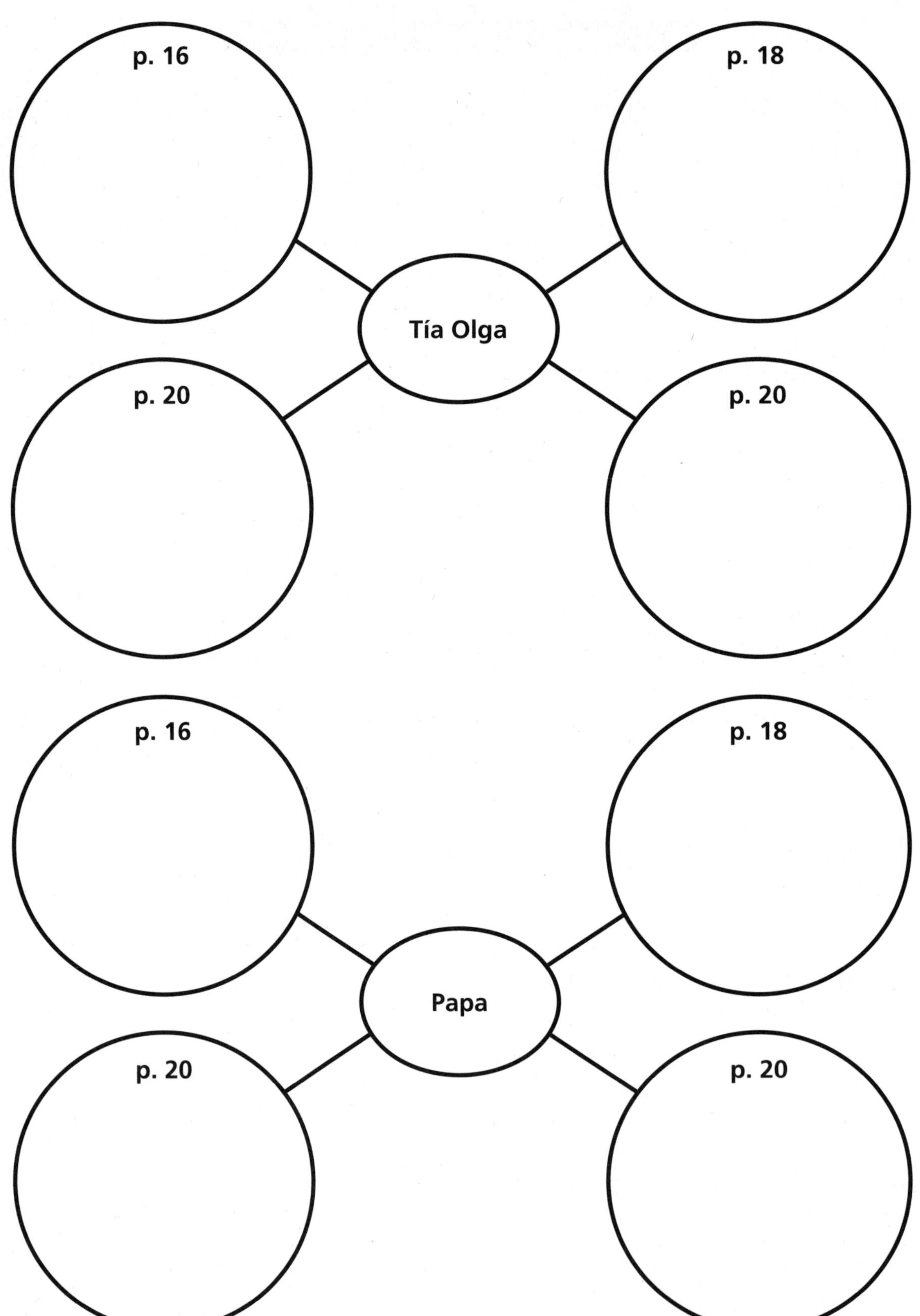

   La Festival Calabaza

Name: _______________________

Draw Inferences Chart

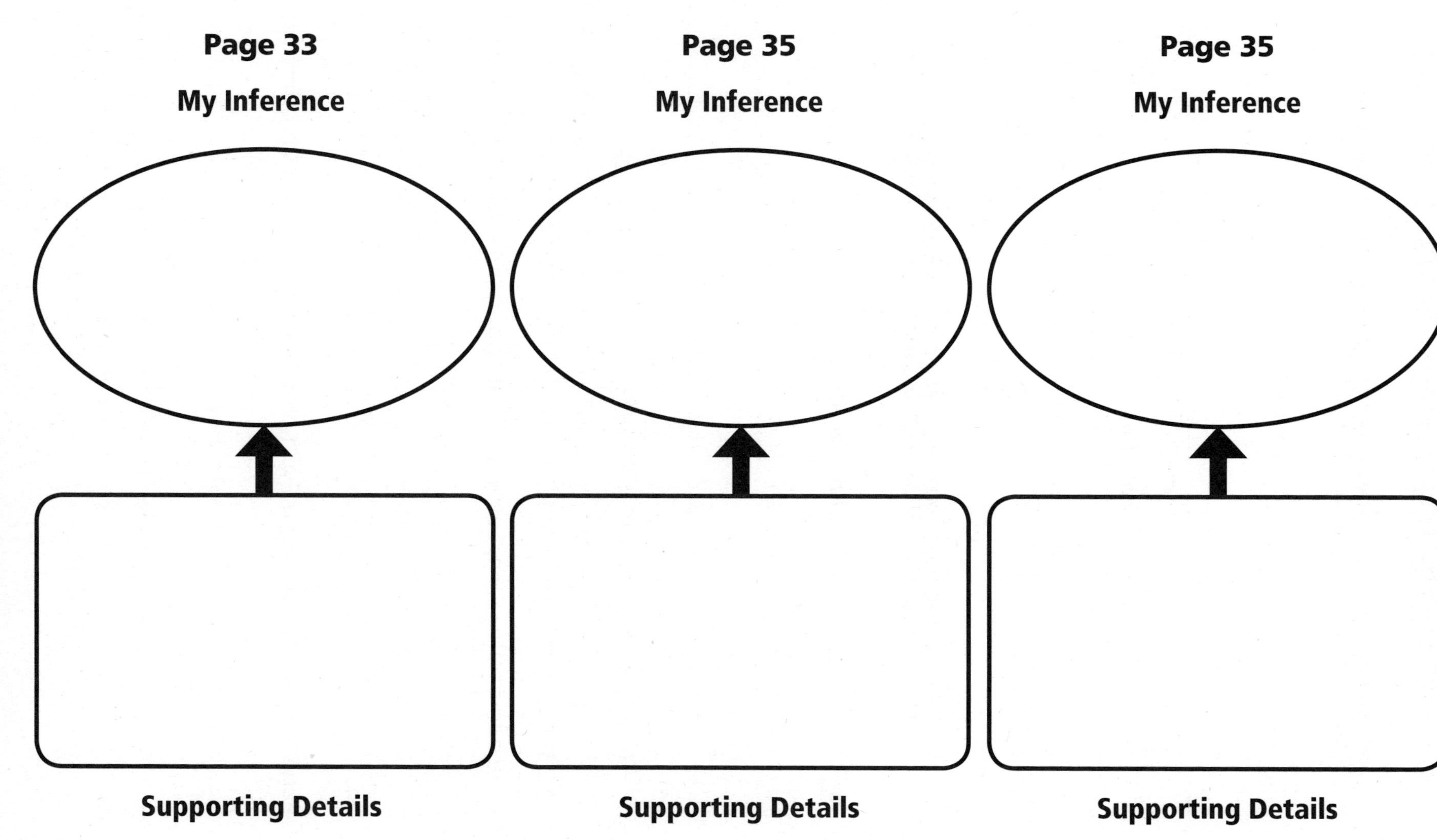

Name: ____

✏️ Close Reading Worksheet

Second Read: Figurative Language (green boxes)

Page 33: Similes Lee Doryong uses are ___________________________________

____.

Page 36: The figurative language shows that ______________________________

____

____.

Third Read: Critical Thinking (blue boxes)

Page 33: I think Ch'unhyang is critical of Lee Doryong's poetry because __________

____

____.

Page 34: Lee Doryong corrects himself because _____________________________

____.

Page 35: At the end of the scene, Lee and Ch'unhyang are weeping because _________

____

____.

Contrast—Page 36: Lee Doryong and Pyon feel differently about Ch'unhyang in that

____

____.

Summary and Important Details Chart

	Summary	Important Details
Act 2, Scene 1 (pages 40–41)		
Act 2, Scene 2 (pages 41–42)		
Act 2, Scene 3 (pages 42–43)		
Act 2, Scene 4 (page 44)		

✎ Close Reading Worksheet

Second Read: Dramatic Structure (green boxes)

Page 40: This scene is set in _______________________________.

The scene adds to the development of the plot by _______________________

____.

Page 42: The first two scenes of act 2 are similar in that _______________

____.

Page 43: The reappearance of Lee Doryong might affect the events of the play

because ____

____.

Third Read: Critical Thinking (blue boxes)

Page 41: The effect of the line is _______________________________

____.

Page 42: Ch'unhyang sees through Lee Doryong's disguise because _______________

____.

Interpret—Page 44: Lee Doryong says that he will leave the poetry to Ch'unhyang

because ____

____.

Name: ____

✏️ **Close Reading Worksheet**

First Read: Poetic Structure (orange boxes)

Page 58: This stanza develops the _______________________ of the poem because it

____

____ .

Page 59: These two stanzas focus on developing _______________________ . I know this

because ____

____ .

Page 60: The truth or insight about the woman's action that the stanza develops is

that ____

____ .

Third Read: Critical Thinking (blue boxes)

Page 58: Count de Lorge is specifically mentioned because _______________________

____ .

Page 59: The woman decides to drop her glove because _______________________

____ .

Interpret—Page 60: King Francis feels _______________________________________

____ .

What I think will happen next: _______________________________________

____ .

Name: ______________________________

Figurative Language Chart

Figurative Language	Onomatopoeia	Personification
Definition		
Example(s) from poem	**Page 59:**	**Page 59:**
My own examples		
My sentences		

Name: _______________________________________

Visualization Chart

Detail from "Ozymandias," page 64:

My visualization drawing:

Detail from "A Sphinx," page 66:

My visualization drawing:

✏️ **Close Reading Worksheet**

Second Read: Compare and Contrast Poetic Forms (green boxes)

Page 64: "Ozymandias" is a _____________________ because _____________________

____ .

Page 66: "A Sphinx" is a _____________________ because _____________________

____ .

The one similarity in structure that both poems share is _____________________

____ .

Third Read: Critical Thinking (blue boxes)

Page 64: The traveler feels that Ozymandias _________________________________ .

I think this because ____

____ .

Page 66: People are fascinated by the Sphinx because _____________________

____ .

Contrast—Page 66: The two statues in "Ozymandias" and "A Sphinx" are different in

that ____

____

____ .

Textual Evidence Chart

Page	Textual Evidence	Inference
80		
81		
82		
84		

Name: ____

🖎 Close Reading Worksheet

Second Read: Word Choice and Tone (green boxes)

Page 80: Yun is in awe of the statues. Regarding the warriors, the narrator's tone is

____.

Page 81: The words ____________, ____________, and ____________ tell me that

Yun feels ____.

Page 83: The tone of the scene after Yun drops the clay head is ___________

____.

Page 84: The narrator has a (positive / negative) view of the inspector.

Third Read: Critical Thinking (blue boxes)

Page 81: The craftsmen vary the appearance of each warrior because

____

____.

Page 82: Yun's uncle says, "This is very bad" because ___________________

____

____.

Evaluate—Page 84: Over the course of the story, Yun has changed

____

____.

   The Warrior Makers

Name: _______________________________

Make Predictions Chart

Page	Details from Story	What I Predict	What Actually Happened
88			
89			
90			
91			

Name: ____

✎ Close Reading Worksheet

Second Read: Point of View (green boxes)

Page 88: The point of view is ______________ and the narrator is ______________.

Page 89: This part of the story would be different with a third-person

narrator in that ____

____.

Page 91: Told from the third-person point of view, these scenes would be

different in that ____

____.

Third Read: Critical Thinking (blue boxes)

Page 88: Cleopatra likes the idea of the royal family being gods in human

form because ____

____.

Page 90: Cleopatra (is / is not) surprised that she had to rule with her brother

because ____.

Page 91: Caesar probably falls in love with Cleopatra because ______________

____.

Analyze—Page 92: Cleopatra is ____

____

____.

Name: _______________________________

Central Idea and Details Web

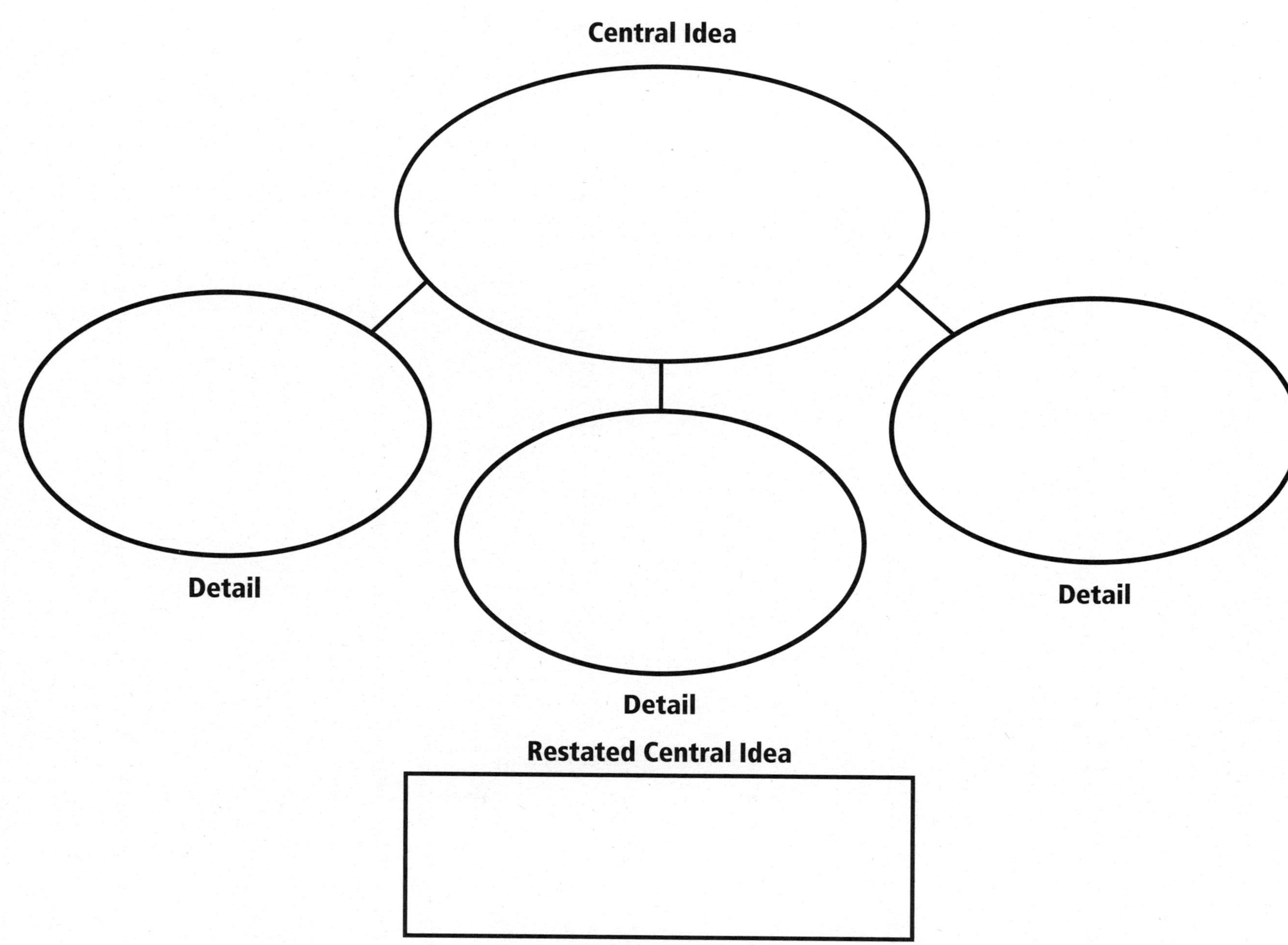

Shackleton: An Enduring Leader

Name: ____

✏️ **Close Reading Worksheet**

Second Read: Secondary Sources (green boxes)

Page 104: This passage is a secondary source because ________________________________

____.

Page 106: The quotation from Amundsen reveals ____.

The quotation from Scott reveals ____.

The author includes these quotations in order to ____

____.

Page 107: The quotation affects my understanding of the selection in that ______________

____

____.

Third Read: Critical Thinking (blue boxes)

Page 105: Exploring the South Pole was so difficult because ________________________________

____.

Page 106: The three explorers were so determined to be the first because ______________

____.

Page 108: Shackleton's story is interesting to today's readers because ________________

____.

Evaluate—Page 108: Shackleton (was / was not) a good leader because ________________

____.

  Shackleton: An Enduring Leader

Name: _______________________________

✏ Close Reading Worksheet

First Read: Ask and Answer Questions (orange boxes)

Page 112: Crossing the mountains was difficult because _______________________

____.

Page 113: The boys reacted oddly because _______________________________

____.

Page 114: Mr. Sorlle acted this way toward Shackleton because _______________

____.

Page 115: Shackleton didn't help rescue the men on South Georgia Island because

____

____.

Page 116: Questions I still have: ____

____?

Third Read: Critical Thinking (blue boxes)

Page 115: The details about the time and place of the passage tell me that

____

____.

Analyze—Page 116: Based on Shackleton's writing, he was _________________

____.

Analyzing Primary Sources Organizer

Primary Source	How a Secondary Source Might Differ
Page 112:	
Page 113:	
Page 114:	
Page 116:	

 from *Escape from the Antarctic*

Name: _______________________________

✏️ Close Reading Worksheet

First Read: Summarize (orange boxes)

Page 128: The big idea of this page is that _________________________

____

____.

Page 130: I would write a postcard that explains _________________

____

____.

Page 132: The main idea of this selection is _____________________

____

____.

Third Read: Critical Thinking (blue boxes)

Page 128: It is likely that the Romans (were / were not) known as great navigators

because ____

____.

Page 129: To be an underwater treasure hunter, you would need to be __________

____.

Page 131: Canceling the permits matters because ___________________

____.

Support—Page 132: The Brazilian government seems to think that __________

____.

When in Rome ... or Brazil

Sequence Chart

EVENT 1 The Brazilian government charged Robert Marx with illegally taking artifacts.

↓

EVENT 2

↓

EVENT 3

↓

EVENT 4

 When in Rome . . . or Brazil

Name: _______________________

Steps in a Process Chart

Steps Taken to Build the Colosseum

> **STEP 1**

> **STEP 2**

> **STEP 3**

> **STEP 4**

> **STEP 5**

> **STEP 6**

Name: ____

✏️ **Close Reading Worksheet**

Page 137: The additional information in the diagram is _______________________

____ .

Page 138: The events that fill in the blanks are _______________________________

____ .

Page 139: According to the scale on the map, the Romans had to carry the stones

____ .

Third Read: Critical Thinking (blue boxes)

Page 136: Two reasons the Colosseum plans had to be precise are because __________

____

____ .

Page 137: The existence of a fourth level tells us _________________________________

____

____ .

Page 138: Using the Colosseum as a quarry was harmful because _________________

____ .

Contrast—Page 140: The Colosseum's uses are different because _________________

____ and similar because

____ .

Name: ___________________________________

Cause-and-Effect Chart

Cause	Effect
Page 153	
Page 154	
Page 156	This increases the risk of damaging gemstones.

Name: ____

✏️ Close Reading Worksheet

Second Read: Scientific Texts (green boxes)

Page 152: The scientific process described in paragraph 3 is that ________________

____

____.

Page 156: In the context of this scientific text, *vein* means ____________________

____.

Page 156: Based on the heading, I expect this section is about __________________

____.

Third Read: Critical Thinking (blue boxes)

Page 153: Potch opals have ____

____.

Page 155: The history of the inland sea is important to opal formation because

____

____.

Page 155: As a miner, it would be a (good / bad) idea ______________________

____

____.

Describe—Page 156: What makes opals so valuable is ______________________

____.

    Opals: Rainbows in Stone

Name: ____

✏️ Close Reading Worksheet

Page 160: There is debate about where the Rapanui were from originally because

____.

Page 161: Polynesian rats arriving on the island would harm native land birds because

____.

Page 162: Scientists would have found out that the *moai* represent Rapanui ancestors

____.

Page 164: The government doesn't forbid tourists to see the *moai* because

____.

Third Read: Critical Thinking (blue boxes)

Page 161: The first humans to settle Easter Island might have destroyed the forests

because ____

____.

Page 162: Tribes might have knocked over their rivals' *moai* _______________

____.

Page 163: People spent so much time doing experiments to figure out how the *moai*

were moved because _______________________________________

____.

Describe—Page 164: Three ways scientists have studied Easter Island are __________

____.

Visual Information Chart

Visual	Question and Answer
Map on page 161:	Looking at the map, I think scientists theorized that the Rapanui came from Chile because
Diagram on page 163:	The most effective method for moving the *moai* is because

Problem/Solution Chart

Details	Problem or Solution?	How It Contributes to the Selection as a Whole
p. 177	☐ Problem ☐ Solution	
p. 178	☐ Problem ☐ Solution	
p. 180	☐ Problem ☐ Solution	

Name: _______________________________

✏ Close Reading Worksheet

Second Read: Technical Texts (green boxes)

Page 176: The natural forces of _______________ and _______________ contributed to the wearing away of the shoreline.

Page 177: The heading is _____________________; it tells me that _______________

____.

Page 178: The steps described on this page are:

1. ____

2. ____

3. ____

Page 179: The author includes the diagram because _______________________

____.

Third Read: Critical Thinking (blue boxes)

Page 176: People might want to save the lighthouse because _______________

____.

Page 179: If all one hundred jacks did not lift at the same time, then _______________

____.

Judge—Page 180: Moving the Cape Hatteras Lighthouse (was / was not) worth the

effort and expense because _______________________________________

____.

   How to Move a Lighthouse

Name: ______________________________

Skim and Scan Organizer

Page	Scanned/Skimmed Feature	Information Gained
184	title and headings	
185	key words	
186	flowchart	
187	diagram	

Name: ____

✐ Close Reading Worksheet

Second Read: Integrate Visual Information (green boxes)

Page 186: The author includes the flowchart because _______________________

____.

Page 188: The flowchart has two branches because _________________________

____

____.

Third Read: Critical Thinking (blue boxes)

Page 184: The major difference between the Kitty Hawk and September 1904 flight was

____. The difference was important because

____.

Page 186: "Wasting runway" means ____

____

____.

Page 187: A plane's tail rudder has the same name as a boat's rudder because _______

____

____.

Connect—Page 188: Knowing about aerodynamics helps passengers because _______

____

____.

Name: ____

✏️ Close Reading Worksheet

First Read: Author's Point of View and Purpose (orange boxes)

Page 202: The author's purpose is to ________________________________

____.

Page 204: The author is (for / against) digital video.

Third Read: Critical Thinking (blue boxes)

Page 202: The author (is / is not) a fan of *Jetmorphs* because __________________

____

____.

Page 203: Moviemakers change things because ___________________________

____

____.

Page 204: The author thinks a true film lover is someone who __________________

____

____.

Page 205: The author (did / did not) convince me that things were better because

____

____.

Evaluate—Page 206: I (agree / disagree) with the author's point of view because

____

____.

Claims and Supporting Evidence Chart

Claim 1:

CGI fixes too many mistakes.

Evidence:

Claim 2:

Digital video has led to the downfall of the theater-going experience.

Evidence:

Does the evidence presented by the author give enough information to support the argument? Tell why or why not.

____

____

____

 Technology Is Killing My Movies!

Name: _______________________________

Connotations Chart

Words to use: newfangled (p. 210), reactionary (p. 210), worrywart (p. 212), symptoms (p. 212), mere (p. 214)

Positive (+)	Neutral (+/−)	Negative (−)	notes

Thank You, Technology!

✏️ Close Reading Worksheet

Second Read: Evaluate Author's Claims (green boxes)

Page 211: The claim about social media is based on (fact / opinion). I know this because

____

____.

Page 212: The fact the author gives to support the claim that technology has made

people smarter is ______________________________

____.

Third Read: Critical Thinking (blue boxes)

Page 210: I (do / do not) believe that technology will provide greater opportunities

because ______________________________________

____.

Page 212: Another way technology helps students learn is ______________________

____.

Page 213: Seeing a doctor would be the next step because ______________________

____.

Defend—Page 214: The author would (agree / disagree) that smartphones are bad for

society because __________________________________

____

____.

Name: _______________________________

Paraphrase Chart

Paraphrase of page 226, paragraphs 2 and 3:

Paraphrase of page 227, paragraph 6:

Paraphrase of page 228, photo caption:

Paraphrase of page 229, paragraph 14:

✏️ Close Reading Worksheet

Second Read: Primary Sources (green boxes)

Page 226: What makes this blog entry a primary source is that __________________

____.

Page 227: Sequence is an effective technique for a primary-source account like this one

because ____

Page 228: The blogger posts the primary-source photo of the fire to ______________

____.

Page 230: The reason a secondary-source photo couldn't capture the details I circled is

because ____

____

Third Read: Critical Thinking (blue boxes)

Page 227: From reading a first-person, real-time blog account, what I might learn that

I couldn't learn anywhere else is ____

____.

Page 229: When the smoke jumpers arrive on the scene, the blogger feels ___________

____.

Page 230—Analyze: The motivation for a dangerous job like smoke jumping might be

____

____.

Name: _______________________

Venn Diagram

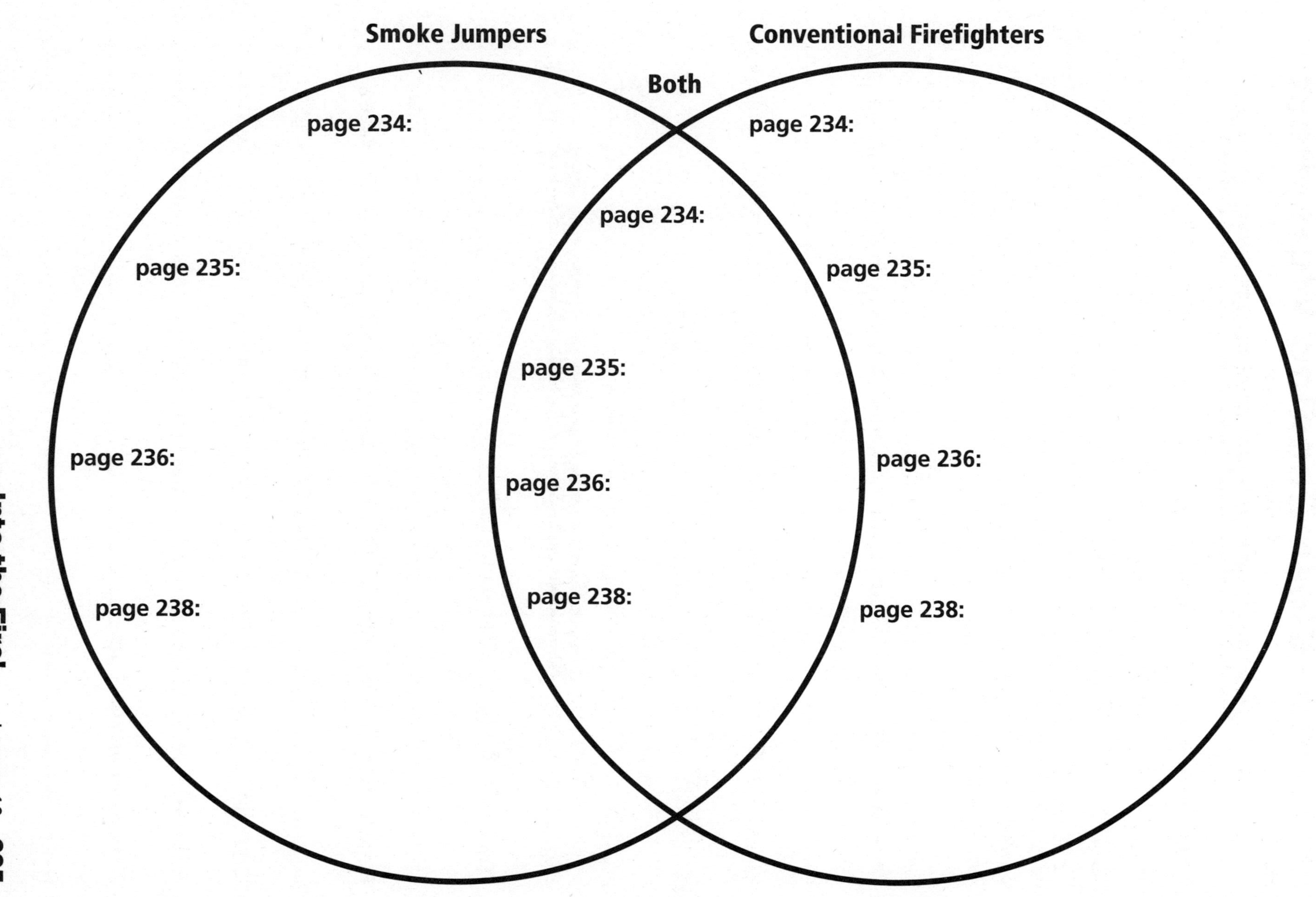

Name: ____

✏️ Close Reading Worksheet

Second Read: Secondary Sources (green boxes)

Page 234: I can tell this article is a secondary source and not a primary source because

____

____ .

Page 235: The photo on this page is a primary source because it shows _______________

____ .

Page 236: The primary-source quotation adds to the secondary source by ___________

____ .

Page 237: For the section "A Smoke Jumper's Toolbox," the writer might have

consulted sources such as ____

____ .

Third Read: Critical Thinking (blue boxes)

Page 235: The fire shelter is probably _______________________________________

____ .

Page 237: In "Hello Blogheads!" the language, word choice, and tone are ___________

_____________________ . In "Into the Fire," the language, word choice, and tone are

____ .

Apply—Page 14: Some ways I might use "Into the Fire" to increase my understanding of

"Hello Blogheads!" are ____

____ .

   Into the Fire